Paul █████████████████████ as the *Financial Times'* Bridge correspondent. He has written six bestselling books on Bridge and Poker, including *The Right Way to Play Bridge, Bridge for Complete Beginners, Texas Hold 'em Poker: Begin and Win* and *The Mammoth Book of Poker*. He is an all-round mind-sports guru, having won gold and silver medals in the Mind Sports Olympiad and The Scottish National Championships.

The Mammoth Book of
Casino
Games

Paul Mendelson

ROBINSON

RUNNING PRESS
PHILADELPHIA · LONDON

Constable & Robinson Ltd
3 The Lanchesters
162 Fulham Palace Road
London W6 9ER
www.constablerobinson.com

First published in the UK by Robinson,
an imprint of Constable & Robinson, 2010

A copy of the British Library Cataloguing in Publication
Data is available from the British Library

UK ISBN 978-1-84901-271-3

1 3 5 7 9 10 8 6 4 2

First published in the United States in 2010 by Running Press Book Publishers

9 8 7 6 5 4 3 2 1
Digit on the right indicates the number of this printing

US Library of Congress number: 2009929936
US ISBN 978-0-7624-3847-1

Running Press Book Publishers
2300 Chestnut Street
Philadelphia, PA 19103-4371

Visit us on the web!

www.runningpress.com

Printed and bound in the EU

Typesetting and editorial: Basement Press

Contents

Introduction

WELCOME to *The Mammoth Book of Casino Games*. It has a simple aim: the next time you play in a casino – whatever your game of choice – I want you to enjoy it more and have a better chance of coming out a winner. It is no exaggeration to say: don't go into another casino until you've read this book, especially the sections on the games you play regularly.

Having played in many casinos all over the world, it always amazes me how incredibly generous players are to the casinos. As if those corporations – which they nearly all are – didn't make enough money already, punters everywhere boost the casino profits with uninformed play, reckless money management, and ignorant attempts to buck the odds. The fact is that nowadays the odds of every casino game can be established by running computer simulations over hundreds of millions of plays. This technique started back in the 1950s when the game of Blackjack, or "21", was first studied by Edward O. Thorpe. He used the early IBM computers to analyse the correct way to play every hand, and then he created a simple count system that, not only cancelled out the casino's advantage, but actually provided the players with an advantage. This cannot be achieved for every game, but the correct play will reduce the house edge to a minimum, increase your enjoyment of the game, and greatly improve your chances of making a profit. In short, there is no place for superstition and feelings, just hard facts and optimum play.

At the start of my *Mammoth Book of Poker*, I ask one simple question, but it is truly the most important of all: Do you want to play, or do you want to win? There is a massive difference between the mind-set for the former and the focus required for the latter. Working at anything usually helps to improve your skills and better results will follow. When it comes to a pastime where you might be risking large sums of money, it strikes me that a little gentle work is scarcely much of a burden when the result could be worth hundreds, thousands, even hundreds of thousands of dollars in your pockets. However, if you feel that you can't be bothered to read up the right ways to play casino games, the best ways to enjoy complimentary accommodation, meals, show tickets and gaming credits, the correct mental approach to gambling, and the best way to behave in a casino, then put this book down, grab your wad, and prepare to lose it. The obvious indicators for this loss are the gigantic monoliths of corporate headquarters, the massive dividends to shareholders, and the huge annual profits earned by the casinos.

Las Vegas is not only the world centre of gambling, it is also probably the best place in the world to gamble. The games are strictly regulated and security is excellent. The most profitable rules for the players are usually applied; bonuses and incentives are superb. But – and it is a huge but – just take a look at the place. Those multi-million dollar hotels, the snazzy boutiques, the massive explosion of up-market real estate are all funded by one thing alone: gambling revenues – in other words, the money lost by the punters in the casinos. In the old days, casino-hotels used to rely on gaming revenues for everything; nowadays, the hotels and resorts may bring in over half the company's revenue, but it is still the promise of gambling, and the bling-bling with which it is associated, that lures in the punters and powers the city's glittering lights. The next time you see pictures of Vegas, or you find yourself walking down The Strip, look up and ask yourself whether you really want to be a major contributor to the global organizations that built them? Or would you rather enjoy yourself for a cheaper price, even leave Vegas in profit?

Let me give you one example to explain how powerful the casinos really are. When Vegas visionary, Steve Wynn, built the first of Las Vegas's mega-resorts, The Mirage, no one would invest in him or the business. He borrowed huge sums using the now discredited junk bond market, and he built the prototype for all new hotel-resorts in Las Vegas. The accounts made for scary reading: just to break even, The Mirage would have to make one million dollars every day! Every day! Did they do it? Absolutely. The first month they made just short of 40 million dollars, and they're still in business, thriving on The Strip today.

So, that's what you are up against when you enter a casino. It is a glamorous, seductive, hypnotic world where you could win a fortune... but you'll probably lose all the money in your pocket.

However, in this book, it's time to turn the tables. We'll look at each game in turn, describe the best approach to each, the one that gives you the best chance to lose as little as possible or to win as much as possible. We'll look at the way to handle your bankroll, manage your money, build up your confidence, seek out the most generous deals, the best games and the strongest chance of you leaving the casino a winner.

As a Poker player, I have spent some time in Vegas playing, not against the house, but against other players. If you are better than average at Poker, over time you can be an almost guaranteed winner. However, even excluding Poker, at the time of writing, I can confirm that I am on a winning streak against the Las Vegas casino games. I leave Vegas with a profit more times than with a loss, and it is a record that I want to maintain. If you would like to join me, read on, and learn the secrets to being a winning gambler in casinos worldwide.

Paul Mendelson
London

1
Preparations for Gambling

P ERHAPS you're thinking: I don't want to prepare, I just want to go and have fun in the casino, maybe win a little money, and come home having been entertained. The casinos love your kind of attitude because they know that, however lucky you may get one day, you play so poorly and recklessly that you will lose it all back to them again very quickly. If you can afford it, then why waste time: just go out, enjoy yourself, and no one will be worried, least of all the casinos. However, if you become frustrated when you lose so much – every time – then the fault really is yours.

The good news is that you can win – not consistently, but regularly enough to take home the casino's money from time to time and use it to fund your next attempts at a big score.

If you want to win, then I urge you to hunker down, read through this chapter and follow the suggestions.

They are an amalgam of real-life experiences from professional gamblers (people who rely on gambling to feed their families and educate their children), psychologists who have studied thousands of actual cases concerning gambling problems, and straightforward science.

Do You Want to Play, or Do You Want to Win?

They are two completely different concepts. You must decide which it is to be. If you just want to play, be prepared to lose – consistently – the more you play. If you genuinely decide that you want to win, prepare to make some simple, but vital, changes to your approach to gambling. I guarantee you that in the long run you will lose much less, and stand the chance to win much more.

Nick Dandalos, more commonly known as Nick-the-Greek, was a famous Poker player and gambler. It was his month's-long epic Poker match with Johnny Moss in the foyer of Binion's Horseshoe Casino in Las Vegas that launched the World Series of Poker, and the billion-dollar business it is today. Nick-the-Greek was a true high-roller and, even though he ended up a low-roller and wiped out, for him any gambling action was good. "The best feeling in the world," he is quoted as saying, "is gambling and winning. And the second best feeling? Gambling and losing."

I love gambling but, for me, the first emotion and the second are world's apart.

Do You Feel Lucky?

No matter what the odds, luck plays a vastly important role in how well you will do when you gamble. Indeed, the less you gamble, the more luck plays a part. For example, the best way to gamble at a game like Roulette is to put your entire bankroll on an even-money chance, spin the wheel once and, if you win, take away your winnings and never return to a casino again. There's a famous story about a man and two suitcases full of cash who got lucky in Las Vegas back in the 1970s, and I'll tell you all about it in the Craps section.

Positive feelings of being lucky, although unquantifiable, are very important for gamblers. If you are in a negative frame of mind; if you are worried about money, feeling depressed about other elements of your life, frustrated, anxious or impatient, I urge you not to gamble today. Save your time and money for another day.

If you approach gambling in a negative frame of mind, you are unlikely to make the correct decisions when it comes to bet size, frequency, and choice of game. Ask yourself this question: have you ever seen a negative, grumbling, moaning player ever turn his day around by winning in a casino. I can honestly tell you that, over many, many years, I never have. I have witnessed people

Please do not gamble if you are worried about money, feeling downhearted or depressed, or have a bad feeling about your luck.

fed up, pessimistic and down-hearted, rally for a while and perhaps even move into profit, but I have never seen them hang on to that profit. They just continue until they are losing again, and usually until they have lost every last cent. There are psychological reasons for this: our brains are programmed in certain different ways and, for many gamblers, losing is a vindication of their view of the world, and their place in it. No one acknowledges this, few are even aware of it, but there is very strong evidence to suggest that this affects a large percentage of gamblers.

I have gambled at the wrong time, either because I started gambling in the wrong frame of mind, or because, through a combination of bad luck and stupidity, I got myself into a position where I felt very downhearted. Every time I do this, I lose – every time, without exception.

If you follow this first tip alone, you will lose less money than before.

Bankroll

Later on, we'll talk about how to use your bankroll, how to protect it, how to build it, and how to enjoy it. For now, let's talk about forming it.

The biggest and most dangerous development in gambling is, without doubt, the ability to use credit cards to provide cash. This is fundamentally against the vital principle of only gambling with money you can afford to lose. You can see how obvious it is: a credit card extends credit to you – for money you may or may not be able to pay back – and it is so simple that the cash arrives in your hand without any discomfort whatsoever. Until I carried credit cards in my wallet, I never gambled with money I couldn't afford, and I never exceeded my bankroll. I never woke up in the morning and thought: "What the hell have I done?". I genuinely implore you, more strongly than you can imagine: never take credit cards to a casino. This is so important, I'm going to make this stand out:

Never take credit cards to the casino.

If you are travelling abroad, take a card which does not provide cash on demand; speak to the credit card company in advance and tell them that no cash is to be permitted from your card. If you think that you do not need to take these precautions, I counsel you: do not take the risk. I have seen successful, professional people lose more money than you can imagine by using credit cards. Please do not fall into the same trap. Take cash or Travellers' Cheques, and use only those for gambling.

Once you have decided how much you can afford to lose – because even if you play correctly there is still a chance that you will lose it all (just as there is an increased chance that you'll make a 500 per cent profit) – put that aside and promise yourself, better still, compel yourself, only to gamble with that amount. If you are going to Vegas, then divide up your bankroll into the amount with which you can afford to play each day. If you don't do this, you will do what most people do when they arrive in Vegas: they gamble all their money and lose most, or all, of it on the first evening.

If you decide to take $2,000 with you for a four-day stay, that gives you $500 per day with which to gamble. This isn't a huge amount and you will have to be disciplined about sticking to it. Put the cash in the safe in your room, take out only what you are prepared to gamble with in any one session, and leave the rest behind. This is very important because, if you have a losing session, it is vital to take a short break, clear your mind, and return to the tables refreshed and renewed and ready for battle. Even if you have to take the elevator back up to your room, open the safe, take out another wad, and go back down to the casino floor, at least you will have time to reflect on whether you should take a longer break, try gambling somewhere else, try another game, or just treat yourself to that massage you have been dreaming about all day long.

We'll talk more about how to live life on holiday in Vegas later on, but this is an essential, so please stick to it.

Understand the Casino Challenge

James Bond, in Ian Fleming's first novel, *Casino Royale*, admits that although there is much luck in gambling, the more you put into it, the more you are likely to get out from it. And, he's right. However, I have to say that Bond rarely gambles very sensibly, either in the novels or in the movies, but I guess when you're Bond, you don't really need to do the sensible thing.

For us, if you want to win, you need to be in the right mind-set: to acknowledge to yourself that your prime concern is to win, and then your behaviour will echo that. Let's be 100 per cent candid here. When you enter a casino, you should be feeling good. The casino should look after you: the staff should be welcoming and friendly, the drinks should be free, there should be bonuses if you play for more than an hour or two, or for high stakes. These should include cash-back points, a free meal, free accommodation. It will vary from casino to casino. If the house is doing its job properly, you should feel pretty good about life as you sit down at your chosen table and start to play.

But, be aware, this is not generosity on the part of the casino, it is just good business. If you are enjoying yourself, if you feel big and important and spoilt, if you feel luxurious, then you are unlikely to worry too much about whether you are winning or losing. You are having a good time. Let's be clear: the casino has only one aim – to squeeze every last dollar and cent from your wallet and, given half a chance, money from your savings and money you don't even have from your credit cards. These people have no shame: they are money vacuum cleaners and they want everything from you – absolutely everything. Don't think the staff are on your side. They may be charming people, but they have a job to do. That job is being monitored by supervisors and bosses, cameras and anonymous inspectors. Most staff rely on tips and a staff bonus at the end of the year: the bigger the casino's profits, the bigger the bonus. The happier they make you feel – winner or loser – the bigger the tips are likely to be. So, don't be taken in, or lulled into a false sense of the casino being on your side.

I have played in plenty of casinos around the world which make you feel awful: the staff are bored and impolite, the managers stingy and unhelpful, you are expected to pay mean-looking cocktail staff even for soft drinks, and then tip them. If this happens, immediately ask for the manager, politely explain that you have never paid for a drink in a casino in your life and you are sure there has been a mistake. If you don't get the reply you want, just smile, and get up. If you find yourself in a place like this, leave. Really, just do it. There is probably another casino nearby where the staff will look after you better. You are doing them a favour risking your money in their casino. You have every right to expect to be treated well; if you are a medium, or high-roller, expect to be treated like a king, or queen. That's the deal here: they give you a good time and you risk your money. If they can't offer you the basics, then get out.

Once you go into a casino – or a casino city, like Vegas – knowing that they are after every last cent and imagining them dipping their greedy fingers into your wallet and pulling out your hard-earned cash with an evil look on their faces, then the battle between you and the casino becomes fun. You know the deal – they are the devil and you are with the angels. Your aim is to beat them at their own game, enjoy all the perks, and leave a winner.

There is a myth about casinos that should be dispelled. Many people think that casinos hate winners. They don't. Unless you are cheating (and casinos have some very weird interpretations of that word), casinos are just fine about you winning. Firstly, they feel that it is good for other players to see some winners around – it makes them believe that everyone can do it. Secondly, since you won, the casino expects you to return to their casino floor again soon, when they hope the expected odds will come to bear and you will lose your profits back to them – and then some more – and, finally, they hope you will increase the size of your bets and therefore risk losing far more in the future.

The fact is that all well-run casinos have a statistical expectation of what they will win from you over time. Your job is to reduce that expectation either to close to zero, or even to swing it in your favour, and to stop betting when you are ahead so that you can cash in your winnings and leave. If you are prepared to do this – to stop when you are winning, or at least lock away part of your profits – then you will thwart the casino at the game they play so very strongly. With a detailed examination of the correct strategy for each game, and a winning mind-set, you will leave with profits and those profits can build to a significant sum.

Set Yourself Sensible Targets

One of the biggest problems of casino gambling is that you enter a viciously tough competitive arena without any clear goals. This leads you to continue the battle to the death – usually of your entire bankroll.

A casino is not the place to get rich quick, unless you are playing the Slot machines (or "Slots") – and even when you do this, if you play merely for the jackpot, you will be disappointed all but once or twice out of the many thousands of times you play.

When you play Table Games, the best of which are almost even-money chances (where the casino has less than a 3 per cent edge against you on the bets I'll recommend), your goal should be to make a 50 per cent profit. However, ask people who visit a casino with $1,000 if they would leave happy with $1,500 and almost all of them would tell you that they are seeking a bigger win than that. Maybe $3,000 or $5,000. To make 300 per cent you have to be exceptionally lucky and your chances of achieving it are very small. In the meantime, you lose your bankroll session after session.

If, instead, you set yourself a reasonable target, not only are you more likely to achieve it – and with that, a feeling of satisfaction – but you are far less likely to move into profit and then, in a vain attempt to increase that profit, lose what you have just made. Sessions which involve doing well early on and then losing all your profit and your original bankroll, are particularly hard to take, and often stimulate the urge to gamble more when it is clearly time to stop.

When playing Slots, a target of any profit is a good one to have, since the house edge (the advantage for the casino) is nearly always so substantial. But even here, you can set a responsible limit – of, say, a 25 per cent profit – and, if you achieve it, walk away. I have studied and watched Slots players and I have seen no one ever do this – and that is just one reason why Slots make such fortunes for the casinos.

Blackjack and Selected Video Poker Machines

If it is played following the strategies shown in this book, Blackjack is almost an even-money game. Aim for a 50 per cent profit and, when you have achieved that, lock away half the profit, plus your original bankroll. Continue to play – if you wish – with the remaining half of your profit, and continue to lock away half of it if you successfully double it.

If you lose the extra profit, leave the table and take a short break. Playing this way, you are guaranteed a 25 per cent profit at the end of your session.

If you choose to be more aggressive, aim for a 100 per cent profit, before locking half away, plus your original stake, and continuing to play the remaining half of your profit.

Select the best Video Poker variations (the Video Poker chapter tells you how) and aim for a 50 per cent profit, locking away half your profit if you achieve this goal and playing only the remainder.

Craps, Baccarat, Spanish 21

Played correctly, these games all offer the house a minimal percentage edge against the player. A 50 per cent profit is a reasonable target for which to aim, after which, lock away half that profit, or leave the table for that session and take a well-earned break.

Roulette, Three-Card Poker, Caribbean Stud Poker, Pai Gow Poker, Blackjack Switch

These games, even when played using the optimum techniques, offer the house too big an edge for you to expect a profit, unless you are very lucky. Aim for a 25 per cent profit and lock away half when you achieve this. Ideally, take that profit and run. If you must continue to play, do not touch the money you have set aside. This way, you are assured a profit from your session.

Other Table Games and Slots

Other Table Games and most Slot machines offer the player very poor odds, with the house edge ranging from 5 per cent right up to 30 per cent – odds against which you will almost never prevail. If you must play these games (or place these highly unfavourable bets at other games), ensure that you are making bets as rarely as possible and at a minimum level. If you succeed in making any profit, get out as fast as you can. You have done very well indeed and you must bank those profits quickly.

Leave With Your Profits

This may seem banal, but you must leave with your profit. By leave, I mean the table at which you are playing, your sessions for the day or, best of all, the casino itself. If you record a big profit and then continue playing the same game, or move to a higher-stake game, and lose those profits, you have achieved nothing (but heartache).

If you do make a profit, I urge you not to use this increased bankroll to supplement your stake. While there is a chance that you will hit a hot streak and that increasing your bets will lead to massively enhanced profits (this is a frequently re-occurring dream for most gamblers), the odds favour that you will lose, slowly or otherwise, at this higher stake and your profit will be wiped out far more quickly than if you had played another session at the same stake and tried to build your profit level slowly.

This is a situation I see repeated day in, day out in casinos all over the world, from players who arrive at the table with $20, to those who roll up to a grand London casino with half a million pounds to play with. Resolve to make all increases in your stake slowly and in response to a gentle run of good fortune (if you are tracking cards at Blackjack, there may be other factors to influence your bet size – see page 62).

Never increase your bet in an attempt to get even – this results in very few successes and a huge number of disastrous sessions for players.

Casino Hold

To beat the casinos at their own game, you need to understand their game. Let's take Roulette, and simplify the odds a little so that I can illustrate this example to you. The exact odds and strategies appear in the chapter on Roulette.

Let's say that, if you bet on even-money chances, the house has an advantage of 3 per cent. This means that for every $100 you bet, you will, in the long run, lose $3. It is easy to think, therefore, that if you visit your favourite casino with $1,000, then you will usually lose only $30, or 3 per cent of your bankroll. That, together with some drinks, maybe a free dinner, all sounds good value.

However, this would only be true if all the bets you made came to a total of $1,000. The more likely scenario is that, over the course of the session, you bet $10,000. Not because you have that amount of money, but because you win and lose a little on each spin and continue to bet – that's what most gamblers do. Let's say that you play Roulette for two hours and, on each spin, you bet $100. The wheel spins 100 times in those two hours and you end up betting $10,000. Now you can expect to lose 3 per cent of $10,000 (not $1,000), which equals $300.

A casino does not estimate its profits on how much you actually win or lose. It looks at the bets you are making, the size of your stake, and the frequency of your betting, and then it works out what the "Casino Hold" (what the casino holds onto) should be. Generally, this figure will range from 30 per cent upwards. Of course, if you played that same game of Roulette for 20 hours in a row (and people do, especially in Las Vegas), then you would expect to place $100,000 of bets, and 3 per cent of that is $3,000 – or more than you actually brought to the table in the first place. On that basis, you are wiped out, and you leave with no money. This makes the casino's expected hold 100 per cent. Frightening, isn't it?

So be aware that your bankroll is under attack from a far more vicious assault than simply the percentage edge the house may hold. For this reason, reducing the house edge is paramount. Even reducing it by as little as 1 per cent can make a vast difference to how much you lose and, far more importantly, your chances of leaving a winner. That's what we'll be doing in this book: paring down the house edge, learning to gamble intelligently, and acquiring the discipline to leave the table just when the casino hopes that you won't. Once you see the faces of the casino staff when you leave with your profit, you'll want to do it again and again.

Casino Behaviour

If you are not familiar with casinos and you go to one, anywhere in the world, you will find that the best way to become accustomed to the atmosphere, and understand how to behave, is to watch everyone around you. This may seem blindingly obvious, but all too often the lure of the tables overtakes common sense. Take time to drink in the atmosphere, to watch how people behave, to see how people exchange cash for chips, place their bets, receive their winnings, cash in their profits or nurse their losses. This will allow you to blend right in, feel relaxed and concentrate on the matter in hand.

In the sections that follow, we will talk about how to behave and what to do when you arrive at, and leave, the table. But, for now, watch what is going on, and enjoy the experience. You are in for an exciting time!

2
Blackjack

BLACKJACK, or "21", or "Vingt-et-un", is the all-time classic casino Table Game. The premise could not be simpler. A player (or players) takes on the dealer. You win if your hand total gets closer to 21 – without exceeding it – than the dealer's hand. The payout is 1–1: even money. For a $10 bet, this means that you receive your $10 bet back, plus $10 in profit.

If your total exceeds 21 you go bust and lose; if the dealer makes a hand closer to 21 than yours, you lose.

If the game stopped there, the casino would enjoy a massively destructive edge (an edge of close to 7 per cent), but to make the game more enticing for players there are a number of options which most – if not all – casinos provide for the player.

The first, as the name of the game suggests, is that you get a bonus for making a Blackjack. This hand consists of two cards, one of which must be a "ten card" (a 10, a jack, a queen or a king), the other an ace – which counts as 1 or 11. When these two cards are dealt to a player, the ace always counts as 11 and so the player has 21 in just two cards, and this is Blackjack. The house pays this hand off at the rate of 3–2 (for a $10 bet, this means that you receive your $10 back, plus $15 in profit).

Other profitable opportunities, which we'll look at in turn during the course of this chapter, include: double down, pair splitting (with subsequent double-down chances), and early surrender.

Many Blackjack players have seen the game played in the movies and on television, have dealt themselves or their friends Blackjack hands at home, and glanced at a book on the subject. However, the general standard of Blackjack play that I have witnessed in casinos all over the world is appalling. All too often, players are sitting down at a Blackjack table without the slightest idea of what to do. I watch players giving their money to the house, without even trying. Why play a game of skill, risking large sums of money, and not learn even the simplest rules for playing it?

There is a right and a wrong way to play every hand of Blackjack. It's not a matter of feeling, intuition or luck, but down to a Basic Strategy. This fact has been proven by computer simulations, for over half a century, playing billions of Blackjack hands and showing that, in the long run, there is a correct thing to do and no other sensible option.

If you are a card player and someone with an average memory, who wants to play Blackjack for money, then to play without adhering to these basic rules is madness.

In a moment, we'll examine this Basic Strategy, and ensure that you are confident about it, and all the other elements that will lead to a more successful – and profitable – approach to playing Blackjack. However, first let's take a quick look at the history of the game and how it influences our approach to beating the house in the twenty-first century.

The Game that Nearly Broke the House

In the 1950s, Edward O. Thorpe and IBM consultant, Julian Braun, set about analysing the game of Blackjack using an early model of the modern computer. They quickly discovered that, not only could Blackjack be played far more efficiently than anyone had ever realized, but that the game could also be won, consistently, by applying a counting system to discover the times when situations existed that benefited the player.

The simple principle of a count system is this: when there is a higher concentration than usual of ten cards and aces left in the deck or dealer's shoe (card holder), this is beneficial to the player. He is more likely to make Blackjack, or 20, or to be successful in double-down situations; the dealer is more likely to bust from low teen totals. In this situation the player should increase his bet size considerably.

If the remaining cards in the deck or shoe boast a higher concentration of low cards, this is bad for the player, and he should reduce his bet or leave the table. Not only are bet sizes altered, but playing strategy is also adjusted, making the player's knowledge very powerful.

In the first exposé of Blackjack, *Beat the Dealer*, Edward O. Thorpe popularized these theories and published a count system, which allowed all dedicated players to play against the casinos and enjoy a statistical advantage over them. When enough players put in the work required, casinos suddenly found that certain players were winning consistently, and that the Blackjack tables generally were losing their profits – and, in some cases, were just plain losing.

The casinos reacted with countermeasures, some of which were so extreme that they put off just about everyone from playing, even those who had no concept of what card-counting could achieve. Once again, the casinos changed their minds and the game reverted to its old form, but this time the casino bosses were on the lookout for the counters – and the tell-tale signs of big bet-size changes – and, when they were found, they were expelled, none too subtly, from the premises. These skilful, innovative players were now branded as "cheaters" and there was no place for them on the casino floors.

In Atlantic City, the counters took the casinos to court, and won their battle: counters could not be expelled. So, the casinos changed the rules again, and since that day, card-counting is permitted in Atlantic City, but the rules are such that, in its basic form, it can never be successful.

Since counting was considered cheating, skilful players had to find a way to continue their battle with the casinos without attracting the attention of eagle-eyed supervisors or, from the 1980s onwards, the all-pervasive eye-in-the-sky (the cameras which watch every move, every chip, every card, in most big casinos). They came up with a simple, but brilliant solution: counting teams.

In this format, a group of, say, six players entered a casino. Five started playing minimum-stake Blackjack, never altering the size of their bets, but carefully counting the ratio of high and low cards which appeared from the deck or shoe. When the situation became favourable to the player, a secret signal was made and one high-rolling player seemingly randomly wandered over to the table. There, he played a few hands at a very high stake, often winning, and then wandered off looking for another table at which to graze. Because he bet only for high stakes, no one observed any change in bet size; because he wasn't watching the table, he could have no idea (from the casino's point of view) what the count position might be. Card-counting teams, from institutions such as MIT (Massachusetts Institute of Technology) and leading US Colleges claim to have beaten the casinos for millions of dollars. Certainly, they were highly successful before the casinos discovered them.

Next up came a technique so remarkable that you might not believe it if you hadn't seen it for yourself: shuffle tracking. I have played cards all my life, primarily Bridge and Poker, and seen players who have been dealt brilliant cards every hand – card manipulators who have known exactly where a given card lies in the deck. I know that, with skill, there is almost nothing you can't do with a pack of cards. Shuffle tracking just about proves this. You study when key cards appear, such as aces, and you study the cards just before the ace is dealt out. You study the human shuffle (which is not truly random) and then you can work out when an ace card is coming – or a ten, or whatever it is that you wish to track. If you know that an ace is going to appear as the first card on your hand, then you pour on the money: you have a high chance of Blackjack (paying 3–2), and, failing that, an excellent chance of making a big hand. And this is what the card manipulators did. They waited until they knew what cards would appear and manipulated their play to ensure that they got the card just where they wanted it; either on one of their own hands or, more commonly, on the dealer's hand – perhaps busting him, and so winning all their hands. This system could not work perfectly, but it worked often enough that the casino's small edge was completely wiped out, and the players gained a sizable advantage.

What next? Computers had revealed that Blackjack could break the house and now they were used to protect the casino. The eye-in-the-sky systems in place in Vegas casinos today are state-of-the-art. They can compare your play on one day to that on another; they can check your usual bet sizes, your usual style of play. There is face recognition software that can see through complex disguises. If you try to beat the casino at Blackjack by counting or shuffle tracking, the casino will try to spot you. However, if you do not alter the size of your bets dramatically, if you follow the guidance which follows, you will be able to play Blackjack against the house where the casino has no percentage edge against you whatsoever (in fact, you have a tiny statistical advantage) – it will be a genuinely 50–50 gamble. This, on top of benefits and perks, will make Blackjack a highly profitable game for you.

In my own experience, the several count systems I learnt were complex and difficult to apply in casino conditions, as they involved altering your bet size, so that it was virtually inevitable that you would be spotted. With these systems you had to play for high stakes to record much profit because you couldn't stay at the same table for any length of time for fear of being caught out. The methods I now use allow me to play in casinos all over the world, for hours at a time, having a great time. I win a little and lose a little. Over a long period of time, I am ahead. Considering how much I've played, it's not a huge profit, as I've never played for very high stakes. But it is a significant profit – more than enough to have been able to pay for some of life's luxuries, all courtesy of the Vegas casinos.

Words of Warning

The feeling of wanting to beat the casinos is very strong, but don't be tempted to take a computer onto the casino floor. There are plenty of online companies offering miniature gadgets to help you win at Blackjack, Roulette and other games. There are programs for your computer, applications for your iPhone, weird and wonderful devices you strap to your body, wires to wind around your torso and up and down your legs and into your shoes. In Nevada, for example, if you are caught with an electronic device designed to aid your Blackjack skills, you won't just be thrown out of the casino: you'll be thrown into jail for ten years! Other jurisdictions are less draconian, but the penalties are still severe.

One more warning: scam systems. If you gamble online, you will be bombarded with offers from people who can sell you the only system on the planet to win at Roulette, or Blackjack, or to help you to cheat at Poker. These are snake-oil salesmen: they have nothing, because if they really had something that could do these things they would be keeping it to themselves and killing the casinos for millions of dollars. So, please never waste even one dollar on this rubbish. Incidentally, many of the games played in casinos have been around for decades and plenty of brilliant men and women have tried to find cracks in the casinos' immutable house edge. With discipline, and without cheating, the casinos' hold over the players' money can be broken, although it can't be beaten long term.

Before Playing Blackjack

Take some time to observe the casino and run a few checks on the type of Blackjack games that are being offered. These are the key elements to look out for:

- Check the minimum stakes at each table. If the minimum bet is $100 and you try to bet $10, you'll look at bit silly – it's not the best way to start your evening.
- Is the dealer using a shoe, or is there a dealing machine in operation? If it is the former, count systems will work; if there is the latter, they will not. In theory, there is no difference between these two methods of shuffling for the Basic Strategy player – which is what most readers will be.
- Find a table with one or two other people on it. This allows you a bit more time to settle down and relax, but also means that not everyone is focused on you. Avoid crowded tables, because the game can be very slow and the more betting boxes in use the harder it is to follow the action.
- Pick a stake to match your bankroll. Ideally, you should sit down at a Blackjack table with 40 times the stake you wish to bet. So, if you want to play $10 Blackjack, you should sit down with $400. As an absolute minimum, sit down with 20 times your stake. Don't play with less than this, because Blackjack, like most basically 50–50 games,

is very "streaky" (has stretches of good and bad patches). You could win consistently, but you might lose a lot of bets before you hit a hot streak.

- Does the house pay 3–2 for Blackjack? Some casinos are now offering only 6–5 (for a $10 bet, if you make Blackjack you get your $10 back, plus $12 profit – instead of $15). This is a really bad deal, since it swings over 1 per cent back in the casino's favour. It is also disgusting: Blackjack was invented to pay a decent bonus if you made the magic hand. However, Strip casinos in Las Vegas have discovered that most people don't realize that 6–5 is worse than 3–2. In fact over 40 per cent of people surveyed a couple of years back thought the 6–5 payout was better! The majority of casinos are still paying the 3–2 bonus out correctly, but if the casino you are in offers 6–5 then walk away.

- Does the dealer stand (take no further cards) on "soft 17" (a hand that adds up to 17 and includes an ace – see page 34), or does he have to hit it (take another card)? If the dealer stands on soft 17, which is what you will find at the majority of tables, this is best for you. Note that you, as a player, should never stand on soft 17 – you should always try to improve your hand from it. Since the dealer cannot do this where house rules dictate that the dealer should stand, this favours you. At tables where the dealer hits soft 17, this benefits the house, increasing its edge by approximately 0.2 per cent. However, you may find that there are compensating rules that benefit you, such as the game being a single- or double-deck game (see page 61), or having preferential doubling rules (see page 37). In general, you should look for tables where the dealer stands on any total of 17.

What other player options does the house offer? The most important ones, which will be explained in the pages that follow, are:

- Early surrender
- Double down after splitting
- Soft doubles
- Re-splitting of aces

Some casinos display all their house rules on signs at each table, usually beneath the table minimums and maximums. If you cannot see these rules, go to an empty table and ask the dealer or supervisor there to tell you which rules are in force in the casino. They'll be happy to help you.

Each of these house rules reduces the edge the casino holds against you when you play Blackjack. Many casinos now offer all these rules, plus some others – and to show consistent profits you need to take advantage of them all.

Finally, ask yourself whether you feel confident that you know the Basic Strategy for Blackjack. If necessary, watch others play and revise the main principles (as given on pages 34–47) before risking your own money. To play without knowing the best approach is the best way to lose.

If you are unsure as to whether you know the strategy, test yourself with the questions on page 76. If you get them all correct, go and play – and expect to win. Get any wrong, and you will be giving your money to the casino.

Playing Blackjack

This is what a standard Blackjack table layout will look like. The dealer's shoe, or dealing machine, will be positioned to the far right of the table, with details about rules and betting minimums and maximums on the left. There will usually be seven betting circles or boxes in which to place your bets. Any side-bet opportunities can be placed in additional betting boxes, which will be clearly marked on the layout. If you are uncertain about how and where to place your bets, ask the dealer.

Once you've picked your table, checked the stake, the house rules and your bankroll, sit at the table and place your cash in a position past the betting box towards the dealer. I like to greet the dealer and nod at my table companions, but it's up to you. The dealer will probably ask you in what denomination you would like your chips. It is best to ask for them in the same denomination as the size of bet you want to place. The cash will be pushed through a slot in the table and the dealer will give you your chips.

If there are other players at the table, I usually ask whether they mind if I open a new betting box(es). Sometimes, players have built up a "rhythm" with a certain number of boxes and like to maintain it. There is no scientific reason to do so, but everyone is entitled to their own feelings, and when a player is winning it feels right to leave things as they are. Usually, players won't mind what you do, but sometimes they ask you not to open a box for a while. You can choose to watch the game, place a bet behind theirs on a betting box and let them make the decisions, or just ignore them and do what you want. (If you are going to opt for the latter, don't even ask them about opening new boxes.)

You may have the feeling that you are in league with the other players at the table, against the house, but this is not the case. It is you versus the dealer, and your responsibility must lie with yourself at all times.

To play, you place one or more chips in the betting box in front of you, and await your cards. You can play more than one box if you wish, although if you are new to the game it's better, at least to begin with, to play only one.

Some old-school Las Vegas casinos still deal a "down-game", which means that your cards are flicked towards you face down and you look at them privately and make your own decisions. However, almost every other casino in the world deals an "up-game", which means that the cards are placed next to your bet, face up, and you are not supposed to touch them at all. Moving from the dealer's left to his right, he will ask each player in turn what action he wishes to take on his hand. Finally, he will play his own hand, and make the payouts, or collect your losing bets.

When it comes to telling the dealer what you want to do, you can tell him by speaking clearly: "Hit me" or "Card" if you want another card; "Stand", "No more" or "No card" if you want to stand – you want no further cards. ("Stick" is a Pontoon term, not used in Blackjack.) Or, you can gesture, using traditional signals. A hand, palm down, over your cards, means that you want to stand. A bending finger (a come-hither gesture) or hand stretched towards you means that you want another card. Some casinos like one or the other; many don't mind so long as you make your intentions entirely clear.

Here are some further tips to ensure that you look like a cool, experienced gambler when you sit down at the tables:

- Don't touch the cards in an up-game – the casino may think you are trying to mark the cards for future identification.
- Once you have placed your bet, don't touch your chips until you've been paid out. There is a cheating move called "past-posting", which is where players try to increase or decrease their bet size once the result of the hand is known. Casinos get very up-tight about that kind of thing.
- Don't abuse the dealer if the cards run badly. It's rude and illogical. If you want to get annoyed, curse the cards, the casino, or your own luck. The poor dealer has nothing to do with it.

- Don't start to play badly just because playing correctly has failed to deliver results. Stay calm and in control. There can be long streaks where the cards seem to defy the odds. In a 50–50 game, it is usual to encounter long losing streaks, as well as long winning streaks.
- *Never* increase your bets when you are losing. Occasionally, you may get away with it; more often than not you will simply lose more and more.

Hole Card, or No Hole Card

In American casinos, the dealer always deals himself one card face down, and one card face up, before the players' hands are played out. This hidden card is known as a "hole card" (because it is "in the hole"). If the card showing (the up card) is a ten or an ace, using a tiny mirror, or more commonly now, a laser reader, the dealer will check whether he has dealt himself a Blackjack. If he has, all losing bets are collected and the hand is over. If he has not, you continue to play out the hand in the knowledge that the dealer does not have a Blackjack.

In most other countries, the dealer takes one card which he exposes, but does not take his second card until all the players have finished playing out their hands. This means that you do not know whether the dealer will make Blackjack or not and, if you double down, or split pairs, you lose all the bets you have placed. There is a small statistical advantage to the house in not having a hole card, but it is slight, and if you cannot find a game where the dealer takes a hole card it need not prevent you from playing.

The Dealer's Up Card

Once you can see the dealer's up card, you immediately get a feeling of the way the hand may play out – although strange things can, and frequently do, happen. The best card for the dealer to have, from the player's point of view, is a 5. It is from a 5 that the dealer is most likely to bust (i.e. go over 21 so have to pay out all players still in the hand). Almost as good is a 6 or a 4, and still decent, a 3. This is why, when the dealer holds an up card of 3, 4, 5 or 6 you should not risk taking a card and busting your hand – there is still a good chance that the dealer will bust.

If the dealer shows	Chance that he will bust (per cent)
2	35
3	38
4	40
5	43
6	42
7	26
8	24
9	23
10, J, Q, K	21
A	12

The moment the dealer holds a 7 or better, the chance of him busting falls to roughly one in four. That is why you *must* try to improve your hand – to a total of at least 17 – when the dealer holds a 7 or better.

Overall, the dealer should bust (or "break") on average a little under one time in four (although it always seems much less than that when I am playing!).

Basic Strategy

This is what you *must* know before you play Blackjack ever again. There is clear evidence to show that this is the correct way to play every hand of Blackjack, unless you are following a count system. A simple count system is explained on page 62, together with the few differences in playing strategy that you would adopt with this system.

Hit or Stand Rules

The most important element to the game is what card the dealer is showing in front of him. This will have a considerable impact on how you play your hands. Here are the two most basic and essential rules. Time and again I see players breaking these rules and losing hand after hand.

- If the dealer's card is 7 or more, you must continue taking cards until you have a total of 17 or more.
- If the dealer's card is a 3, 4, 5 or 6, do not risk busting, since there is a decent chance that the dealer will go bust and you will be paid.

The principle on which this is based is simple. On the table in front of you, there are words printed on the baize. "Dealer must stand on 17 and must draw to 16" means that he cannot stop taking cards until he has at least 17, at which point he will stop. Assume that the dealer will take a ten as his next card, and examine his position.

If he has a 7, 8, 9 or ten, his next card will give him a "made hand", and he will not take any more cards. If you have not continued trying to make a hand totalling 17 or more, you will lose.

On the other hand, if he is showing a 3, 4, 5 or 6, and he then takes a ten, he cannot stop at that point. He must take another card. If this second card is also high, he will make a total exceeding 21 and go bust. All players still in the hand will therefore get paid.

You may notice that there is no mention of the 2. This is a dangerous card for the dealer to hold from the point of view of the player, roughly on a par with a 9 (which looks far more threatening). When the dealer is showing a 2, follow this rule:

- If the dealer shows a 2, continue taking cards until you reach 14. With a total of 14 or higher, stand, and hope that the dealer busts.

This action is necessary because the chance of you busting by taking a card when your hand totals 14 or more is greater than that of the dealer busting from his 2.

In some situations, it may not be clear what to do. For example, the dealer shows a 6, and you hold a total of 12. Do you take a card, or do you stand?

Following the second rule, you should stand on 12, declining to take another card. This is because, since the dealer holds a 6, he is quite likely to bust when he takes further cards. You should not risk busting first. Remember that you always have to play your hand out first before the dealer. If you bust and he busts, he wins, because you lost your money before the dealer played his hand. This is the big house edge.

- From your (the player's) point of view, the dealer's best cards are: 3, 4, 5 and 6, since these are the cards from which the dealer is most likely to bust. In fact, the 5 is statistically the best card for the dealer to hold from your point of view, since if he holds a 6, he can pull an ace to make 17. From a 5, he is most likely to bust.

- From your (the player's) point of view, the dealer's worst cards are: 9, 10, J, Q, K and ace, since these are the cards from which, if he draws a ten card, he will make a better than an average hand, which is likely to beat yours.

- 7 and 8 are neutral cards for the dealer to hold, but are still likely to yield totals of 17 or more.

- The average Blackjack hand is 18.3. This means that if you were dealt 17 or 18 every single hand, you would still lose in the long run, which is why you must know the Basic Strategy and play with more skill than the casino is bargaining for.

These are the first few rules of the Basic Strategy. Following these rules reduces the house's edge massively, yet the vast majority of Blackjack players fail to apply them. It is hard to believe that people are willing to risk their money while not knowing the most basic rules of proper play.

Soft Totals

Here are the next Basic Strategy Hit or Stand rules, and these are pretty straightforward too. They concern what we call "soft hands" – those hands which contain an ace. Because an ace can count as either 1 or 11, this often gives you two chances to improve your hand, rather than just one.

- If you hold A2 (i.e. an ace and a 2), A3, A4 or A5, just assume that the ace is worth one and continue to hit (take more) cards until you make a hard total of 17 or better.

- If you hold A6, although this is worth 17, you have extra chances to improve your hand and you should always hit this hand (take another card). Continue to take cards until you make a hard total of 17 or more.
- If you hold A7, this is worth 8 or 18. 18 sounds really good, but if the dealer is showing a 9 or a 10 the chances are that your 18 will lose the hand. For this reason (only if the dealer is showing 9 or a 10), you should ask for a card and continue hitting until you make 17 or better. You may only make 17; you may even bust. However, since you are odds against winning the hand with 18 versus the dealer's 9 or 10, you are making the correct play. Expect everyone at the table to express surprise as many people don't understand this rule.
- If you hold A8 or A9, you have 19 or 20, and these are decent totals on which to stand. It is way against the odds that you can improve your total, and you would be mad to try.

Doubling Down – Hard Hands

A "hard hand" is a hand that does not contain an ace. Most casinos permit you to double your bet after the first two cards, and receive one further card on your hand. This is very good news if you time your doubling down wisely.

The best times to double down are when you hold a total of 9, 10 or 11 with your first two cards and you hope that you will receive a ten card on top of this to make a really strong total. At the same time, ideally the dealer should have a poor card showing, such as a 3, 4, 5 or 6. This doubles your chances of success since, even if you do not receive the high card you were hoping for, the dealer may still go bust.

To double, you place a bet equivalent to your original bet next to, or sometimes behind, your original bet and say "Double". The dealer will now give you one – and only one – further card.

It is very important that you double down at the right moments, and avoid any "sucker bets" (i.e. foolish bets) which the dealer may try to offer you. All dealers are trained to offer you the chance to double down at any time, but you must turn them down, except in the following beneficial situations:

- If you hold a total of 11, double down against any dealer card except ace.*
- If you hold a total of 10, double down if the dealer shows 2, 3, 4, 5, 6, 7, 8, 9.
- If you hold a total of 9, double down if the dealer shows 3, 4, 5, 6.

    * If the dealer deals himself a hole card, checks it, and does not have a Blackjack, you should double down against *all* dealer cards, including the ace.

These rules are logical. With 11 in your hand, you hope that you will score a 10 and make 21. If this occurs you cannot lose the hand, and you will almost certainly win it. If you hit a 9 or an 8, you still have a good chance of winning. If you draw a lower card, there is still a small chance that the dealer will bust and you will win.

With 10 in your hand, you hope for a ten card. In this instance, you double down when the dealer holds a card which, if he draws a ten, will not beat your hand. Do not double down with 10 against a dealer who is showing a ten card or an ace himself.

With 9, the double down only becomes worthwhile if the dealer is showing a card from which he is likely to bust. Even if you take a 10, your total of 19 is not impregnable, and you may still lose. However, since you are doubling down only when the dealer has his worst possible cards showing – 3, 4, 5 and 6 – there is a good chance that he will bust.

A common trap to avoid is doubling down on 9 when the dealer shows either a 2 (which, as explained earlier, is a strong card for the dealer, roughly equivalent to a 9) or when the dealer holds 7 or 8. This looks tempting but if you do not receive a 10 you are odds-on to lose the hand.

That's all there is to doubling down. Anyone interested in playing Blackjack should be able to learn these rules in two minutes flat. You can cut out the chart on pages 79–80 as a reminder, or write the rules down on the back of a piece of card, or on your hand. Casinos rarely mind players bringing in an aide-memoire.

Doubling Down – Soft Hands

A "soft hand" is a hand that contains an ace. It has two values: for example, A6 counts as either 7 or 17, depending upon whether you use the ace as a 1 or as an 11.

Doubling with these hands provides a small edge for the player, but it is not nearly as important as the doubles of hard hands. If your game is running badly, or you are not confident about on which hands you should double, it would not cost you much to ignore this section. However, to get the best out of your skill, you should have these bets as part of your artillery.

- If you hold A2, A3, A4, A5, double down if dealer holds 4, 5 or 6.
- If you hold A6 or A7, double down if dealer holds 3, 4, 5 or 6.

Do not double on any other soft total. Stand or hit depending on your total and the dealer's up card.

Notice that you are doubling your bet when the dealer is holding his worst possible cards. In the case of A2, A3, A4 and A5, you put more money down when you hope that the dealer will bust. With A6 and A7, you have a good enough total to have two decent chances yourself; you may either receive a 10, which will maintain the value of your hand, or a very low card, improving your hand. Whatever happens, because the dealer is showing a low card, you still have the chance that he will bust himself.

Splitting Pairs

When you see Blackjack in the movies or on television, the hero always splits a pair of cards and makes two winning hands with them. In reality, the split is usually used to avoid losing the hand by winning one of the split hands and losing the other, thereby making a stand-off between player and dealer. Once again, correct use of this strategy will result in smaller losses and bigger profits for the player.

Almost all casinos now allow you to double down on split hands as well, and this can provide a fantastic opportunity to forge ahead.

- If you have two cards of the same value, you may opt to split those cards into two separate hands, and play each of them individually. Some casinos allow any two ten cards, whether they are 10s, jacks, queens or kings, to be split. Since you should *never* split tens, this is of no interest to you.

To split, you gesture split, or say "Split", and place a bet equal to your original bet next to it. Do not touch your cards, or your original bet – this may upset the casino if they think you are either marking the cards somehow, or changing your original bet size. The dealer then divides your two cards, and begins playing each hand. Some casinos get their dealers to deal a second card to each hand and then play them out one by one; others deal a second card just to the first split hand, and only when you have completed playing the hand do they then deal to the second split hand. It makes no difference which they do.

   You will only want to split when the split hand offers a better chance of making decent totals than the first two cards you have received. Otherwise, play normally. These are the times it is proven to be correct to split:

Your hand	Split if dealer shows
22	2, 3, 4, 5, 6 or 7
33	2, 3, 4, 5, 6 or 7
44	5 or 6
55	Never split
66	3, 4, 5 or 6
77	2, 3, 4, 5, 6 or 7

cont...

Your hand	Split if dealer shows
88	Always split *
99	3, 4, 5, 6, 8 or 9
10 10	Never split
AA	Always split **

* Unless surrender against 9, 10 or ace.

** Do not split AA if you are playing a no hole-card game and the dealer shows an ace. You could make 21 on both your hands and still lose to a dealer's Blackjack. However, when there is a hole card, the dealer will start by checking if he has a Blackjack and, if he has not, then you must definitely split your aces.

If you split, say, two 7s and on the first split hand, another 7 appears, then you must split again. If it was the correct strategy to split the first time, then it is the correct strategy to split again. Most casinos allow you to split as many times as you wish, whereas some limit you to one or more splits. My personal record is splitting 9s seven times. Not only that, I doubled down on two of the hands, making a total of nine bets placed on the one hand. The dealer busted, and I moved firmly into profit for that session.

If, on your split hands, you make a total of 9, 10 or 11, most casinos then give you the opportunity to double down. Take up the opportunity whenever it is the correct time to do this. Double downs and splits are the best possible positions for the player, where you can make serious money with the odds in your favour – a rare situation to find in a casino.

Let's take a quick look at why each of these split decisions is logical:

22   4 is a lousy total to hit, whereas 2 is reasonably strong. When the dealer holds a bad, or a medium, hole card (2 through to 7) this makes the split a sound move.

33   6 is an even lousier total, whereas 3 is okay. When the dealer holds a bad, or a medium, hole card (2 through to 7) this makes the split sensible.

44   8 is a decent total, but if the dealer is showing a 5 or 6 – the two cards from which he is most likely to bust – this is a good time to get more money into your betting box. If the casino does not permit a double down after splitting, you are better simply to hit your 8 and hope to make 18 and win the hand. However, if you receive a 5, 6 or 7 on your 4, you then have a double-down opportunity at the best possible moment, and you have a chance to win a big hand.

55   10 is an excellent total. Against all but a dealer's 10 or ace, you should be doubling down, not splitting.

66   12 is a pretty feeble total, but then two hands starting with 6 are fairly awful too. However, if the dealer is showing his four worst cards (3, 4, 5 or 6), then it is worth splitting to try to make at least one strong total. This is a loss-reduction exercise.

77   14 is a horrible total and 7 is not a bad one to start with. All dealer cards matching lower than 7 make the split a good idea and put you ahead of the dealer.

88   16 is the worst possible total; two hands starting with 8 are not bad. Your aim here is modest. You would like to win one hand and lose the other to break even.

99   This is the only slightly strange one. You shouldn't split against a dealer's 2 because 18 is a decent total and, even if you made two 19s, the 2 for a dealer is a threatening card and he might make 20 or 21 and beat both your hands. Against a 7 in the dealer's hand, you hope that your 18 is enough to win the hand. You shouldn't split against a dealer showing a ten, since you might convert one losing hand into two losing hands.

10 10   20 is a great total and you would be mad to split these cards. Although many players do, and sometimes it works, in most cases it is equivalent to handing wads of your cash to the casino. The casino would love you to split, but our strategy is simple: anything they want us to do, we do the opposite.

AA   This is a special one. You only receive one card on each ace and, if you make Blackjack, it only counts as 21 – you do not get the 3–2 bonus payment because it is not based on the original two cards of your hand. Nonetheless, always split aces, unless you are playing in a no hole-card game and the dealer is showing an ace – in which case, just hit until you make 17 or better.

Hopefully, all these explanations will seem logical to you. If they do, then you will find it easier to remember the rules. You will find charts illustrating all these rules on pages 79–80. You can take them with you to the casino, or use them to help you learn the rules.

Surrender

Many casinos now offer the players an opportunity to surrender their hands after they have been dealt their first two cards and seen the dealer's up card. This is a benefit to the player who uses this facility correctly.

Most casinos do not permit surrender against an ace in the dealer's hand, although some permit surrender if the dealer takes a hole card and checks that they do not hold Blackjack.

Ask the dealer if you are uncertain which rules are in force.

If you decide to surrender, indicate this by announcing "Surrender" when the dealer offers all the players this option, before he starts to play out the first of the players' hands. You must take surrender at this point; you cannot wait until it is your turn to play your hand before taking surrender.

The dealer will take your hand out of play, and take half your bet, returning the other half to you. You play no further part in this "coup", or hand.

You should take advantage of surrender only when it is statistically correct to do so, unless you are counting (see page 62). The casino offers this benefit for one simple reason only: more players misuse it, adding to the casino's profits, than utilize it properly.

- If you hold a two-card total of 15 or 16, and the dealer shows a 9 or a ten card, this is the correct time to surrender.
- If you hold a two-card total of 15 or 16, and the dealer shows an ace, check if surrender is available and, if it is, grab it!

It is not correct to surrender at any other time.

Late Surrender

This is available in very few casinos and offers you the chance to surrender at any time against the dealer. It is a great advantage. Wait until you play your hand to announce that you wish to surrender. You may do this after two cards, three cards, or even four cards have been dealt to you. Follow the advice given above for the only times it is correct to surrender.

Insurance

Emblazoned across the baize in front of you, in block capitals, are the words: "Insurance pays 2 to 1". The reason why it is advertised so heavily is because insurance is a bet the casinos would love you to take. This is what it is about:

If the dealer's up card is an ace, you can place a bet – equal to half your original bet – that the dealer has made, or will make, Blackjack. If he does, you win 2–1 on your money, meaning that you get back your insurance bet and your original bet and end the hand even. If the dealer does not make Blackjack, you lose the insurance bet and continue to play the hand with your original stake.

The moment a casino's up card is an ace, the dealer will bellow "Insurance?" and look you firmly in the eye. When you have made a Blackjack yourself, they may offer you "Even Money", which means that before the dealer discovers whether or not he has, or will make, Blackjack, you can take a 1–1 payment on your Blackjack and get out of the hand. Alternatively, you can reject this offer and wait to see what happens. If the dealer does then make Blackjack, the hand is a stand-off for you because it is a tie, or "push" (in all cases where the hand is a tie, the player's money remains in the betting circle); if the dealer doesn't make Blackjack, you get paid properly at 3–2. What should you do?

Never take insurance.

Is that clear enough? If you are an expert card counter, taking insurance is almost never the right move (see page 70 for one exception). If you aren't counting cards it is *never* going to be right in the long run to take insurance.

Even if they call it "Even Money"– *do not take it*.

It is very important that you realize exactly what this bet is. It has nothing to do with the Blackjack hand that has been dealt. It is a side bet, an irrelevance. You are simply betting on whether the dealer has, or will draw, a ten to go with his ace and make Blackjack. This bet is popular with the casinos because it has a built-in edge of 8 per cent to the house. *Eight per cent!* Compare this with the house edge of less than 1 per cent against you in a game of Blackjack and you will understand why insurance is a nonsense.

Of course, sometimes you'll wish you'd taken it. However, since you have no idea whether the dealer will make Blackjack or not, just trust the figures. It is a rotten bet. Give your money to charity instead.

In general, my advice is follow this rule: anything the casino wants you to do, you should do the opposite. The louder they advertise something, the better it will be for them, and the worse for you.

Side Bets

Why do you think the casino is offering side bets? They do it, not to give you a chance to win, but for more player action; to offer a game that is worse odds for you and take your mind off one of the games which, if played skilfully, can lead to profits for you, session after session.

Let's look at some of the more popular side-bet games on offer to the Blackjack player. Just remember: like insurance, these have nothing whatsoever to do with Blackjack – they are completely separate bets. Their only saving grace is that most casinos allow you to place minimum bets, often as little as $1. However, these dollars soon add up, and they add to the casino's profits, year after year.

Under or Over 13

This is a bet which allows you to guess whether your first two cards will total more or less than 13. An ace is always counted as 1 in this bet (not as 1 or 11 as is usually the case), so a Blackjack is 11. If you bet on lower than 13, you get paid a bonus for two aces, usually 7–1.

Sounds like a 50–50 game? Crucially, if the hand total is exactly 13, both bets lose. And that's where the house makes its edge – a thumping big 6.5 per cent.

If you are an experienced card counter and you find this option at a casino, then by all means use your great skills to punish the casino. For the rest of us, forget it.

Perfect Pair

This is a bet that is becoming very popular at Blackjack tables. You bet that your first two cards will be a pair. The payouts will vary from casino to casino, but the standard format is as follows:

Mixed pair	5–1
Same colour pair	12–1
Perfect pair (same suit)	30–1

Considering that you are playing a game which is, basically, even money, these payouts sound very attractive. The dealers will enthusiastically ask you whether you want to place this bet every time, since it pays 7 per cent and upwards to the house – once again, a bet that is best avoided.

Five-Card Trick

This is now only rarely offered. A bonus is paid if you create a hand containing five cards which does not bust. It is more usually offered as part of the game, requiring no extra bet from the player. The inducement of a payout may encourage you to hit your hand when you really should stand. You must judge whether it is more important for you to win your Blackjack hand, or whether you wish to go for the bonus. If in doubt, play the Blackjack hand correctly, and ignore the bonus.

The reason why casinos offer this bet is to persuade you not to split low pairs, like 22 or 33, or not to split aces, in an attempt to make the five-card trick. Anything that stops you from playing correctly is to the casino's benefit and should be ignored.

Magic 7s

This is offered at casinos all over the world. You are betting on your first card being a 7, on your second card being a 7, and then, for the jackpot wins, for your third card also being a 7. If you make three 7s of the same suit, you win the jackpot, which is usually, although not always, an accumulating "Progressive Jackpot" (i.e. a jackpot that continues to rise by tiny increments while people are playing the game, until a player wins the jackpot, or part of the jackpot). The odds vary, but here are the usual payouts and why it is such a bad game for the player.

One 7	5–1
Two 7s	50–1
Three mixed 7s	5,000–1
Three 7s, same colour	10,000–1
Three 7s, all same suit	15,000–1 or Progressive Jackpot

Let's go through this quickly, taking basic figures, to illustrate why this is such a bad deal for the player.

- The chance of your first card being a 7 is 1/13 – you are offered 5–1.
- The chance of your first two cards being 77 is roughly 1/139 – you are offered 50–1.
- The chance of having three same suit 7s is, roughly 1/139,000 – you are offered 15,000–1.

These pay-outs are appalling, giving a massive edge to the house, well in excess of 10 per cent and much higher without the cumulative jackpot. Unless the Progressive Jackpot is at least 100,000 times the stake, don't even think of playing the game. Ignore it and concentrate on your Blackjack.

Tipping

This can be far more than just a courtesy; it can benefit you in many ways. The bottom line is that most casino staff are poorly paid and many rely on customer tips to supplement their wages. This is especially true in Vegas and the rest of the United States, where there is an ingrained tipping culture.

Dealing with the public is not easy, and the job is made harder because the vast majority of punters are losing (often through their own mistakes). Usually, they will blame the dealer, or the casino, or their fellow players. Being a dealer is a very tough job indeed and so if the dealer is friendly and welcoming I am usually happy to tip him or her as the session proceeds. If you are losing, the dealer won't really expect a tip, but if you are winning a tip is very much in order.

The best way to tip casino staff is to place a bet for them right next to your own bet. Most casinos allow you to bet below the table minimum when you are betting for the dealer, and that is usually what you should do. If I am playing $25 Blackjack, and I want to tip the dealer, I will place a $5 chip next to my bet, which counts for this hand. If the hand demands a double down, I will usually double down for the dealer too. If I lose the hand, the dealer loses their tip; if I win the hand, the dealer wins double the tip (or even 3–2). Most dealers like this method of tipping because they love gambling (some get off shift and go straight to the tables to play). It also involves the dealer in your fate, and that is no bad thing.

When the bet wins, gesture to the dealer to take the bet tip. He will tap on the table and put it into a tip box or into his apron.

Obviously, if your dealer is unfriendly and grumpy, don't tip.

I continue to tip while I am doing well, even sometimes by just betting $1 – anything to show that I am interacting with the dealer. After all, he is doing his job and it is nice to acknowledge him. There are now thousands of Blackjack machines in casinos the world over – you don't have to talk to anybody; you don't have to tip anybody. But, for me, Blackjack is a social game.

Tipping can benefit you in many different ways:

- If you make a mistake and call for a card when you meant to stand, or vice versa, when you try to correct it the dealer will call for the supervisor. If the dealer likes you, he will defend you and say it was an honest mistake; if he doesn't, he'll stay quiet and the ruling will probably go against you.
- If you forget to double down, the dealer who likes you will remind you; the dealer who doesn't won't.
- You are being rated for your play (see pages 474– 480). If the supervisor has been busy, he may ask the dealer how long you have been playing and for what stake. A dealer who likes you will be generous with his estimate of your play and the size of the stake; one that doesn't won't be so positive. This can make a big difference to the number of perks you receive at the end of a session.
- Happy dealers seem to be able to attract cocktail waitresses effortlessly; unhappy ones seem to lose the knack and your beer never arrives.
- You feel like a meal at the casino. You ask the supervisor for a line pass and free buffet, and he looks at your play record. Although dealers have no official influence, it is not uncommon for them to say: "Yes, have a little break, and then come back to my table. We'll look after you." Sometimes the supervisor will offer you dinner. Now, that's nice.

Here's a little story from Las Vegas a few years back. I doubt that it would happen now, but it might. It harks back to the good old, bad old days of Vegas, when the town was a lot more edgy and dangerous and exciting than it is today.

I was in town with a Canadian friend of mine, by the name of Russell. We had been playing Blackjack on the Strip for some time and we decided to go downtown to Glitter Gulch (or Freemont Street, as it is now) to sample the down-home gambling, with less tourists and more of the locals. Although it has now been jazzed up, this area is still well worth a visit as it retains a little of the old Vegas atmosphere.

We walked into Binions Horseshoe Casino, the original home of the World Series of Poker, and scoped out the Blackjack tables. They still dealt single-deck hand-held games then, and Russell had never played old-style Blackjack before. Eventually, we sat down at a table with two elderly American men and threw down some money. I managed to elicit a weak smile from the elderly lady dealer with my cheerful banter. As the game progressed, it became clear that the two Americans were the rudest pair of grumpy old codgers I could remember meeting. They played badly, and they moaned about their luck. They moaned at the dealer, and they moaned at us. We weren't worried because we had started by winning, and continued to do well. We both tipped the dealer, placing little bets for her, and she kept winning.

An hour later, the two Americans got up and left the table, and we started to chat with the dealer. She told us that she had been dealing to them for six hours, with the occasional break, and they hadn't stopped moaning from the moment they had arrived. They had frightened away other players and hadn't given her a single tip. We chatted some more and continued playing. I cracked a few jokes and she began to relax with us. After a few minutes, I noticed two remarkable things. Firstly, the dealer was dealing until almost the last cards of her single deck: this gives counters a big advantage as we can determine the make-up of the remaining cards with reasonable accuracy. Secondly, from time to time, the dealer was flashing us the top card off the deck with a flick of her wrist. The advantage of knowing the next card is enormous and we could adjust our bets and plays accordingly. I tipped a bit bigger, and so did Russell.

"I'm off home in half an hour", she told us. The message was clear: make hay while the sun shines. Between us, we won a lot of money and the dealer made plenty from us in tips. Everyone went home happy.

So, quite apart from the fact that I believe in trying to be courteous and friendly to dealers, sometimes a little generosity can be rewarded many times over.

Dealer Advice

This is very important. Dealers, supervisors and pit bosses have been known to offer advice to players, either because they are asked, or because they see a player is uncertain what to do. But I must caution you: the advice offered is usually wrong!

I find it incredible that a person could deal a game like Blackjack, for eight hours a day, every working week, and not pick up the plays that work and those which fail. If I were a dealer I would research the game in its entirety to ensure I knew every last aspect of it. But, sadly, this is not the case with many dealers. Here are some of the key pieces of advice I have heard: they are *all* wrong!

- "If you hold a Blackjack and the dealer shows an ace, you should always take Insurance." **Wrong!** The insurance bet has nothing to do with what you hold, it is a simple bet on whether the dealer holds a ten card with his ace. It is a bet which offers 8 per cent to the house and should be avoided. *Never take insurance!*

- "If you hold A7, that is a great total of 18; why hit it?" **Wrong!** If the dealer is showing a 9 or a 10, you should hit this hand, because 18 is unlikely to be enough to beat his total.

- "If you play exactly like the casino does, it is an even-money game." **Wrong!** If you matched the casino and hit every hand until you had 17, regardless of what card the dealer was showing you, you would be offering the casino over a 10 per cent edge – and that is massive. You would hardly ever win, and your losses would be astronomical.

- "If you hold 15 or 16 on the final box before the dealer takes his second card, you should stand, because if you hit a 5 or a 6, you will wish the dealer had taken that card instead." **Wrong!** This is one of the biggest myths associated with Blackjack. I have heard it repeated all over the world. It is nonsense, and you must reject it wholeheartedly. Just because you make a decent hand doesn't make it any more likely that the dealer will make a winning or a losing hand. You have no idea what the next cards are and there could be two 5s in a row, in which case, if you stood on 15 or 16, you would give the dealer 20, and you would lose your hand.

Incidentally, you are not playing as a team against the
dealer: your job is to make the best hand possible for
yourself. You have no idea what will happen to the
dealer, so don't waste any time thinking about it.

- "The average hand for the house is 17." **Wrong!** The
  average hand for the house is 18.3. You must try to
  play correctly to overcome this frightening statistic.

- "Eight little cards have come out in a row, the next
  card must be a ten." **Wrong!** In a standard six-deck
  shoe, just because a series of little cards have appeared,
  the chances of the next card being a ten are only a
  minuscule better than if the previous eight cards had
  been a mix of high and low cards. The chance is so
  minuscule as to be statistically unimportant. You
  cannot tell what the next card will be from looking
  at the preceding cards.

You can see how easy it is to be influenced by the rubbish
spoken at the Blackjack table. And, by the way, the dealers
are far from being the only sources of gross misinformation.
The other players at your table will tell you the most
amazing gobbledygook and present it as hard fact. Once you
know the game you'll learn to ignore it. Don't bother to
argue the point: how they play makes no difference to you.
You will just know that your way is statistically, scientifically
proven to be correct and their's isn't. I just smile at them.

Betting Patterns

In the long run, it will make no difference to your results if
you bet one chip per hand, every hand, or whether you vary

your bet from one chip to ten chips. You are equally likely to win or lose when you make a little bet as you are when you make a big bet. Unless you are tracking the cards, varying your bet is simply for your own entertainment.

However, there are good reasons to vary your bet, from the protection of your bankroll to the stemming of losses during a particular session, to the acceleration of profits.

The biggest mistake I see players make when varying their bets is to increase the bet size having just lost the previous hand. This chasing of losses is doomed to failure in the long run because, eventually, a bad streak will outlast your bankroll and you will leave broke. I've seen it happen so many times, and I don't understand it. Your job, as a semi-serious player, is to maximize your profits from the good times and to minimize your losses during the bad times. There is a simple way to achieve this and that is with wise money management.

As mentioned earlier, Blackjack is a very streaky game. You may suffer long periods of the dealer turning dreadful hands into 21, or simply dealing himself all the Blackjacks and you none. At other times, the player(s) can hit a hot streak, when the dealer busts repeatedly, deals out strong "pat hands" (i.e. those which do not need any play, and on which you can stand pat: 18, 19, 20 and 21) over and over again, and produces big, fat ten cards every time you double down. The key is to be betting small during the first period and big during the second period.

Playing Basic Strategy, my money management plan is simple. When I win, I increase my bet by a small amount; when I lose, I continue to play my base stake, whatever that might be. So, at a $25 table, I start with $25. If I win, I increase it $35, win again, I might go to $50, and so on. If I hit a hot streak, I bet a little more each time and I benefit from those increased bets.

If I hit a long bad period, I am betting the minimum all the time and so limiting my losses.

Let's look at an eight-hand losing streak. These happen far more often than you might imagine. I lose eight bets in a row at $25, I've lost $200. I win the ninth bet when the streak ends, and I'm down just $175.

If I enjoy an eight-hand winning streak, and I increase my bets as follows: $25, $35, $50, $75, $100, $150, $200, $200, I win $835!

I'm going to lose $200 on the ninth bet when the streak ends, but I've still recorded a win of $635.

Increasing your bet when you win, or "parlaying" (putting the chips you've just won back on the table to increase your bet) is standard play by many gamblers, and the casinos don't bat an eyelid.

Streaks like this don't come along as often as you would like but, when one does, this simple method of bet control ensures the you lose the minimum and win the maximum. When you do hit a hot streak and win a lot of money, that's the time to leave the table, or lock away part of your profits.

If there is a long session of choppy results – the dealer wins, the player wins, the dealer wins – then this strategy is no more or less efficient than betting the same amount every time. But, when you are winning – and that's why you play – it increases your winnings.

This money-management system has served me well for a long time. On the occasions when I hit a really hot streak, I can win a seriously large sum of money. When I next play, I start small again and test the waters.

Bankroll Management at Blackjack

Everyone who visits a casino thinks that they want to win, but they don't really. Many make no effort to win and show no discipline to retain profits. All they want to do is to gamble. And, that's fine. It is certainly fine for the casinos – that's just what they want.

Instead of taking a haphazard approach, why not set yourself some realistic targets. When I play Blackjack, I like to aim to make a 50 per cent profit. When I have played for a while, I assess my chip position. If I find myself 50 per cent in profit, I don't stop (though maybe I should). What I do instead is to lock away half that profit.

Imagine I start with $1,000. After an hour of play, I check my chips and find that I have a total of $1,500 in front of me. I'm enjoying the game and I'm doing reasonably well. Now is the time to lock away some profit, so that I cannot leave the table other than a winner. That is what is required: to want to leave the table a winner – and to have the guts and self-discipline to do it.

I take half the profit and put it to one side. Put the chips in your pocket if you want to, get them changed up to a higher denomination by the dealer – whatever it takes for you to put them out of play. This leaves me $250 of profit with which to play. If I lose that, I leave the table; if I continue to win, I re-assess the position a little later. I cannot leave the table other than as a winner. It is a great feeling.

I have enjoyed evenings in Vegas where all I have done, all night long, is put away profits, continue playing and make more profits. I have put chips in my trouser pockets, my jacket pockets, in my shoes... And I have enjoyed other evenings where I locked away some profit, had some dinner, played my profit afterwards and lost it, but still enjoyed my evening without losing anything. But, you have to have the determination to lock away the profit when you have it.

Stop-Loss and Stop-Win

Some players swear by these methods. A Stop-Loss simply means that once you have lost a pre-determined proportion of your session bankroll, you leave the table. Perhaps you decide that if you lose 50 per cent of your session bankroll, you will seek a new game at a different table. If you stick to this, it can be effective. Statistically, however, you are no more likely to get a better game at another table than you are at the one you are at.

A Stop-Win situation means that once you have reached a pre-determined win, you stop playing and go elsewhere. Again, you are no more likely to find a better game elsewhere. The advantage of the method of locking away some of the profit as already described is that, if you, or the players at your table, are enjoying a prolonged hot streak – and these streaks do happen – then you are staying at the table to benefit from it and not walking away.

If you are counting, then you will not move away from a table that offers you a positive expectation of winning, whatever your Stop-Loss agreement might be in advance. In general, I am in favour of any system that helps players to leave tables with their profits, and to reduce overall losses, so whatever works for you is fine.

Dealing Machines

In the good old days, there were hand-held single- and double-deck games all over Las Vegas. For players who could count cards, these games offered by far the best chance of beating the game and, for a time, the skilful players did. The casinos reacted by introducing dealing shoes, holding four or six decks of cards. This dilutes the effect of the count early on, but is no more difficult to track than a single deck. In Atlantic City, they moved to eight-deck shoes – all in an attempt to thwart the counters. Nowadays, the casinos have the ultimate weapon: dealing machines. Inside a solid plastic gadget, the cards are mixed and dealt. A card that was in a hand a few moments previously can re-appear. It renders counting impossible, and the casinos know it.

Some scientifically-minded characters have devised ways of anticipating the shuffle and the cards which might appear, but even they admit that it's a hit and miss method. The manufacturers tell me that the next generation of dealing machines will have as close to completely random shuffling as it is possible to produce. This is good news for the casinos, and bad news for the skilful, counting Blackjack player.

The better news, however, is that many casinos realize how much all Blackjack players mistrust machines and many retain shoe-dealt Blackjack games. Casino surveillance is so good nowadays that they believe they can spot counters a mile off and warn them away from their Blackjack games. Historically, whenever learned works on card counting have been published, the casinos have seen their Blackjack profits rise (yes, you read that right, *rise!*) because so many people have suddenly believed that that they can beat the game. The truth is that if you count cards you have to be very accurate, have a large bankroll, disguise your actions very carefully, and move from table to table and casino to casino on a regular basis, often many times per session.

Simple, Powerful Count (SPC)

To make a living counting cards at Blackjack is, these days, virtually impossible. I have met a number of card counters who, as late as the 1980s and 1990s, were making a lot of money from Blackjack. All those people have now retired.

However, there is a simple count system which anyone who is determined to win at Blackjack can learn. It turns a game where the house has a small advantage – a touch under 1 per cent over the Basic Strategy player – into a game where the player has a tiny statistical advantage over the house. This advantage is not sufficient to treat the game as anything other than an even-money game, but if you were to play thousands of hours of Blackjack you would expect to make a small profit and not the inevitable losses of those playing against the house edge.

Be aware that although it is 100 per cent legal, honest and fair to count cards at Blackjack, all casinos consider counters to be "cheaters". This is not only ridiculous, but it is also an abuse of the English language. However, most casinos are considered private clubs – even if you can walk straight into them – and so you are at the mercy of the casino's own systems. If a casino suspects you of counting, they will usually, either try to put you off from playing by making the game very slow, or uncomfortable, or they will approach you and tell you not to play Blackjack at their casino. This is not a major problem, but most players would prefer to avoid this.

Let's look at what is involved in SPC, how to apply it successfully, and what you can expect from using it.

Table Choice

Pick your table carefully. Ideally, select a table with one or two other players already playing. Observe them for a few minutes to check that they play Blackjack following Basic Strategy reasonably accurately (you'll be surprised how many mistakes you see people making). Although, statistically, how others play at your table makes no difference to your chances, because of our SPC methods you may need to involve others in your plans and you want them to play decently. Also, there is nothing more frustrating, distracting and upsetting than sitting with players who take ages to make every decision, and then make the wrong decisions, either for themselves or, as it pans out, for you.

Pick a low-stake table, because you want your base bet to be modest. You can always increase your bets, on a scale from 20 times the base bet, right up to several hundred times the base bet.

Where to Sit

I like to sit at one or other end of the table, so that I only need to glance in one direction at the cards on the table. If you sit in the middle, you will look like a spectator at the Wimbledon Tennis Championships and you may draw attention to yourself. Seat one, by the shoe, is probably best, because most counters prefer seat seven, at the opposite end, and this seat is sometimes watched more carefully than the others.

How to Behave

I have seen people trying to track cards moving their lips as they count. This is a bit of a give-away! If you can't count in your head quickly, this is not for you. Relax, watch the cards, and when there is a pause (during shuffles, cash changes, player decisions) chat away merrily with the dealer, the supervisor, the pit boss, the cocktail waitress, and your fellow players. It really isn't tough to keep one figure in your head while you do this. And, remember, if the shoe starts negatively (I'll explain this in a moment), you can switch off for the remainder of that shoe and play minimum stakes with Basic Strategy. While playing, get up from the table, wander around (without looking at other people's hands), and enjoy yourself. In this way, no one will believe that you are tracking the cards.

Counting

Unlike any other casino game, Blackjack dealt out of a shoe is a game which develops during the course of that shoe. The cards that appear on the table will never re-appear for the duration of the shoe. This is completely different from a game like Roulette, where each spin is entirely independent of the previous ones.

When people hear about the principle of card counting, they assume that you have to track every card that is played. Although you are looking at every card, you are not trying to remember what has gone. Instead, you are keeping track of the ratio of high cards that have been dealt, compared to that of low value cards which have appeared. This is because, in general, the more high cards remaining in the shoe, the more favourable the position for the player; the more small cards remaining in the shoe, the less favourable this is for the player.

A vast number of counting methods are available, most of which are more accurate than the one I recommend. However, all are virtually unusable, and contain significant drawbacks. The most important drawback, in my view, is how difficult they are to learn. I can attest to this since I spent months learning several count systems, and I have been playing cards, remembering cards, tracking cards, since I was about 13 years old. On top of this, to remember a difficult count system when you are under pressure in a casino environment is extremely hard. The second downside of all these systems is that they require huge bet variations, sometimes expecting you to multiply your base bet by 20 times! If you did this in a casino you would attract so much attention that you would be expelled from the casino before you had time to draw breath.

So, what I present is a usable, achievable count system which provides a very small advantage to the player. This means that you can enjoy your Blackjack over a long period of time – expecting, over that long period, to record small, but tangible, profits. Bear in mind that even if you play Basic Strategy perfectly, you will still lose more the more you play. But if you use this achievable count system, you will win more the more you play – and when you are receiving player benefits this all adds up to a happy casino experience; a chance to live like a high-roller, even if your actual cash profits are modest.

The easiest way to count the ratio between high and low cards is as follows:

High Cards:	9s, all tens, aces
Low Cards:	2s, 3s, 4s, 5s and 6s
Neutral Cards:	7s and 8s

Every time a high card appears, you subtract 1 from the count total. Every time a low card appears, you add 1 to your total. When 7s and 8s appear, they do not count, since they are considered neutral cards. For example, at a table of four players, the first hand dealt is as follows:

	Dealer		
	[8]68		
Q54	4466	K53	485

There are eleven low cards and two high cards, so the count stands at +9. If this is the first hand from the shoe, this is a good start for the players. The dealer has broken with a total of 22 and you have lost a lot of low cards and won all four hands.

Adjusting the Count for Decks Remaining in Play

If this was a single-deck game, I would increase my bets and anticipate a promising end to the deck. However, if the shoe from which the cards were being dealt contained six decks, the effect of all these low cards appearing in the first hand would be lessened, and the way to allow for this would be to divide the count figure by the number of decks still in play. So, if this was the first hand dealt from the shoe, you would say that there were still six decks in play, and you would divide the count total by six. Nine divided by six equals +1.5. This would be a positive shoe for you, but not to the extent that you should increase your bets or change your playing strategy.

Since casinos place cards which have been dealt into a discard tray, you can estimate how many cards, and therefore decks, have been dealt, and adjust the figure by which you must divide your count as more cards are dealt out.

If casinos dealt all the cards down to the very end, you would have a very accurate idea of the make-up of the final deck. Sadly, casinos cut off the last 1–2 decks as a defence against counters and this, once again, dilutes the effect of the count. So, for example, you might estimate that the remaining three shoes in the deck are very rich in high cards but find that the next 52 cards to be dealt are mainly low. You would then know that the last two decks are *very* favourable to you, but just as you are about to receive all those lovely high cards the dealer produces the cut card and the shoe ends, leaving those high cards undealt, stranded at the end of the shoe.

Cutting the Cards

When the dealer has finished shuffling, a player will be handed a cut card, usually a red plastic card, to insert into the stack of decks. Having done this, the dealer will take the cards on one side of the cut card and place them at the other end of the stack of cards, showing everyone that the player has made the decision as to where to cut. He will then remove the cut card and insert it again, between one and two decks from the end of the stack of cards.

Since it benefits you to have as many cards dealt from the shoe as possible (because your information about the final third of the shoe is far more accurate than from the first third), you should try to induce the dealer to cut off as few cards as possible from the end of the stack. Tipping the dealer may help but, for me, a gentle psychological hint often works well. When you first cut the decks, cut off just a small fraction – maybe half a deck – from the end of the stack. You might even glance up at the dealer while you do it. Your hope will be that, seeing the narrow portion you have cut off when cutting the cards, the dealer will be influenced, when he places the cut card in the stack, to indicate the end of the dealing portion of the shoe. I have found that this works quite well, and I can often induce the dealer to cut off only one deck rather than one and a half or two decks.

Incidentally, in casinos where the dealer still has to shuffle the cards, he will instinctively want to cut off as few cards as possible, whatever casino policy may be, because the more cards he deals from each shoe, the less shuffling he has to do. Most people, given half the chance, would like to work a little less, not more.

Action Count

When the count reaches a score of +8 (i.e. the count, divided by the decks remaining in the shoe) this is the time to change your playing style. There are almost an infinite number of ways to change your playing style, but the purpose of this count method is to keep things simple, and to increase your winnings. Therefore, the most important thing to do, when the count has become markedly favourable to you, is to increase your bet size. As discussed earlier, casinos are suspicious of players who raise their bet size unnaturally, so you must endeavour to achieve this discreetly. Here is the method I recommend:

Firstly, double your bet size on your own betting box and, secondly, place bets of equal size behind those of other players at your table. This is why it is important that you play with people who have some idea of the game. Your money is now under their control. However, as I always tell myself, if they are dealt 19, 20, 21 or Blackjack, there isn't much they can do wrong!

Assuming that you have a total of four betting boxes in play at your table, you have now increased your bet by eight times the base bet, spread over four boxes, attracting no attention from the casino. Win or lose, if the count remains in the range of +8 or greater you can double all your bets again. Within two hands, you have increased your bet by 16 times over the base bet and still no one is likely to take much notice of you. I like to accompany my bet increases by rubbing my hands with glee and announcing that I'm feeling lucky and my horoscope told me that "when I saw two queens of spades…" (or whatever else I think of) "I should bet big…". Anything superstitious, silly and illogical. Casinos are used to looking for quiet, introverted types who are card-counting. I like to make a lot of noise and distract everyone from the matter in hand. For me, this is part of the game.

What you have achieved here is to increase your coverage and bet size by up to 16 times your original bet, when the action is potentially favourable to you. It's simple, effective, and is unlikely to draw adverse attention.

Strategy Changes for Positive Positions

A positive position for you is when the count, divided by the number of decks remaining, is +8 or better. This situation will not occur often, but when it does you can consider altering your play. Basic Strategy during this time would serve you perfectly well, but you can add some extra plays and make some simple changes to enhance your position, as follows:

- **Stand on 12 and 13 against dealer's 2.**
  The dealer is more likely to break from a 2, since there are more high cards outstanding.
- **Double down with 9, against dealer's 2 or 7.**
  You are more likely to make 19 with extra tens available; the dealer is more likely to make either 17 or to bust with the extra ten values.
- **Double down with 8, against dealer's 5 or 6.**
  You are more likely to make 18, and the dealer is more likely to bust.
- **Take surrender with 16 against dealer's 8.**
  There are fewer small cards with which to make you a winning hand; the dealer is less likely to break, and more likely to make 18.
- **If surrender is not available, stand on 16 against dealer's 10.**
  Your best chances of winning the hand are now for the dealer to break. You have about a 20 per cent chance of winning in this situation. This is why surrender is such a valuable benefit to the player who is counting.
- **If the count is +12 or better, and only then, take insurance.**

> The odds now favour you for this bet. Counts of +12
> rarely occur; if they do, break the habit of a lifetime
> and take that insurance bet.

Do not get overexcited when the count is favourable for
you. You are not certain to win, but you are more likely to
win, which is why you are increasing your bet size. The
dealer will also benefit from the higher proportion of high
cards remaining, so when you make 20 on all four of your
hands, and the dealer makes Blackjack, you can only reflect
that you were very unlucky. However, in the long run you
will win more hands when the count is very positive for you
and, if you are betting much more money on those
occasions, you will see your long-term profits increase.

I remember the first time I put my counting skills to use
at the Blackjack tables many years ago in London. After two
hours, I finally found a shoe that got positive and I increased
my bet. I also bet on other people's boxes. The hands came
out as follows:

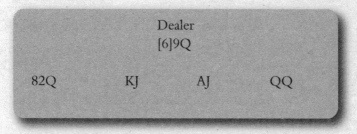

The dealer showed a 6 – the best card for the players. We
doubled down on the final box on a total of ten and received
a big, fat picture card, just as I had expected. Then the dealer
drew a 9 and a queen to bust. From betting one box at a

base bet of £10, I had bet four boxes at £20, and doubled down on one of them. On that single hand, I made 11 times my base bet – £110 – and I thought to myself: this is it, I'm going to get rich!

Well, to get rich at Blackjack, you need to play a great deal, very accurately, at high-stakes and without being discovered. You have to enjoy your fair share of luck, consistently. That's not for me, but I have enjoyed my Blackjack, sometimes losing a little, sometimes winning a lot, ever since.

Strategy Changes for Negative Positions

If you find that the count comes naturally to you, then there are some strategy changes which you can invoke when the count is very negative for you, i.e. the high cards have appeared early, and in high quantity, and your count equates to -8 or worse. During this period, you will be playing minimum stakes at Basic Strategy. However, there are some minor adjustments you can make to increase your chances:

- **Do not double down on 9, except against dealer's 5 or 6.**

  Doubles on 9 against dealer's 3 and 4 are marginal anyway and if there are many low cards outstanding the chances of you making a decent total with one card, or the dealer busting, are both greatly reduced.

- **Hit not only 12 but also 13 and 14 against a dealer's 2.**

  The 2 remains very strong for the dealer, who is unlikely to bust. You must therefore strive to improve your total from the low teens to something better.

With low cards outstanding, you have a better chance to improve your hand than usual.

- **Do not surrender 15 against dealer's 9.**
  With the shoe now rich in low cards you stand a better chance of making a working hand from 15 than losing half your bet from a surrender.

When the shoe ends and the dealer shuffles, take away all your bets, make a show of counting your chips and, if you have recorded a decent profit, lock away some of that profit so you cannot lose it again.

If you play Blackjack like this, you will be a long-term happy gambler. I cannot guarantee you profits, but I can assure you that you will lose less and win more. Together with player benefits and bonuses, you will *definitely* be a winning player in the long-term. I don't know about you, but a holiday to Las Vegas, where your accommodation and food are paid for, and your flight is redeemed by some small profits, sounds good to me. For details of player benefits, see page 474.

Blackjack
Summary of Strategy

Check Out the Tables and the House Rules:

- that a Blackjack pays 3–2 (not 6–5 or some other lower payout).
- whether soft doubles are available.
- whether you can double down after splitting.
- whether the dealer hits soft 17, or stands on soft 17.
- whether surrender is offered.
- whether the game is dealt from a shoe, or from a dealing machine.

Check Yourself That:

- you are in a positive mood, and that you want not just to play, but to win.
- you know Basic Strategy perfectly, so that you will not make any money-wasting mistakes.
- you have a bankroll set aside with which to play ideally 40 times your base stake (a minimum of 20 times your base stake) and that you are totally resolved not to change any more money for chips.
- you have set yourself a profit limit – say 50 per cent – at which point you will set aside your original stake, plus half the profit, which you will not touch – ensuring that you *will* leave the table a winner.
- you take no credit cards with you to the casino.

Revise:

- Basic Strategy, using the questions and the charts on pages 76–80.
- SPC (Simple Powerful Count) so that you can produce an edge in your favour over the long term (see below).

Blackjack Charts

1 Hit or Stand, and Surrenders
2 Hard Doubles
3 Soft Doubles
4 Splitting

Simple Powerful Count

- Establish how many decks are contained in the shoe (usually 4 or 6).
- Pick a seat at the table where you can see all the cards of every player without having to squint to see them. Ideally, pick seat 1, 2, 6 or 7. Count:

9s, all tens, aces	-1 for every card dealt
2s, 3s, 4s, 5s and 6s	+1 for every card dealt
7s and 8s	0 neutral card

Divide your count by the number of decks remaining. When the count, divided by the remaining decks, hits a figure of +8:

- Double your own bet and open two new boxes, or place bets behind existing boxes controlled by other players, and place matching bets on those boxes.
- If you win, parlay each bet (add your winnings to each bet) so that you now have 12 times your base bet in play. Maintain this level while the count stays at +8.
- Alter your strategy as outlined on pages 70–72.

21 Questions
Answer these correctly before you risk your money at the tables

Answer hit, stand, double, split or surrender to each of these questions. You should be fluent in Basic Strategy before risking your money at the tables if you are to reduce the house edge against you to a very beatable 1 per cent. If you answer these questions incorrectly, you are handing over your hard-earned cash to the casino without a fight.

1   You hold Q4; the dealer shows a 3

2   You hold 88, the dealer shows a 7

3   You hold 96; the dealer shows a K

4   You hold 72; the dealer shows an 8

5   You hold A7; the dealer shows a 9

6   You hold A6; the dealer shows a 5

7   You hold J4; the dealer shows a 2

8   You hold Q3; the dealer shows a 4

9   You hold QQ; the dealer shows a 7

10   You hold 99; the dealer shows a 7

11   You hold A8; the dealer shows a 5

12   You hold AJ; the dealer shows an ace;
     do you take insurance?

13   You hold 87; the dealer shows an 8

14   You hold 22; the dealer shows a 2

15   You hold K2; the dealer shows a 2

16   You hold Q6; the dealer shows a K

17   You hold 66; the dealer shows a 6

18   You hold A4; the dealer shows a 5

19   You hold 10 6; the dealer shows a 7

20   You hold A6; the dealer shows a 7

21   You hold J2; the dealer shows a 5

Answers on page 80

Basic Strategy Hit/Stand and Surrender (where permitted)

Player	Dealer shows									
	2	3	4	5	6	7	8	9	10	A
12	H	H	S	S	S	H	H	H	H	H
13	H/S	S	S	S	S	H	H	H	H	H
14	S	S	S	S	S	H	H	H	H	H
15	S	S	S	S	S	H	H	H*	H*	H*
16	S	S	S	S	S	H	H	H*	H*	H*
17	S	S	S	S	S	S	S	S	S	S
18	S	S	S	S	S	S	S	S	S	S
19	S	S	S	S	S	S	S	S	S	S
20	S	S	S	S	S	S	S	S	S	S

*Surrender if available H = Hit S = Stand

Basic Strategy Double Down on Hard Totals

Player	Dealer shows									
	2	3	4	5	6	7	8	9	10	A
9	H	D	D	D	D	H	H	H	H	H
10	D	D	D	D	D	D	D	D	H	H
11	D	D	D	D	D	D	D	D	D	H*

* Double on 11 against an ace, only when dealer has taken hole card and has checked that he does not hold Blackjack
D = Double down H = Hit

Basic Strategy Hit/Stand and Double Down on Soft Totals

Player	Dealer shows									
	2	3	4	5	6	7	8	9	10	A
A2	H	H	D	D	D	H	H	H	H	H
A3	H	H	D	D	D	H	H	H	H	H
A4	H	H	D	D	D	H	H	H	H	H
A5	H	H	D	D	D	H	H	H	H	H
A6	H	D	D	D	D	H	H	H	H	H
A7	S	D	D	D	D	S	S	H	H	H
A8	S	S	S	S	S	S	S	S	S	S
A9	S	S	S	S	S	S	S	S	S	S

H = Hit S = Stand D = Double down

Basic Strategy Pair Splitting

Player	Dealer shows									
	2	3	4	5	6	7	8	9	10	A
22	SP	SP	SP	SP	SP	SP	H	H	H	H
33	SP	SP	SP	SP	SP	SP	H	H	H	H
44	H	H	H	SP	SP	H	H	H	H	H
55	D	D	D	D	D	D	D	D	H	H
66	H	SP	SP	SP	SP	H	H	H	H	H
77	SP	SP	SP	SP	SP	SP	H	H	H	H
88	SP	SP	SP	SP	SP	SP	SP	SP*	SP*	H*
99	S	SP	SP	SP	SP	S	SP	SP	S	S
1010	S	S	S	S	S	S	S	S	S	S
AA	SP	SP	SP	SP	SP	SP	SP	SP	SP	SP**

* Surrender where available
** If no hole card, do not split, just hit
H = Hit S = Stand D = Double down SP = Split

Answers

1   **Stand**. Do not risk busting when the dealer holds a 3, 4, 5 or 6.

2   **Split**. 16 is a lousy hand, but two hands of 8 might produce two winning hands.

3   **Surrender**. If this is not available, hit.

4   **Hit**. Only double down on 9 if the dealer shows a breaking card (3, 4, 5 or 6).

5   **Hit**. As the dealer is likely to make 19, your 18 probably will not win. Try to improve your total.

6   **Double**. The dealer holds a good card for you; double your stake. If soft doubles are not permitted, hit.

7   **Stand**. The dealer is more like to bust, than you are to improve your hand.

8   **Stand**. A 4 is a breaking card for the dealer.

9   **Stand**. *Never* split tens.

10 **Stand**. You have 18, against a likely 17 from the dealer.

11 **Stand**. 19 should be sufficient against the dealer's worst card.

12 **Stand** and no, **don't take insurance**.

13 **Hit**. Do not stand, do not surrender. Your best hope is to play out the hand.

14 **Split**. To hold 4 against a dealer's 2 is poor, but two hands of 2 will provide a better chance of making winning hands and, if the casino permits double downs after splits, you may get the chance to increase your bet size if your split hands total 10 or 11 after their second cards.

15 **Hit**. A 2 is a dangerous card for the dealer. Try to improve your hand.

16 **Surrender**. If surrender is not permitted, hit.

17 **Split**. 12 is a lousy total, whereas you may get double down chances after splitting and make a big score on this deal.

18 **Double**. The 5 is a busting card for the dealer; double your bet. If soft doubles are not permitted, hit.

19 **Hit**. You have barely a 20 per cent chance of the dealer busting; you must try to improve your total.

20 **Hit**. You have a chance to improve your total. You must take it.

21 **Stand**. The dealer holds the card from which he is most likely to break. Do not risk busting yourself.

3
Craps

ALTHOUGH Craps is massively popular in the United States, only a few casinos offer the game elsewhere in the world. This is a great shame because Craps is not only dynamic and exciting, it also offers the informed gambler a really decent shot at beating the casino. If you find yourself on your own in Las Vegas, there is no better way to get invited to a party than to join a busy Craps game. If the house is winning, there is a bond among the losers; when the players are on a hot streak, the atmosphere can be electric, with high-fiving, cheering, screaming, shouting and celebrating. Chips fly all over the place. It is a gambling experience unlike any other, and I recommend it highly.

One of the problems with Craps is that if you don't know the rules it appears impenetrable. In fact, the game itself is simple and, if you know the best way to play, the number of bets about which you need to worry is actually very small. The secret of Craps' appeal is that the table is covered in what look like tempting bets, but which are, in fact, terrible bets – some of the worst in the entire casino. If you avoid these distractions and stick to the Basic Strategy, you can play a game where the house has less than a 1 per cent edge against you, where you can win a lot of money quickly in a great atmosphere and get well rewarded for your play with casino benefits. And, there is one further amazing deal on offer at the dice tables: the chance to place bets where the house has no edge against you whatsoever – genuine "correct-odds" payouts! There is no other chance in a casino to get paid at the correct odds – for both big and small bets. Of course, if you play Craps for long enough, you will slowly lose a small percentage of your bankroll – that is the long-term edge the casino exerts over any game which carries an edge against the player. However, before that happens you may have won yourself a lot of money and you will certainly have enjoyed a fantastic bang for your buck. In terms of sheer excitement, Craps beats the crap out of any other game in the casino!

The Simple Game of Craps

Before looking at a Craps table and describing all the bets, let's see what the game of Craps is all about because, once you know that, you will understand that it is actually a very simple game.

The game involves two dice on a table that is like a sunken pit with groovy rubber-studded walls. The player who throws the dice – and everybody has the option of being the Shooter as the game progresses – must throw them so that they hit the studded walls, since this ensures that the throw is honest and is not being manipulated by the Shooter.

With two dice, the totals that the dice can show vary between 2 and 12. Let's take a quick look at which totals are most likely to occur, since this will form the basis of the game:

Number	Combinations	Ways to roll that number
2	1&1	1
3	1&2 – 2&1	2
4	1&3 – 2&2 – 3&1	3
5	1&4 – 2&3 – 3&2 – 4&1	4
6	1&5 – 2&4 – 3&3 – 4&2 – 5&1	5
7	1&6 – 2&5 – 3&4 – 4&3 – 5&2 – 1&6	6
8	2&6 – 3&5 – 4&4 – 5&3 – 6&2	5
9	3&6 – 4&5 – 5&4 – 6&3	4
10	4&6 – 5&5 – 6&4	3
11	6&5 – 5&6	2
12	6&6	1

You can see that 7 is the easiest number to roll, whereas the extremes, 1 and 12, are the hardest numbers to roll, since they can both be achieved by only one of the 36 possible combinations.

The betting opportunities at Craps break down into two defined areas:

The first is the **Come-Out Roll**. At the start of the game, the Shooter rolls the dice. His intention at this point is to roll a 7 or an 11. If he does this, everyone who has bet with him wins their bets at even money. If the Shooter rolls "Craps" – 2, 3 or 12 – everyone loses their bets. If the Shooter rolls a 4, 5, 6, 8, 9 or 10, then this number becomes "the Point" and the game moves into its second stage. A small white disc is placed on this number on the layout to remind everyone that this is now the key number.

Throwing the Point is the second stage. The Shooter must strive to throw the number which has become the Point, before he throws a 7. If he succeeds in doing this, all the players win – at various beneficial odds. If he rolls a 7 before he repeats "the Point" number, the players lose their wagers.

Incidentally, these bets are known as playing *with* the table. On a Craps table, you can opt to play *against* the table too. In this scenario, in the first instance you are betting that the Shooter will not throw a 7 or 11 – and you want him to roll a 2, 3 or 12. In the second instance, you want the Shooter to throw a 7 before he repeats the Point.

You will find that the vast majority of players decide to bet with the Shooter, since this builds camaraderie between players. However, betting against the table is quite legitimate and offers virtually the same long-term odds.

Those are the two stages of a Craps game, and I hope you can see that there isn't really anything very complicated about the game. What makes it look so complex are the vast number of betting options available. In the James Bond movie *Diamonds Are Forever*, Sean Connery rolls up in Las Vegas and makes straight for the Craps tables. The moment he gets a chance to bet, he instructs the dealers to place a wide array of bets all over the table. Most of these bets are very poor ones and they would normally result in big losses, but Bond, being Bond, manages to win big immediately and end up with the girl.

However, for us mortals there are some simple, statistically correct bets to place, and all the others should be ignored. We'll look at the bets that should be ignored so that you can see why you should not place them. Our strategy will be simple: to reduce the house edge to well below 1 per cent.

Table Layout

Printed on the baize (the colour varies from standard casino green or blue, to psychedelic purples and screaming pinks) is a complex-looking layout of betting boxes and sections, lines and circles. The first thing to appreciate is that, if you are playing at a vast, full-size Craps table, each end is a mirror image of the other: in effect, you have two tables joined in the middle.

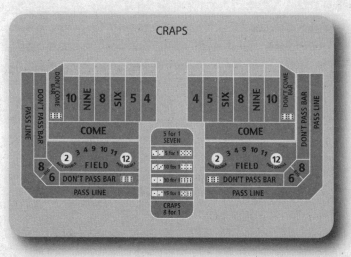

There are more staff manning the tables than you will find at any other game in the casino, which may be one reason why it is not so popular with some casinos. There is a Boxman, who is in charge (unless a big boss comes by) and keeps guard of the massive piles of chips, of many denominations, that are required for the game. He watches not only those chips, but also the other casino staff at the table. He settles disputes and, when the dice leave the table (as they often do during a frantic roll), he checks that the same dice are in play and that no one has substituted loaded dice.

The Stickman, so-called because he holds a stick with which he can push the dice around the table, stands opposite the Boxman. He never touches the dice, but directs them towards the Shooter for the next roll. He also calls out the result of each roll, reminds everyone of the Point number, and controls the "Proposition Bets" (see page 99) in the middle of the table.

Finally, there are two dealers, who stand on either side of the Boxman. They change up cash for chips at the outset, place almost all the players' bets on the layout, and pay each player his winnings. It is a good idea to get to know all the staff, since the Stickman and the dealers often rotate around the table, taking it in turns to perform various tasks. You can ask any of them for advice at any time and, generally, a Craps crew is among the most friendly and entertaining of all casino personnel. Tipping is appreciated and is best performed by placing small bets for the crew. We'll look at that later.

Playing the Game Correctly

During the course of this chapter, we will look at every possible bet on the Craps layout. However, since so many of them are terrible bets, we'll start by running through the only bets you really need to know, so that when you visit a Craps table you will have the very best chance of winning.

Arriving at the table, check the table minimums – they usually start at $3 upwards – and also the opportunities for "Odds Bets". These are the no-edge bets the casino offers and they are the best bets available in the casino (unless you are tracking cards at Blackjack). In Las Vegas, you will see signs advertising "Up To 100X Odds Bets!" – and this is brilliant for the player – but most casinos offer standard Odds Bets of X3, X4 and X5. We'll look at how they work shortly. In London, the casinos only offer X1 Odds Bets, which are not so good.

Assuming that you will bet with the table, once you have your chips I recommend waiting until the dealers tell you that it is a "Come Out Roll". This means that the last Shooter has just rolled a 7 and the game is starting anew. You place your bet – let's say $10 – on the Pass Line in front of you. This bet is for the Come Out Roll. If the Shooter rolls a 7 or 11, you will win even money on your bet (usually, this means that your $10 bet will be left on the layout, and you will have $10 placed next to it by the dealers). It is normal practice to take this profit off and place it with the rest of your chips in the grooved rail in front of you. Guard your chips carefully, because swindlers have been known to slip their hands over your chips during an exciting roll and whip away a few of your chips while you are distracted.

If the Shooter rolls a 2, 3 or 12, there will be a collective groan and you will lose your initial bet. The Come Out Roll will start again, and so you can place another bet on the Pass Line.

If the Shooter rolls a 4, 5, 6, 8, 9 or 10, this becomes the Point and the game enters its second phase. At this stage, you can place your Odds Bets – and you should certainly do this, since your initial bet will only be paid at even money if you/the Shooter makes the Point. For any Odds Bets placed, you will be paid at the correct odds, offering you a genuine chance to beat the house.

In most casinos on the Las Vegas Strip, the standard odds available are as follows:

- If the Point is 4 or 10, you may place up to 3 times your initial bet in an Odds Bet.
- If the Point is 5 or 9, you may place up to 4 times your initial bet in an Odds Bet.
- If the Point is 6 or 8, you may place up to 5 times your initial bet in an Odds Bet.

If you are not sure what you can do, you can always ask the dealers. Whatever you do, take the maximum Odds Bet you are permitted, since these bets will be paid back to you at the statistically correct odds. For example:

- If 4 or 10 is the Point, the chances of rolling that number again, before a 7 is rolled, is 2–1 against. If the Shooter does roll that number, you will be paid 2–1 on your Odds Bet.
- If 5 or 9 is the Point, the chances of rolling that number again, before a 7 is rolled, is 3–2 against. If

the Shooter does roll that number, you will be paid 3–2 on your Odds Bet.
- If 6 or 8 is the Point, the chances of rolling that number again, before a 7 is rolled, is 6–5 against. If the Shooter does roll that number, you will be paid 6–5 on your Odds Bet.

At this stage, if you do not want to place any more bets, you can enjoy watching the Shooter trying to roll the Point number before he rolls a 7 again. He can try as many times as he likes until he either rolls the dreaded 7, or he succeeds. If he fails, you will lose your bets and the table will wail; if he succeeds, you will be paid even money on your initial bet, and the full, correct odds on your Odds Bets. When the Shooter rolls a Point, the table usually explodes in celebration. Be as wild as you like; it is a real chance to let off steam and have some fun.

Once you have placed your Line Bet for the Come Out Roll, you cannot remove it, or increase or decrease it. It is there until it wins or loses. Most other bets, however, can be increased, decreased, or removed after each roll of the dice. This is one of the reasons why a Craps Pit can look so chaotic – there is always lots of action.

Play the Best Odds Always

I am amazed at how often, when I play Craps, no one at the table takes the opportunity to place their full quota of Odds Bets. These are the best bets on the table, the best bets in the entire casino, and people ignore them. Perhaps they don't know that they are the most profitable bets for the player, or maybe they are distracted by all the other bets with higher payouts. I just don't know, but I hate to see players hand over their money to the house without having a fair shot at taking the casino for big bucks.

I have seen players ignore the Odds Bets and cover the table layout with bets, some of which offer the house a 16.67 per cent edge – 16.67 per cent! It's unbelievable. To have any chance of success in a casino you must know the best bets and place them consistently.

Take this example – and this happens regularly at the tables. A player walks up to the table and places $60 on the Pass Line. The Shooter rolls a 6 and this becomes the Point. Now, the player leaves his initial bet and places no odds at all. On the very next roll, the Shooter throws another 6, and the table wins. The player gets paid even money on his $60, and he walks away with $60 profit.

If you had played, what would have happened? You would have placed $10 on the Pass Line and, when the Shooter threw a 6, you would have placed 5X Odds Bet behind your initial bet. When the Shooter rolled another 6, you would have been paid even money on your initial bet ($10) and 6–5 on your Odds Bet ($60). So, you would have walked away with $70 profit. That's $10 more profit just because you knew the correct way to play at the tables – nearly a 20 per cent better payoff! Yet, time and time again I see players ignoring Odds Bets and costing themselves thousands of dollars in profits.

The two bets already discussed, the initial Come Out Roll on the Pass Line, and the Odds Bets which you place behind your initial bet, are bets which you place yourself on the layout. There is one further bet that you can place yourself – a "Come Bet". All the other bets are placed by the dealers: in between rolls, you announce to your dealer what bets you would like to make and he ensures that you give him the correct amounts with which he can place your bets.

Come Bets

A Come Bet is very similar to the original Pass Line Bet, but it occurs only once the Shooter has established a Point. It allows you to place a wager in the big box on the table called the Come Box. Let's say that you place $10 in the Come Box once the Shooter has rolled an 8. On the next roll, if the Shooter rolls a 7 or 11 you win your bet in the Come Box at even money. If he rolls a 2, 3, or 12 – Craps – you lose your Come Bet. If he rolls another number, 4, 5, 6, 8, 9 or 10, your bet gets transferred to the number box in front of each dealer. At this point, you have the option of placing Odds Bets at the same limits as on the original Line Bet and, once again, if you are sensible you will take those Odds Bets since they are the best bets in the casino. You can continue to place Come Bets and then place your Odds Bets as often as you like. My recommendation would be to play your Line Bet and then one or two Come Bets, and then stop. You will now be covering three numbers for big payouts and you don't need to risk any more money. If you win one of those bets, whether it's the Point or one of your Come Bet numbers, you can then make another Come Bet later.

If the number on which you placed your Come Bet is repeated, you will be paid at even money on your original Come Bet and at the correct odds for the Odds Bet. Both your initial bet and your profit will be paid out to you and the bet will be taken off the table.

Some casinos allow you to retain your initial Come Bet on the number which has just been rolled, and stack up your Odds Bet behind it again. This is a good offer and is worth accepting.

I almost never see players taking Come Bets and then placing full odds behind them. Instead, once the Point is established, they scatter chips all over the layout. This is simply terrible play. Once again, if the Shooter rolls the number on which you have made a Come Bet, you will be paid at the correct odds on your Odds Bet; the players who have placed their bets without using the Come Box will get paid at incorrect odds, offering the casino anything from a 1.5 per cent edge on 6 and 8, 1.52 per cent on 5 and 9, and a massive 6.67 per cent on 4 and 10. Why would they do that? I guess, because they don't know the best bets. Would you really want to risk a lot of money at a game where you don't even know the best odds?

Money Off on Come Out Roll

There is one further key situation which you should know about when you are playing the best strategy for Craps. When the Shooter makes the Point, and everyone at the table celebrates, the game starts anew. At this moment, there will be another Come-Out Roll. You must now choose whether to leave your Come Bets, and the Odds Bets that you placed with them, in play, or "off"?

If you leave these bets in play and the Shooter rolls a 7 you will lose all your bets, and the Odds Bets with them. If, however, you call for them to be "off", the dealer will mark your bets as off, and if the Shooter then rolls a 7 you will lose only your original bets; the Odds Bets will be returned to you.

There is no particular reason to opt for one decision or the other but since, on a Come-Out Roll, you are hoping that the Shooter rolls a 7, I would recommend calling for your existing bets to be "off". That way, you can celebrate with the rest of the table if the Shooter does roll a 7 during the Come-Out phase of the game.

Generally, dealers will ask players whether they want their bets left in play, or out of play (off), whenever this situation occurs. Bear in mind that no one will mind if you ask questions or need help at the table – everyone has to learn the game somehow. Armed with the information in this book, you will not only have a head start, but you will be playing the optimum strategy from the outset. Just don't be surprised if you find that you are the only person who knows it!

To Shoot, or Not To Shoot?

Do you want to be the Shooter? At a Craps table, the role of Shooter is offered to players in a clockwise direction. When you establish a Point and you fail to make it, rolling a 7 first, you lose the dice and they are offered to the next player. Most people who bet against the table (or the "wrong way", as it is often called) reject the dice. Many people who are shy also turn down the offer to be the Shooter. However, it is Vegas lore that if a lady who has never played dice before is given the chance to shoot – especially if she has no idea what she is doing – she will roll brilliantly and bring the table the dreamed-for hot streak.

In Vegas, it is not unusual to see brides – in full white flowing dresses, their veils swept back over their heads – shooting Craps with their newly-wed husbands. Of course, in Vegas nothing should really surprise you. I have played Craps at a table with 11 Elvis impersonators, and I have also played Craps at six in the morning with Hollywood actress Halle Berry, just as the foyer of the hotel filled up with a Harley Davidson bikers' convention!

But, should you shoot? Yes, definitely. For a few moments, you get to be the centre of attention as all eyes are on you and what you do with those mystic cubes. There are some simple rules for ensuring that you give a good impression:

- There is always a selection of dice from which to choose when you start out. The Stickman will push dice, usually five, in your direction. Pick any two and move them towards you. The remaining dice will be removed from the layout.
- Hold the dice in one hand. Do not move them from one hand to the other, which is a cheater's move and the Boxman may ask you to place them down on the table so that he can examine them for changes.
- When you throw the dice, try to ensure that they hit the studded rubber side of the Craps table at the far end from you. This way, the casino staff will be satisfied that the roll is a legal one. If you fail to do this, the Stickman will probably accept your roll but ask you to try to hit the end wall the next time.
- If one or both dice fly off the table – as sometimes happens – you can ask for the "same dice". A player or supervisor will collect the dice, return them to the Boxman, who will check that they are the same dice (each set carries a unique serial number) and then they will be returned to you. If you are not bothered about changing dice, you will be offered a choice from the remaining dice.
- If one (or both) dice lands against a pile of chips or the back wall of the table, and is not lying flat, the roll will have to be repeated. Both dice must lie flat for the roll to be considered complete and fair.

- Be as superstitious as you like. Arrange the dice on the table in whichever way you prefer. You can hold them in your hand in any way but make sure that they don't go beneath the level of the table and that the casino staff can see your hand at all times. Blow on them, pray over them, massage them, call something out if you like; throw them high, roll them low. Roll them however you want, just so long as you roll 7 or 11 on a Come-Out Roll, or the Point number afterwards. Remember that 11 is a good roll for everyone at any time (except for the "wrong" bettors).

- If you make your Point, the table will cheer you; if you fail to make it, there will be a groan and the dice will move on. If you make two or three Points, the table will really get behind you and start asking your name, shaking your hand, high-fiving you, offering you cigarettes and drinks. If you get into a really hot roll, where everyone is winning money, high-rollers may even throw you chips. Enjoy every minute – these prolonged hot rolls don't happen often.

- My longest hot roll was in Las Vegas – nine Points made over an hour and twenty minutes. I've never felt happier, or richer, in a casino in my life. A high-roller was chucking $100 chips at me every time I rolled him a number he had covered. He was winning about $5,000 each time, so I guess he felt I was worth rewarding! The dice were on fire and everyone – even the dealers who were enjoying big tips – was smiling and laughing and happy. I'd have loved to see the look on the pit boss's and casino manager's faces while this was going on.

Other Bets on the Craps Table

I strongly recommend that you don't place any other bets on the Craps table. They all offer poorer odds than the Come-Out Roll and bets placed via the Come Box. However, you will see almost everyone else at the table placing a huge variety of bets, so you may be tempted to follow them. Here are those other bets, together with the house edge each one offers.

Place Bets

Instead of placing Come Bets to bet on numbers other than the Point, you can make direct bets – via the dealer – onto any of the Point numbers. You will find that, because of the payouts, you may be asked to increase or decrease your bet size so that it is easy to pay should you win.

Placing a Bet on 4 or 10

You will need to place a bet that is a multiple of five, since the payout on these bets, should the Shooter roll a 4 or 10 before he rolls a 7, will be 9–5. This represents a house edge of 6.67 per cent, which is far too high to offer a casino at any time.

Notice that this payout is inferior to the bet placed via the Come Box and backed up by Odds Bets, which would be paid at the correct odds of 2–1.

Placing a Bet on 5 or 9

Again, your bet will need to be a multiple of five, since the payout on these bets, should the Shooter roll a 5 or 9 before he rolls a 7, will be 7–5. This represents a house edge of 4 per cent – still too high to offer the casino. A bet placed via the Come Box, and then backed up with Odds Bets, would be paid at the superior rate of 3–2.

Placing a Bet on 6 or 8

This time, your bet must be a multiple of six, since the payout on these bets, should the Shooter roll a 6 or 8 before he rolls a 7, will be 7–6. This represents a house edge of 1.5 per cent – just about acceptable, but not as profitable for you as betting via the Come Box and placing full odds behind your bet, which pays at 6–5.

Place Bets are the impatient gambler's way of covering all the numbers as quickly as possible. These directly placed bets offer the house an edge of between 1.5 per cent and 6.67 per cent compared to the 0.6 and 0.8 per cent edge offered through covering numbers via the Come Box and taking Odds Bets. Why would you do that?

Frequently, the moment that a Point is established, you will hear gamblers tell the dealer to cover all the numbers with Place Bets, shouting "Across the board" and throwing down large sums of money. This shows an uninformed gambler, out of control, impatient to play – and not focused on winning.

If you do succumb to the lure of making direct Place Bets, stick to the 6 and 8 where the house has the least edge. You can increase, decrease or remove Place Bets at any time, and the default position for them during the Come-Out Roll is for them to be "off" – out of play. You can opt to have them in play at this time if you wish.

Buying 4 and 10

This is a rarely used, but slightly less rash, way of placing bets directly on numbers 4 and 10. To do this, you state that you

would like to "Buy 4" or "Buy 10" and you then provide the
dealer with your bet, plus a 5 per cent commission, which the
house takes from you immediately. Having paid this
commission you get paid at the correct odds (2–1) should the
number appear before a 7 is rolled. This nets the house an edge
of 4.75 per cent and is therefore far worse odds than going
through the Come Box and placing full Odds behind your bet.

Field Bets

The Field Box is usually located next to the Come Box and
is just as big. It is filled with what seems to be almost all the
possible numbers and offers a one-roll chance to double
your money, since all bets are paid at even money should
you win. You can bet on the Field during a Come-Out Roll,
and indeed at any time. Your bet remains for just one roll of
the dice and you are then either paid, or, more likely, the
casino collects your bet. Some casinos offer bonus payouts
if the Shooter rolls a 2 or a 12 – sometimes paying double
money (2–1) for either of these rolls, and sometimes offering
3–1. Even with these bonuses, the Field Bet is a bad one,
since the house is taking between 2.7 per cent and 5 per
cent, depending on the bonuses paid for 2 and 12.

The reason for this substantial house advantage is this.
The Field offers to pay out if the Shooter rolls 2, 3, 4, 9, 10,
11 or 12. There are 16 ways to roll these numbers (if you
are getting paid 2–1 for 2 and 12, you can round this up to
18 ways), while there are 20 ways to roll the remaining
numbers 5, 6, 7 and 8. The key here is that all those numbers
shown on the Field layout come up less often than those
which are not covered by the Field – this is the intrinsic
house edge and why you should not place Field Bets.

Having said that, I did see a young couple in Vegas bet on the Field relentlessly for an entire session and win a lot of money. This is the attraction of casino gambling. You can make all the wrong moves and still win! But – and this is the key – in the long run, if you make the wrong moves you will definitely lose, and lose big, whereas if you follow the correct strategies, even in the long run you have a decent chance of winning, and winning big.

Proposition Bets

In the centre of the Craps table layout there is a densely laid-out section featuring many different combination bets. This section is not repeated for both sides of the table, but shared by players wherever they are standing. The most prominent of these Proposition Bets are the "Hardways Bets".

There are four numbers that can be made by the "hard way": 4, 6, 8 and 10.

- 4 can be rolled with 3&1 or 1&3, or the hard way: 2&2.
- 6 can be rolled with 5&1, 4&2, 2&4, 1&5, or the hard way: 3&3.
- 8 can be rolled with 2&6, 3&5, 5&3, 6&2, or the hard way: 4&4.
- 10 can be rolled with 4&6 or 6&4, or the hard way: 5&5.

As you can see, in the case of 4 and 10, there are two ways to roll the number easily, and one way to roll it the hard way. In the case of 6 and 8, there are four ways to roll the number easily and only one way to roll it the hard way.

Often, when the Point made is one of these even numbers, players back that Point to come up the hard way; sometimes they cover all the even numbers to appear the hard way. These bets remain on the layout until either a 7 is rolled, when all bets are lost, or until the number is rolled the easy way, when you lose your bet on that particular number.

If you do succeed in rolling the number the hard way, you are paid out as follows:

- On 4 and 10, you are paid at 7–1.
- On 6 and 8, you are paid at 9–1.

These sound attractive payouts, but in fact they offer the house an enormous edge: slightly over 11 per cent on the 4 and 10; slightly over 9 per cent on the 6 and 8. You can see why these bets *must* be avoided if you are to expect to win at Craps.

American Terminology

This is very important. Since Craps is originally an American game, even outside America you may find that Craps tables use the American terminology. This can be very misleading – and costly – to the unwary. Let me explain what I mean.

On the Hardways Bets just described, you will usually see the payouts advertised as "8 for 1" and "10 for 1" respectively. This is not the same as being paid 8–1 or 10–1.

- 10 for 1 means that for your one chip, if you win you will receive ten chips.

- 10–1 means that for your one chip, if you win you will receive eleven chips (your original wager returned, plus ten chips).

Be aware of this difference, or you may be in for a nasty shock.

Other Proposition Bets

If you thought that the odds against you were bad for the Hardways Bets, just wait until you hear about these other, almost unbelievably bad bets offered enthusiastically to you by the casino.

Big 6 and Big 8

Many casinos have removed this betting box from the layout because it was so rarely used. Even the most uninformed of gamblers recognized instinctively that these must be bad bets and avoided them.

If you were to bet on this box, you would be paid at even money if the Shooter rolled a 6 or 8 before a 7. The casino would love you for this bet because they would enjoy an edge of just over 9 per cent every time money was placed in this box. If you want to cover 6 and 8 together, make a Place Bet instead and you will be paid at 7–6, reducing the house edge to 1.5 per cent. Better still, make bets via the Come Box, take full Odds, and reduce the house edge to 0.6 per cent!

Any 7

This is a one-roll bet that the Shooter will hit a 7 on the next roll. If you are playing with the table, you certainly don't want to see a 7, since you will lose all your other bets. If you suddenly become convinced that the next roll will be a 7, then place a big Come Bet. However, any such thoughts are odds-against, and since the true odds of rolling a 7 at any time are 6 chances in 36, the payout should be 5–1 (6 for 1). On the Craps table, the house offers you 4–1, and is therefore taking a massive 16.67 per cent off you every time you make this ridiculous bet.

Any Craps

This is a one-roll bet that the next number rolled by the Shooter will be 2, 3 or 12 – the Craps numbers. Since there are only 4 out of 36 possible ways to roll these numbers, the house should pay 8–1; they offer only 7–1, and that provides them with a tidy 11 per cent edge. This is another terrible bet.

2 and 12

A one-roll bet, this offers two opportunities to cover the least likely of all the numbers to appear. The chance of appearing for each of these numbers is only 1 in 36, and should therefore pay out at 35–1. The house offers you 30–1, and this provides them with an edge against you of almost 14 per cent.

3 and 11

Another one-roll bet to cover 3 or 11 being the next number rolled. Since each of these numbers can only be rolled in two ways, the payout should be 17–1, whereas the house offers 15–1, yielding an edge for them in excess of 11 per cent.

It should be clear why sensible players who care about money ignore all Proposition Bets. They are the real sucker bets of the casino, and when I see them being played heavily I shake my head in disbelief that players could be so ignorant. But they are, and that is why casinos get ever richer.

Horn Bets

There is one last Proposition Bet that takes the biscuit for sheer, shameless cheek on the part of the casinos: the Horn Bet. A one-roll bet, this covers 2, 3, 11 and 12 with four bets simultaneously. Not only do you give the house between 12.5 per cent of your money every time you make this bet but, should one of those numbers actually appear, you lose the stake on the remaining three that did not appear.

This represents probably the silliest bet in the entire game: four terrible bets placed at the same time!

Hop Bets

Hop Bets are a series of bets that tries to predict the exact outcome of the next roll using Hardways and 2 and 12 bets. These are all horrendously bad bets, paying the house a 16.67 per cent edge. Just ignore them and wish that you had never heard of Horn Bets and Hop Bets!

Betting the "Wrong Way"

If you feel like being a maverick, or you have watched the players betting with the dice lose session after session, you may decide to swap allegiance and start betting against the dice. The odds on playing Craps this way are vitually indentical to playing with the table, so you can choose to mix up your action a little bit if the idea appeals to you. Traditionally, players who are betting against the dice reject the chance to be the Shooter.

Don't Pass

This is a bet placed before the Come-Out Roll. You bet just as you would on the Pass Line, but this time you place your bets in the Don't-Pass section of the layout. On the Come-Out Roll, you win immediately if the Shooter rolls a 2 or 3, and you are paid at even money.

- If a 12 is rolled, the bet is a stand-off.
- You lose your wager if a 7 or 11 is rolled.
- If a Point is established, you win your bet if the Shooter rolls a 7 before making his Point and you lose if the Shooter succeeds in rolling the Point number before rolling a 7.

In other words, you are betting on exactly the opposite outcomes to the standard Pass-Line Bets.

The main difference occurs once a Point has been established. Since it is now more likely that the Shooter will roll a 7 than repeat the Point number, if the Don't-Pass bettor wants to take Odds on his original Don't-Pass Bet this is still the correct play. If he wins he will collect at the correct odds, but these are less than even money. On this basis, Don't-Pass bettors are more likely to win once a Point is established, but they have to lay out more money to do so, and this increases their exposure on the table. So, if the Shooter hits a hot streak, the Don't-Pass bettor can lose a lot of money very quickly.

I was playing at a busy table in Las Vegas a few years ago, where everyone was betting the "right way" with the dice. We were doing pretty well. Suddenly, the two-times World Poker Champion, Johnnie Chan, arrived at our table, changed up $500,000 dollars, and started to play the Don't-Pass Line. Just at that moment, the lady Shooter hit a 5-Point hot streak and the table reaped the rewards. I don't suppose the casino minded one little bit. While the bulk of the players collected around $20,000 between us over the half hour or so, Johnnie Chan dropped $300,000 playing against the table! (Don't feel too bad for Mr Chan: he is a hugely successful, brilliant Poker player. I doubt he shed even a little tear at the luck going against him that day.)

Don't Come

Once the Point has been established, the Don't-Pass bettor can place Don't-Come Bets and back them up with Odds Bets, hoping that the Shooter does not roll these numbers before rolling a 7. As before, the Don't-Come bettor has to stake more money for a lower payout, since the chances of him winning are that much greater.

Laying Bets

In the same way that you can "Buy" 4 and 10 at a 5 per cent commission for the correct odds, you can "Lay Bets" on any of the Point numbers that they will not appear before the Shooter rolls a 7. You still pay the 5 per cent commission, and the house receives edges against the player that are almost prohibitive:

- on 4 and 10: 2.45 per cent
- on 5 and 9:   3.25 per cent
- on 6 and 8:   4 per cent

These bets can be increased, decreased or removed altogether whenever you wish.

You will very rarely see players betting on the Don't-Pass Line, taking Don't-Come Bets with Odds, or Laying Bets. If everyone at the table is betting with the dice and you come in to bet against the dice, you will be a most unpopular winner, since your fortune will be at the expense of everybody else's. Craps is a uniquely sociable casino game and everyone usually enjoys working together to beat the house. The atmosphere during a hot streak when everybody at the table is winning is something to be savoured. My advice is to bet with the table and share the joy of beating the house at its own game.

Tipping at the Craps Table

Tipping casino staff is not universal but in Las Vegas in particular it is still the done thing. This is a city which treats punters based on the value of their custom and nothing else, and although that may seem exploitative it is at least an understandable prejudice. The bottom line for casino employees is that most work for minimum wages and their tips cheque at the end of each month is vital to top-up their meagre earnings.

As with Blackjack, I believe that to tip can save you money. Dealers are more likely to look towards you warmly if you have placed even the most modest tips than if you resolutely refuse to place a bet for them. The advantages may include: reminding you to take Odds Bets behind the Pass Line or behind Come Bets once they have alighted on a number; keeping an eye on your chips if other players start playing very close to you; giving you the benefit of the doubt where minor disputes occur. These are all things you hope would be undertaken by any enthusiastic and diligent dealer but, given the vagaries of human nature – and we all have bad days, after all – they do not necessarily happen automatically.

When placing a tip, players vary their style. I like to place a small Line Bet before a Come-Out Roll and, if a Point is established, back this up with the full Odds Bet. I might be playing $25 behind the line myself, but I can still place a $5 bet for the dealers, or even a $1 bet – most casinos will allow you to bet sub-minimum amounts for dealers. You can announce that you are making a bet for the dealers, or you can just place the bet – they will know that it is for them. Others prefer to place Hardways Bets, or direct Place Bets. All such bets are appreciated and should be acknowledged by the dealers when they bank the winnings.

Since I know the best chance of winning, I opt for the Line Bet method of tipping, since I know that this provides the best chance of a win and a nice, healthy tip for the dealers.

Incidentally, in the old days of Las Vegas, the Craps pits were considered to be most important areas of the casinos and the tips at the Craps tables were the highest anywhere in town. Nowadays, with the proliferation of Slots, there are fewer staff and fewer tips. After all, no one is going to tip a Slot machine.

Craps Lore

If you are visiting Las Vegas and staying in a big hotel on the Strip, I urge you to go downtown to Glitter Gulch – or Freemont Street as it is more commonly known these days – and spend a little time playing Blackjack and Craps in the smaller hotels there. Here, you will find the locals betting minimums and exchanging hard luck stories. It is a rich vein of gambling information and gossip and quite an experience to join these, usually elderly, men, with their cowboy hats and thick cigars, or tartan hats and long drooping cigarettes.

At night, four blocks are covered by an enormous domed ceiling containing a multitude of coloured lights. Remarkable giant lightshows, animated, and accompanied by dramatic music, are presented in the sky above at regular intervals. It's a memorable experience and the modern face of downtown Vegas.

Binion's Horseshoe Casino – the original site for the World Series of Poker – was also the setting for a remarkable Vegas occurrence. Binion's was renowned for having no limits at its tables. The first bet you placed could form your limit so, in theory, you could place a $1,000,000 bet on a Blackjack table and that would become your limit. During the 1970s, an unassuming man arrived at the casino cage carrying two suitcases. From one, he produced $777,000 in cash, had it changed into chips and lugged them all over to a nearby Craps table. There, he bet the entire sum on the Don't-Pass Line (he evidently did not know about taking Odds) and let the Shooter make a Point. That achieved, he now needed the Shooter to roll a 7 before he rolled his Point number again. On the third throw, the Shooter rolled that magic 7 and the man collected all his winnings, had them taken back to the cage and re-filled his first suitcase with his original stake, and the second suitcase with his profit. Then, he walked out of the casino and was never seen again.

There is an unconfirmed report that he returned ten years later with only $150,000 in his suitcase, bet on the Don't-Pass Line once more, and lost the lot.

Both players and casino staff become very superstitious about Craps games. In the old days in Vegas, if a Craps table was losing the casino a lot of money – which, I'm pleased to say, they sometimes do – they would suddenly decide to close it down. Dice which provided a hot roll for a player would be thrown away, or crushed. There is even talk of one pit boss taking a hot pair of dice out into the desert, digging a little hole for them, and burying them. A Mob method for disappearing them!

One downtown casino even brought in a glass case to display a pair of Craps dice that had produced a winning streak of no fewer than 17 Points made in a row. It must have cost the casino a fortune, and made the players there rich beyond their dreams. What a session that must have been for anyone slowly increasing their bets as the hot roll got going. After a few weeks, the casino was astonished to find that the display case had been broken into and the dice removed. A few months later, it turned out to be one of the casino's shift managers. He hated those dice with a passion, and they had to go!

I once spent a long evening chatting with a man dressed in tatty jeans and a frayed shirt. We played dice at Bellagio, in Las Vegas, at the same table for six hours or so, during which he told me of how, when the casino had first opened, he had arrived to play Craps with $50,000. During the course of 24 hours at the table, he turned his original stake into $950,000. At this point, despite being exhausted, he decided to continue playing until he reached $1,000,000, so that he could tell people that he had beaten this new, ultra-luxurious resort out of a million bucks. He played for another 24 hours and, although he got to within $10,000 of the one million mark, he simply could not cross it. Eventually, unable to stand up any longer, he left the table with $850,000 – still a remarkable success over the tables.

When the man left, I couldn't help asking the dealers if they believed his stories. The two dealers both looked up at me and smiled: "Yes, it was at this table, and we won't forget that night." By all accounts, everyone who had stood at that table had won, the gambler had tipped the dealers in excess of $10,000, and others had chipped in too. It was a bumper night for players and the dealers.

Winning Strategy for Craps

Amidst all the odds and edges, and the multitude of betting possibilities, there is actually a very simple set of rules to follow if you want to give yourself the best chance of winning at Craps. This isn't an opinion, or open to debate – it is statistically proven.

For the purposes of this strategy, we will assume that you are playing at a Vegas Strip casino and you are allowed X3, X4 and X5 Odds. Try to avoid playing anywhere that does not offer you these Odds options. To play Single-Odds (where you can only place an Odds Bet up to the same value as your Line Bet) or Double-Odds Craps is loading the dice – so to speak – too much in favour of the house.

Bankroll

To be able to weather the spells of both good and bad luck involved in a random game, you must take a sufficient bankroll with you to the table not to feel pressured the moment anything goes wrong. The best method of assessing your bankroll requirement is to multiply the Line Bet you intend to make by 75. This means that if you are planning to play $5 on the Line, you should arrive at the table with at least $375; for $10 Line Bets, $750, and so on.

Even though you are playing an almost even-money game, it will be by no means rare that you will lose your entire session bankroll from time to time. The good news is, you will also double your session bankroll almost the same number of times. But, you must be ready for this entirely predictable variance.

Betting Strategy

Your strategy is simple. Start with a base Line Bet. Once a Point is established, take full Odds on the number behind your original bet.

I recommend then placing a small bet (perhaps half the size of the Line Bet) on the Come Box and, if this is moved to a number, also taking the full Odds available on that bet. Every time you win a Come Bet with the Odds, place a new bet in the Come Box.

If you want a slightly more ambitious and risky strategy, continue placing bets in the Come Box until you have three numbers, other than the Point, covered with Come Bets and full Odds.

For those wanting maximum profits if a hot roll hits, continue making Come Bets at all times, backing each one up with full Odds bets once they get placed on numbers.

However daring you choose to be, resist the temptation to place even small wagers on the truly awful bets such as Hardways, Place Bets on 4 or 10 (buy a bet on 4 and 10 if you must) and the Field.

If the Shooter makes the Point, this is the time to consider increasing your Line Bet for the next Come-Out

Roll. For myself, if my base bet is $10, I would then move up to $15 after the first Point is made and then continue to increase it as the hot streak, hopefully, continues.

If you lose your session bankroll quickly, do not be tempted to change any more money. Walk away from the tables, have a coffee or a drink, and perhaps walk to another casino elsewhere before you try again.

If you encounter a hot Shooter early on, lock away 50 per cent of your profit from that hot roll and resolve that you will not touch it at this table. That way, you cannot leave the table a loser. Start any new Shooter's action with your base bet once again and move up slowly if he, too, is successful. Remember that dice have no memory, and if they were hot once they may be stone cold now – and vice versa.

The most dispiriting thing to do is to be part of a hot roll at the start of your session and then squander all your money trying to repeat the success soon afterwards. Be wary after a hot roll – your adrenalin will be pumping, and the desire to press on with big bets will be strong. Resist it, take stock, then lock away half your profits and start again in a modest way.

4
Roulette

ROULETTE is one of the most glamorous casino games, and with payouts of up to 35 times the bet placed it may seem an attractive game to play. In casinos throughout Europe, Roulette remains hugely popular, especially in the famed gambling rooms of the grand casino in Monte Carlo. In London, Chinese gamblers flock to the low-stake Roulette wheels, often spending whole days covering the layout with chips. When a table is busy, it can seem a dynamic and exciting game.

Before looking at the game in detail and deciding on the best strategies, there is one simple question to answer: how many zeros are there on the wheel?

In Europe, generally the Roulette wheel contains 36 numbers, plus one zero – this offers the house an overall edge of 2.7 per cent.

In America, generally the wheel contains 36 numbers, one zero and one double zero. This offers the house an overall edge of just over 5.25 per cent.

Before staking a single dollar, euro or pound, it is vital that you check on which wheel you are playing. If the wheel contains one zero, the odds against you are bad; if the wheel contains two zeros, the odds against you are very bad!

How to Leave the Roulette Table a Millionaire

Arrive a billionaire!

Throughout the world, most casinos offer you a single-zero Roulette game. These wheels are European-style, featuring numbers that are read from the inside outwards. In some casinos – in the USA, onboard cruise ships, in illegal gambling halls – the wheels are American-style, featuring a zero and a double zero, with the numbers reading from the outside inwards. However, do not be confused, since many European casinos offer what they call American Roulette, but played on the single zero wheel!

As a gambling game, not only are the players offered poor odds, there are other fundamental flaws with Roulette.

Firstly, unless you bet on just one single number, even if you win you will lose all your bets on other numbers. Secondly, depending on the wheel there are 37 or 38 different numbers on which you can bet – plus another dozen or so alternative wagers. Because everyone tends to bet on different numbers, once the result is known there tends to be just one happy player at the table – everyone else has lost. (In my experience, usually everyone loses, and only the casino is happy.) In games like Blackjack, Craps and Punto Bunco/Baccarat, the players are normally on one side and the house on the other so that when the players win everyone is happy, and when they lose everyone can console each other. Roulette is a very individual game, where you are, in effect, willing all the other players to lose.

Playing the Game

When you approach the table, the first thing to do is to check how many zeros appear on the wheel. The numbers 1–36 are almost always displayed in alternating red and black colours, the zeros are almost always green. So it is easy to spot how many zeros appear on your wheel. If you see a zero (0) and a double zero (00), walk away from the table and either find a casino which offers a single-zero game, or play another game where you will get much better value for your money. To play a game where the casino has a consistent 5.25 per cent edge against you is truly to throw away your money without a decent fight.

Assuming that you have found a single-zero wheel and you are determined to play, you will change your cash at the table. Check the minimum betting limits, which will be displayed (along with the maximum bet size) on the table. As with other casino games, some tables will offer low limits (25c, £1, 1 Euro); others may demand a relatively high minimum bet. When you are changing your cash for chips, if you are alone at the table, you could play the game with the standard casino cash chips. However, it is more usual to change your chips into "colour" chips. These chips are only to be played at this one Roulette table (and are not valid anywhere else in the casino, or even at the casino cage). This system is used because if the table is busy and everyone is playing standard casino chips it would become confusing as to who had placed which bets, and then there would be disputes over who was to be paid.

The colour chips have no monetary value written on them. Usually, they are marked with the number of the Roulette table to which they apply. The default value of the colour chips is the table minimum. However, if you are a high-roller, you can ask for your colour chips at a higher denomination. For example, if I was playing at a $1 minimum table, but I wanted my chips to be worth $10 each, I would say: "Colour at $10". The croupier would note that my colour chips were worth $10 each, and then provide me with the appropriate number of colour chips at that denomination. At many Roulette tables there is a small display (sometimes electronic nowadays) on which the croupier can indicate the value of everyone's colour chips to ensure that there are no mistakes.

When you win, you will be paid in the same colour chips, unless you state that you would like some, or all, of your winnings paid in standard casino chips. Let's say I won $350, and I wanted some of my winnings paid in standard casino chips, I might say: "200 in cash, and the rest in colour". I would now probably be paid 15 colour chips (at $10 each) and two $100 standard casino chips.

Before leaving the table, should you be lucky enough to have any money left over, you can change your colour chips for standard casino chips, allowing you to play other games, or convert them for cash at the casino cage.

Placing your Bets

The attraction of Roulette is that it is a stylish and leisurely game. Seeing the wheel spin and the little white ball whirl around the casing in the opposite direction to the wheel can be very exciting when you have some large bets which might win you a fortune, if only the ball would land in the right little pocket. There are a huge variety of different bets which can be made. Let's run through all of them, so that you can try as many as you like if you decide to play. Traditionally, many Roulette terms are described in French. However, these days English is the global gambling language and we will use the standard English terms for each situation.

Each bet is illustrated by a chip shown on the diagram and described below. The numbers on the chips in the diagram correspond to the numbers in brackets after each named bet.

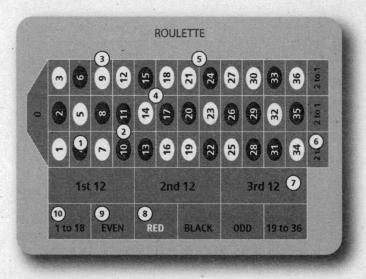

Straight Up (1)
This is a bet on a single number on the layout. On the diagram on the previous page, it is placed on number 4. Position your chip in the middle of the number box on the layout, so that no part of the chip is touching the lines around it. If there are other players who have placed this bet, put your chip(s) on top of the pile in the centre of the betting box.

You may place as many Straight-Up Bets on different numbers as you wish – including on zero (and double zero if you are foolish enough to be playing a double-zero wheel), and as many chips on each number as permitted by the house maximums. If you win, you will be paid 35–1 on your bet.

Split (2)
This bet covers two adjacent numbers. Place your chip on the line between the two numbers you wish to cover. On the diagram, this is between 10 and 11. If you win, you will be paid 17–1 on your bet.

Row (3)
This bet covers three consecutive numbers in a row. You place your chip on the line to the right of the three numbers you wish to back. On the diagram, this covers 7, 8 and 9. If you win, you will be paid 11–1 on your bet.

Four Number – Corner (4)
To cover four numbers with a single chip, you place it on the intersection of the four numbers on which you would like to bet. Ensure that your chip is touching the corner of all four numbers. On the diagram, this corner bet covers 14, 15, 17 and 18. If you win, you will be paid 8–1 on your bet.

Six Number (5)

This is, in effect, a double Row Bet. Place your chip on the line between the two rows you wish to cover on the right of the layout. On the diagram, this covers 19, 20, 21, 22, 23 and 24. If you win, you will be paid at 5–1.

Column Bets (6)

This bets allows you to cover a line of 12 numbers. At the bottom of the layout, furthest from the wheel, you will see three boxes, usually marked "2–1". A chip placed in one of these boxes covers every number contained within that vertical line. On the diagram, this covers the first column. If you win, you will be paid at 2–1.

Dozens (7)

To the left of the layout, you will see three broad boxes, usually marked with "1st Dozen", "2nd Dozen" and "3rd Dozen". These cover the numbers 1–12, 13–24 and 25–36 respectively. A chip placed in these boxes cover the corresponding numbers. On the diagram, the chip covers the 3rd dozen. If you win, you will be paid at 2–1.

Even-Money Bets
Red/Black (8)

To the left of the Dozens Bets, you will see six large boxes on which you can make even-money wagers. In the middle of these boxes are the most popular of the even-money bets: Red or Black. A chip placed in these boxes covers all red numbers, or all black numbers, but not zero. On the diagram, this chip is on Red. If you win, you will be paid at even money, 1–1.

Odd/Even (9)

To the right and left of the Red/Black bets, there are the Odd or Even boxes. A chip placed here will win if you predict an even number or an odd number. On the diagram, the chip is placed on Even. If you win, you will be paid at even money, 1–1.

1–18 and 19–36 (10)

This is, in effect, a High/Low betting opportunity, where you can try to predict whether the next number is low (1–18) or high (19–36). On the diagram, the chip is placed on 1–18. If you win, you will be paid at even money, 1–1.

There are a few further comments to make about these even-money propositions:

Most casinos will not allow you to place a table minimum bet on the Lines, Dozens or Even-Money chances. Usually, they will require you to bet at least five times the table minimum on these wagers. Therefore, if you are playing at a $5 minimum table, a bet on one of these wagers must be at least $25.

Depending on the house rules, how your even-money bet is treated if a zero is spun will vary. In most US casinos and on wheels with two zeros, these bets are usually lost (increasing the house advantage). In Europe, it is traditional to play a version called "en-prison", where, if the number spun is zero, your bet remains untouched on the layout, and if the bet wins on the next spin you have your original bet released – without winnings. If the bet subsequently loses, you lose your bet.

These days, the "en-prison" rule is rarely applied and, instead, half your bet is taken away and the remaining half returned. Where this method is employed, the house edge against you is reduced to 1.35 per cent – making even-money bets at Roulette a decent shot for your money. In many modern casinos, however, the management takes advantage of the fact that most gamblers do not know the history of the game, nor the modern rules, and they simply claim all your money when the ball lands in zero.

If you are going to play Roulette regularly (not recommended), or for considerable stakes, then you should check which payout the casino would offer you in the event of zero being hit when you have even-money bets in play.

Neighbour Bets

Some casinos – most often in Europe – offer Neighbour Bets on a subsidiary betting layout, usually positioned to the left of the main betting layout. The Neighbour layout looks like a small oval racing track, showing all the numbers on the wheel laid out in the order they appear. If you wish to cover five numbers at once, you can ask the croupier to place a Neighbour Bet for you. To do this, you must bet at least five times the minimum bet, since you will be covering each number with at least that amount. You do not place these bets yourself – only the croupier can place them for you. For example, you might say: "14 and Neighbours by five". This would mean that you wish to cover the number 14, and the two numbers both to the right and left of 14, with $5 bets. You would pass the croupier $25 and he would place that on the Neighbour betting layout on 14. This bet also covers (on a European wheel) 1 and 20, 31 and 9. If any of these numbers come up on the next spin, the croupier will transfer $5 of your Neighbours Bet to the main layout and place it Straight Up on the number. You will then be paid at 35–1, and your remaining Neighbour Bets are lost.

There are many other possible bets that can be placed which cover a multitude of different combinations. They are not generally used, and so I will not discuss them here, other than to mention the granddaddy of them all, the Full Complete.

The Full Complete

This bet asks the croupier to cover one number, to table maximums, in every possible way available. I have seen this played in London's Crockford's Club – one of the highest rolling casinos in the world – and it is certainly exciting to hear it being placed and to see the number come up. We are talking here of a bet in excess of £50,000 on a single spin at Roulette. If your number actually appears: a win not far short of one million pounds!

Placing Bets

It is traditional to place your own bets on the main layout – though not on Neighbour Bets. If a table is busy, and there are many players milling around, there will be a fair amount of jostling and you will have to jostle with the best of them if you want to get your bets down.

However, you can, at any time, ask the croupier to place the bets for you. Simply put down all the chips you want to bet in a pile to the side of the layout and state, loudly and clearly, the bets you wish to make. The croupier will then repeat your instructions and place your bets accordingly.

At almost all casinos, you will find that there is a rope preventing players from walking around to the croupier's side of the table. This is to stop people getting anywhere near the store of chips each table must carry in the event of a successful series of spins for the players. Don't try to cross this point, or lean against the rope – casinos really don't like it. At one casino, there was so much jostling that I allowed myself to be pushed into the rope, lost my footing on the shiny carpet and went head-over-heels into the croupier's section. Not only did this amuse everyone hugely – including the staff – it also appalled the management that a client should have been pushed over, and a multitude of people rushed towards me to help me up, offer me drinks and dinner, and generally to tender loving care. While I don't recommend this action, despite a nasty bruise the whole experience turned out most agreeably: I've never been so well looked after in my life!

Betting Strategy

First let's make something very clear to avoid any misunderstanding. Unless the Roulette wheel is biased (which is almost impossible these days due to constant checking of the equipment by casinos), no inference can be drawn from previous spins of the wheel. The wheel does not "know" which numbers it has spun in the past, and it certainly does not know which numbers will come up in the future. No predictions can be made based on previous results; each spin is entirely independent of the previous spin(s). For this reason, no technique or strategy has any advantage over the wheel.

There are tales of the man who broke the bank at Monte Carlo, because he noticed a wheel bias and was able to exploit it, and players who have developed brilliant systems to break the house at Roulette. Again, let's be clear: this has never been done.

The laws of probability are frequently rolled out when it comes to Roulette. For example, if the wheel has spun eight black numbers in a row, is it more likely that the next number will be red? The simple answer is No. If the wheel has spun the number 27 three times in a row, is there a worse chance that 27 will appear again? No.

What people misunderstand about probability is the length of time over which it is measured. Let me give you an example. A coin toss is, assuming that the coin is tossed in a random fashion, a 50–50 bet. Let's toss the coin ten times and see what the result is. It may be five heads and five tails. But, equally, it may be seven heads and three tails. Does that make it more likely that tails will occur subsequently? No.

What the law of probability tells us is: the more times we toss that coin, the more likely it is that the number of heads and tails spins will be the same. It does not say that they ever will be the same, or that one or other will not dominate. Simply, that the more you toss the coin, the closer to the expected outcome it is likely to be. Put it another way: just before the point of infinity, the number of heads and tails spun will be very close!

So, when casinos show you the previous 20 or 30 spins on an electronic display, they do it merely for entertainment, to add to the interest in a fairly dull game. What has occurred in the last 20 or 30 spins has absolutely no relevance to what might happen next. None at all.

Playing in the casino in Estoril, Portugal, a few years back, some of my friends noticed that one Roulette wheel had spun 13 red numbers in a row. They hurried over to join the crowds of gamblers who were piling the Black number box high with chips. These players actually thought that, because the ball had landed in red 13 times, it was now more likely than 50–50 (minus the chance of the ball landing in the zero) that the ball would land on a black number.

If 13 spins ago you had predicted that the ball would land in 13 red numbers, you would be a very rich gambler now. But, just watching 13 spins land on red does not help you – even one tiny little bit – to guess on which number the ball will land next.

The fourteenth spin was a red number and a huge groan went up around the table. Many players doubled their bets on black, which now, surely, must appear. The fifteenth spin was red, and the groan increased still more in volume. This outcome – 15 spins with the ball landing on red numbers – is rare but, over the hundreds of thousands of spins that wheel had made, perfectly understandable. There was now a delay of almost ten minutes as more and more players moved to the table to place bets on black. It was like a feeding frenzy. Eventually, everyone had placed their bets, and when the ball landed for the sixteenth time on red, everyone lost their money. This time, there was no groan: just a collective muffled cry of anguish. Many players lost their entire bankrolls on those three bets, so convinced were they that the odds had turned in their favour.

On the seventeenth spin, a black number appeared, and some tenacious gamblers rejoiced that their "strategy" had succeeded. But, as I hope you can now see, theirs was a mistaken assumption, costing them a fortune.

Betting Systems

When a game has a built-in guaranteed house edge, it makes no difference what system you play. It cannot help you – scientifically – to increase or decrease your bets at any time, nor to change which numbers you back. The bottom line is that you have to be lucky to win. However, many books actually recommend betting systems for Roulette, and this is nothing short of pure, unadulterated lying.

During my continued research for this book, I noticed that a number of online casino sites had betting advice for players on how to beat Roulette, and they made the most extravagant claims. They presented these ideas with a veneer of good sense about them, so I present to you some vital evidence to refute them. Do not be seduced by anyone telling you that you can beat Roulette. You cannot beat this game, unless you are just plain lucky.

The Martingale

This is the most famous system of all for Roulette, although you can apply it to any game where the odds are, roughly, 50–50. This was the "guaranteed method" being promoted by the online casino sites, and it is pure nonsense.

I must repeat myself: there is no system which will beat Roulette. Never pay anyone for a Roulette system because it does not exist. It is a con.

The principle of the Martingale is this: you bet $1 (or whatever your base stake happens to be) on an even-money proposition. Let's say you bet on Black. If this bet wins, you win your $1 and you have made a profit. Well done. The system doesn't tell you what to do now, so I guess you leave with your $1 profit and tell yourself you have beaten the casino. That, or you go straight back and try to do it again.

If you lose, you then bet $2 on Black. If this wins, you have $4 for the price of only $3 in bets – and hence you have made your $1 profit. Then, apparently, you start again. If you lose that bet, you now place $8 on Black, and so on.

This seems, at first glance, a reasonable method of playing. And, indeed, you are very likely to make $1 profit if you continue doubling your bet every time you lose. In fact, you will succeed the vast majority of the time. However, there are several problems.

Firstly, imagine if you were unlucky enough to hit a streak like the one at the casino in Estoril. Had you started at 1 Euro and kept losing and doubling up, you would have lost 65,535 Euros. That doesn't sound such a great system!

More importantly, because all casinos have an upper limit on bets, you would probably have been stopped when you reached, say, 1,000 Euros, meaning that having lost over 2,000 Euros already, you wouldn't be able to bet 2,000 Euros, only 1,000 Euros. So, now you would have to win twice in a row just to get your money back. Call me old fashioned, but to risk $1,000 to win $1 sounds like a crazy idea to me. And that's exactly what the Martingale System is.

It makes no difference whether you bet one chip or ten, unless you can predict the outcome of the next spin. You can't, so don't worry about it. Just bet modestly, hope for good luck and, if Roulette is your cup of tea, enjoy the game.

Cover the Board

Some players become so desperate to see a stack of chips pushed in their direction that they cover every number on the layout. This is not a good idea, since it guarantees that you will lose every single spin. (You would place 37 chips and receive only 36, including the one staked, at the end of each spin).

Others decide that they will cover all but two numbers. Unless these two numbers appear, they are bound to make a profit, every single time. Well, every single time, until one of those two numbers appear. Then, you lose *35 times* the amount you won in each spin previously, all in one spin. Quite simply, the more bets you place, the more money you offer to the casino, from which they, in the long run, take 2.7 per cent (or 5.26 per cent) from every single chip bet.

The Newtonian Casino

In the book of the same name, the story is recounted of a group of MIT students who developed a method to track the spin of the wheel, against the speed and position of the ball, and therefore predict where the ball might land.

In this highly recommended read, the students prove that, in theory, you can do this, using a team of highly trained personnel, some brilliant thinking and low-tech application. Even then, the result is not accurate; it might predict into which quarter of the wheel the ball might land. The problem is that the equipment malfunctioned and had it been tried for any length of time in a casino, the surveillance would have been able to spot them very quickly, based on those present at the wheel, and the style of betting undertaken.

Please never forget that in Las Vegas if you are found with any kind of computer equipment to help you to cheat the games, you are likely to end up in a very hot prison for a very long time!

Chip Exchange

In the days before high-tech surveillance, those with a genius for sleight of hand could arrange to substitute chips in the blink of an eye while the croupier was seeing in which number the ball had landed. Chips could be placed on winning numbers and taken off losing numbers, low denomination chips swapped for high denominations, and so forth. These days, casino surveillance would crack scams like this in two seconds flat, but in the past, these brilliant con artists have been able to rob casinos of huge sums of money. If you are caught attempting this, you will not enjoy the consequences, be they legal or otherwise.

Simple Sensible Betting Pattern

As with all betting ideas, the standard one is the best. When you are losing, keep betting small amounts in order to keep your losses to a minimum. We all have bad days when no matter what we do we seem to lose. At least if you are losing small, the pain will not be too great to bear.

If you are winning, increase your bet a little each time. This way, you take advantage of a winning streak – what all gamblers hope for – by winning a little more each time. However, don't risk all your profits from one successful spin on the next one since the chances are this won't work. If it does, that's great, but then walk away from the table.

In terms of which bets to place, if the casino offers you half your bets back on even-money propositions when zero appears, you are playing against a house edge of 1.35 per cent, which is just about acceptable. Stick to the Odd/Even, Red/Black, and 1–18/19–36 wagers and, with a little luck, you can return a profit.

The problem with playing even-money wagers on Roulette is that it is a slow game and you are likely to be tempted to place other bets at poorer odds – the main layout of numbers all take 2.7 per cent from you whichever way you place your bets.

If the only Roulette game available features a double zero, try to resist playing. At over 5 per cent per spin, the house edge will grind you down very quickly.

In Las Vegas, many of the big casino resorts on the Strip are realizing that it is better to have some action with a poorer house edge, than no action whatsoever. To this end, many of these casinos now offer single-zero Roulette. Often, they insist on higher minimum bets, in order to get back a little of what they might have gained from the much higher-edge double-zero Roulette. However, this has been a change forced on them by necessity. Gamblers were asking for Roulette, but finding only very poor games to play. Ultimately, if gamblers demand better playing conditions and a better chance to beat the casinos, than the casinos will bow to the pressure – but only if gamblers refuse to play the games offering the bad deals.

I cannot really recommend Roulette to you at all. I have seen so many grim-faced Roulette players leaving casinos having lost all their money; it is a sad sight indeed. The problem with Roulette is that you can see the little white ball passing over the numbers you have backed and so nearly dropping into the right pocket. You feel sure that it must do so on the very next spin. It is a massive adrenalin-inducing game. That burst of excitement is part of what makes gambling addictive, and Roulette holds a very powerful grip on those who are attracted to the adrenalin high.

In addition, you can see others – covering alternative numbers – raking in what appear to be huge winnings. Casinos like to pay out winnings at Roulette in massive stacks of low denomination chips because, quite rightly, they think that if other players see a huge monolith of chips being slowly pushed towards a winning player, this will encourage others to come and play. My advice is: bet on it sparingly, and seek out games offering you a superior chance to beat the house.

Summary of Strategy

- Play only at tables with a single zero. Walk away from wheels with both 0 and 00.
- Bet on even-money wagers (Red/Black, Odd/Even, 1–18/19–32) if the casino offers half your stake back if you hit zero. This reduces the house edge to 1.35 per cent.
- If you must bet on numbers, restrict yourself to only a few different numbers per spin. Even if you win a bet on one of them, you lose all your chips placed elsewhere.
- Keep betting minimum amounts until you win. Increase your stake a little and continue doing so until your winning streak ends. Then, leave the table, or return to your base stake until a winning streak seems to be beginning.
- The law of averages does not apply over a few sessions in a casino. It may not even come close to

expectation within a lifetime of spins. Past results on a Roulette wheel have absolutely *zero* influence over future ones.

- No betting system, or predictive system, can work on Roulette. Nor has there been one in the history of gambling that has worked. All these systems lead to placing more bets at higher stakes, and to ruin for the player. If anyone claims to have one that makes money, it is impossible that they are correct. Remember, as with so many things: if it's too good to be true – it's *not* true.

5
Baccarat, or Punto Bunco

THIS IS A casino Table Game rarely played outside Europe and the Far East. Often associated with glamour and excitement, it is a game requiring no skill whatsoever and which offers a house edge that is small enough to give the player a genuine chance at beating the house. James Bond plays a form of this game in several movies, including the iconic gambling scene when we are introduced to Bond in the first movie, *Dr No*, a classic encounter with Largo in *Thunderball*, and Roger Moore playing against the odds in *For Your Eyes Only*.

The modern games are thought to have originated from an Italian card game called "Baccara" (which, in Italian, means zero). From there, it evolved into games called Chemin de Fer, and Chemmy. However, even though it may be possible to find a real Chemin de Fer game offered in the South of France, or in private homes, almost all of the world's casinos offer it in the form which will be described here, calling it Punto Bunco, or Baccarat.

In the traditional game, every player at the table had a chance to act as the Bank – a favourable position to be in. In the modern game, the casino plays the role of the Bank and therefore retains a favourable position for itself throughout the game. Players can choose to bet either on the Bank's hand winning, or the opposition's hand, called the Player's hand.

The Table

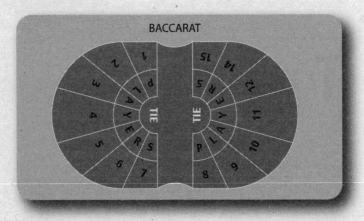

The full-sized Baccarat (or Punto Bunco) table is the grandest of all the tables found in the casino. Traditionally, it is a large oval, several times the width of a Blackjack table, with a slight indent in the middle on both sides, making it look like a figure of eight on its side. The casino personnel sit and stand in the two indentations forming the figure of eight, from where they can survey the action on both sides of the table. In the old-fashioned Chemin de Fer version, the chief official sat in a raised chair, like a tennis umpire's chair, looking down imperiously upon the action beneath him. Although a couple of casinos still retain this position, the supervisor in charge of the table is usually standing up.

With up to eight seats on either side of the table, sixteen players can be sitting down and betting. Standing players are often also permitted to bet at the table.

For the seated players, there will be numbered betting positions corresponding to their seats at the table. If in doubt, check with a dealer that you are placing your bets in the correct boxes. Standing players should check that their bets will be accepted and where they should place them.

Sometimes, there is a friendly rivalry between the two sides of the table, with one side betting on the Bank's hand to win and the other on the Player's hand to win. The casino loves this action because it ensures that, whatever happens, they will win (taking their 5 per cent from all winning bets on the Bank, and never paying out more than they have taken in from those who have bet on the losing hand). However, you are permitted to bet on whichever hand you wish. You do not have to bet on every hand, and you do not have to bet as much as everyone else. The table minimums will be posted clearly on a small sign at the table. Usually, the minimum bet is $25.

Approaching the Game
In London's highest-rolling clubs and the smartest Strip casinos in Las Vegas, the game is considered to be the king of the casino games. Staff are usually attired in tuxedos and

the lady dealers wear long flowing dresses with plunging necklines.

The standards of service at the Baccarat tables will be the best in the house; high-rollers are brought champagne, canapes and even light meals to enjoy while they are playing. Indeed, many of the Baccarat pits in Vegas casinos are in what appear to be Salon Privés – where only the highest-rolling players go. However, in almost all cases, anyone is welcome to join the game, even if they are betting as little as $25 per hand.

At the end of the six- or eight-deck shoe, there is a suitably arcane ritual of bringing back the cards from the discard container (beneath the table), spreading them around the table and placing them all face down. Then, dealers mix the cards roughly on the table for everyone to see (sometimes called a Chemmy Shuffle – one considered the hardest for the casino to cheat), before gathering the cards together, perhaps shuffling them again, and then offering them to a player to be cut. The cards are returned to the shoe, several are "burnt", or discarded, and the game begins once more. Traditionally, the dealer turns over the top card and whatever value it shows is the number of cards to be discarded before the first coup is dealt.

This process can take up to ten minutes, allowing players to head for the rest rooms, or eat a snack, before returning to battle. In some casinos, the management can't bear to think they are wasting valuable betting time, and so a dealing machine prepares an alternative eight decks, and these are cut and put in the shoe quickly. This is a rather disappointing, greedy method, and I hope smart casinos resist this urge.

The grand table, often lit by glamorous chandeliers, can appear somewhat daunting, and if you are new to the game it is probably better to make your way to a table where the game is already in play and join there.

Choose a seat which suits you. Those closest to the dealers sometimes have a limited view of the far ends of the table, since the casino personnel may be standing between you and where the cards are dealt. For this reason, I would pick a seat at the far end of the table, on either side.

As with most Table Games, you place your cash on the table and it is counted and exchanged for chips. Usually, only high value chips ($25 or higher) are in play at these tables, although because of a pay-out anomaly (to be described shortly) you may be provided with some smaller denomination chips to cope with this requirement.

Take a few moments to observe how the game is played at the casino you are in and then, when you feel ready, place your first bets.

Mini-Baccarat

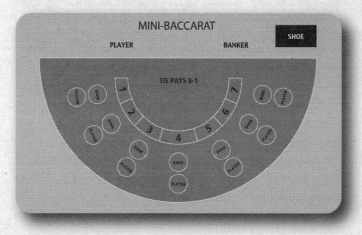

Many casinos have decided that the grand Baccarat table is not used sufficiently to warrant all the space it takes up, nor the minimum of three staff members it takes to man such an operation. Instead, they offer players a Mini-Baccarat game (or Mini-Punto Bunco), which is played at a table similar in size – and layout – to a Blackjack table. This can be manned by a single dealer, plus a supervisor or Pit Boss.

You take a seat, change your cash into chips and bet on the Bank's hand or the Player's hand in exactly the same way as for the big game. The difference here is that all the cards will be dealt face up by the dealer, and all payoffs will be made by the dealer at the end of each hand.

The limits are often lower than at a full-sized table, and the ritual and glamour of the game has been diluted. I don't recommend playing this game in its shrunken form: it's really not much fun.

How the Game Works

The game itself could not be simpler. All gamblers wager on whether the Banker's hand will win, or whether the Player's hand will win. There is an additional option, not offering good odds: betting that the hands will be tied.

Usually, the casino then deals the cards out of a long shoe, which traditionally holds eight decks of cards. In some up-market casinos in Europe, and in the Salon Privés of some Strip casinos, gamblers can take it in turns either to deal the cards from the shoe themselves, or to have the cards dealt to them, so that they examine their values before anybody else gets to see them. Both these "privileges" have absolutely no effect on the outcome of the games, since, the moment the cards are shuffled, cut and fitted into the shoe, every hand is pre-ordained.

Dealing to the Player's hand first and then to the Banker's hand, each player receives two cards. An ace is worth 1; low cards 2, 3, 4, 5, 6, 7, 8 and 9 are all worth the value of the card itself. Tens, jacks, queens and kings are worth zero. The winning hand is the one that gets closest to 9.

If the total of the two cards dealt exceeds 9, then you knock off the 1 (or the 2) from the beginning of the number and take only the second digit as your total. For example:

- An 8 and an 8 totals 16. Knock off the 1 from the front, and the hand value is 6.
- A queen and a 5 equals 5.
- A 7 and a 3 equals 10; knock off the first digit and your hand total is zero (or Baccarat).

On some occasions, the Player's hand, and/or the Bank's hand, is permitted to take a third card in order to improve their hand. When this happens, the actions that follow are shown below, but you don't have to remember them, since the casino will enforce the correct play depending on the position.

For the Player

- If the Player's first two cards total 0, 1, 2, 3, 4 or 5, he draws a third card.
- If the Player's first two cards total 6 or 7, he stands.
- If the Player's first two cards total 8 or 9, this is called a "Natural", and he stands.

- If the Player makes an 8 or a 9, the Banker cannot draw a third card, since a two-card Natural hand beats anything but an equal or higher Natural hand.

For the Bank(er)

- If the Bank holds a total of 3, and the Player has drawn a third card of any value, except for an 8, the Bank takes a third card. Otherwise, he stands.
- If the Bank holds a total of 4, and the Player has drawn a third card of 2, 3, 4, 5, 6 or 7, the Bank takes a third card. Otherwise, he stands.
- If the Bank holds a total of 5, and the Player has drawn 4, 5, 6 or 7, the Bank takes a third card. Otherwise, he stands.
- If the Bank holds a total of 6, and the Player has drawn 6 or 7, the Bank takes a third card. Otherwise, he stands.
- If the Bank holds a total of 7, he always stands.
- If the Bank holds a total of 8 or 9, this is known as a "Natural" and he always stands.

These Hit/Stand moves sound complicated, but they are based around the fact that the Bank has an advantage in acting second, and is always trying to make the correct play to increase his total following any action by the Player. Once you play the game for a short while, you soon get used to the correct plays and you find yourself knowing when the dealers will tell you to stand or to take a third card.

The key hands to look for are the "Natural" hands of 8 or 9 made by the first two cards only. If either player has one of these hands, the other player cannot take any further cards and must stand. A Natural 8 beats everything but a Natural 9; a Natural 9 beats everything (or ties with another Natural 9).

Whether the cards are dealt face up by the house or by a player, or whether the Player's cards are examined first by the player representing that hand, eventually both hands will be revealed and a third card taken where it is required. Once this process has been completed, one of the dealers will announce which hand has won, and to whom winnings should be paid.

The game becomes exciting when the hand values change suddenly. Let's imagine everyone at the table has bet on the Bank's hand. The first card dealt is to the Player. It is a 9 – the best card possible. The second card goes to the Bank's hand. It is a king (zero) – the worst card possible.

So far: Player: 9   Bank: 0

Everyone is now hoping that the Player's second card will be an ace or a low card, to reduce his total. Players may be calling out "Break it!" to the dealer. The second card is dealt to the Player's hand. It is a 3, making the Player's total 12, which counts as 2. The bank now receives his second card: it is a 5. This makes the Bank's total 5.

So far: Player: 2   Bank: 5

This is not the end of the hand, however. Holding a total of only 2, the Player draws a third card. It is a 4, making the Player's total 6. Now, the bank will draw a third card also. He needs an ace to tie the hand, a 2, 3 or 4 to win the hand, and any other card will lose him the hand. The final card is a... Well, you can see how it becomes exciting as the hand develops. In our example, the final card is a... 3! This gives the Bank a hand total of 8. A low cheer rises up; players tap their hands on the table, applauding.

Finally: Player: 6   Bank: 8

The dealer announces: "Bank has 8; the Player has 6. Bank wins. Pay the Bank."

Pay Offs

- If you have bet on the Player's hand, and this is the winning hand, you will paid at even money, 1–1.
- If you have bet on the Bank's hand, and this is the winning hand, you will be paid at even money, 1–1, minus a 5 per cent commission (or *cagnotte*), which is retained by the house. *

  * Some US casinos pay the full even-money amount and do not subtract the 5 per cent commission until the end of the shoe, or when you decide to leave the table. If you have a losing session and still owe the casino commission, this is a horrible position to be in. More and more casinos realize this and they are deducting the commission at the time of the initial payout on the Bank's hand.

The bets are paid this way because it is more likely that the Bank will win. Without the 5 per cent commission, everyone would bet on the Bank's hand and would win an average of just under 4 per cent against the house all the time. This would lead to massive losses for the casino, and is therefore never going to be offered.

The actual odds against the player are quite modest, which makes this game a good one to play if you are not a skilled player in Blackjack, Craps or Video Poker (all of which offer you a better chance of beating the casino).

- Bets on the Bank's hand offer the house an edge of a little under 1.1 per cent.
- Bets on the Player's hand offer the house an edge of a little under 1.25 per cent.

Betting on the Bank's hand is therefore marginally better and it is the default bet of most gamblers at Punto Bunco/Baccarat tables.

Seeking the Best Odds

Although it is rare, it is possible to find both land-based and online casinos offering better odds than those quoted above. This will only occur if the commission on the winning Banker's hands is reduced.

At the time of writing, several online casinos are offering to take only 4 per cent commission (which reduces the house edge to barely over 0.5 per cent), and one is offering high-rolling bettors 3 per cent commission (reducing the house advantage to 0.15 per cent).

If you find any of these offers, this makes the game a much better proposition for the player, but double-check that there are no disadvantages for the players that might compensate the house. As ever, if something looks like a brilliant offer, it's probably got a catch.

Betting on a Tie

You are allowed to bet on the result of the hand being a tie. On the table, there is a betting box marked Tie, or *Égalité*, into which you can place your bet, either as a sole bet on the hand, or in addition to a bet on the Bank or Player. If the hand is tied, bets on Bank and Player are considered stand-offs and your bet is returned to you. Bets placed on a Tie are paid out at 8–1. This sounds a very healthy pay off for a game which otherwise pays even money or below. However, the Tie Bet is one of the worst bets in the casino and offers the house a whopping 14.3 per cent. **Never bet on a Tie at Baccarat**.

Tracking the Shoe

Many high-rolling Baccarat players keep a tally of which hand has been winning and when throughout the shoe. They do this on a card provided by the casino. As with most casino games, the outcome of any particular hand is completely unaffected by the result of the previous hands, so this ritual of filling out the card is just that: a ritual. It cannot help you to predict which hand will win the next coup.

Counting systems have been developed for Baccarat by gaming statisticians, but even they admit that the advantage provided by the most complex methods is marginal and that the situations to exploit such an advantage are very scarce indeed. A cursory glance at such systems leads me to believe that they require a huge duration of play and a massive bankroll to bet very high when you think a favourable situation is about to occur. On this basis, they run the risk of a significant loss for the short to medium term, with only the possibility of sustained success over a very long period of time. For all these reasons, they are not recommended.

Betting Strategy

There is no particular strategy to betting at Baccarat, but there is one key element to remember: never place a bet on a Tie (or *Égalité*). This is the worst bet on the table by far and offers the house an edge of over 14 per cent.

If you plan to play Baccarat for only a short time, it does not matter whether you bet on the Bank's hand or the Player's hand. However, since bets on the Bank's hand attract 0.15 per cent less of an edge against you than the Player's hand, in the long run this will add up against you. Your default position should be to bet on the Bank's hand.

The history of the shoes, previous shoes, even the previous hand, will have no effect whatsoever on the outcome of the next hand. There is no betting strategy that can overcome this.

Money Management

In terms of bankroll, an even-money game can still fluctuate quite dramatically, so for a full session a minimum of 40 times your base stake should be allowed for. This means that if the minimum at the table is \$25, you should bring \$1,000 in bankroll. This will allow you to survive any bad runs of fortune.

For a short session, 20 times the minimum stake is recommended (at \$25, this means a \$500 bankroll).

If you find that you have made 50 per cent profit, lock away your original stake, plus half of that profit. This ensures that you have made a 25 per cent profit when you leave the table. Continue to play as long as you wish with the remaining profit. If you make this up to the original stake amount (tripling your 25 per cent profit), place half of this profit with your original stake and original 25 per cent profit, and continue in this way until you believe it is time to stop, or your extra profit runs out. Do not touch the profit or stake which you have put to one side.

Be aware that if the 5 per cent commission is not collected at the time of pay-out you should keep aside the combined 5 per cent payments on the table, so that this money is not counted as part of your bankroll. It is not your money – and never will be.

Summary

Baccarat is a simple, low-edge game for the house, offering a player a game not requiring any skill, but still providing a decent chance to beat the casino.

- Note the table limits, particularly the minimum bets, as these can be quite high.
- Bet on Bank or Player, but never on a Tie (*Égalité*) which offers the house far too high an edge.
- The dealers will guide you as to whether a third card should be drawn to the Player's or the Bank's hands. You do not have to make any decision yourself.
- If the casino does not collect the 5 per cent commission on the Bank's wins at the time of pay-out, you must keep that money aside to pay when you leave the table (or at the end of the shoe). You are liable for that payment, even if you lose your entire bankroll at the table.
- Seek out land-based and online casinos which may offer a reduced rate of commission to be paid on winning Bank bets. This reduces the house edge dramatically, and improves your chances of winning.
- Do not be put off by the grand impression of the game. It is a friendly, relaxed and slow-paced game which often generates great camaraderie among the players. It is well worth a try in a casino, especially if you do not have the skills to play expertly at Blackjack, Craps or Video Poker.

6
Three-Card Poker

THIS SIMPLE Table Game started to appear in Strip casinos in Las Vegas, and then throughout the world in the 1990s. It has proven very popular both with players and the casino operators, cashing in on the explosive popularity of Poker generally. In fact, the game has very little to do with Poker, other than utilizing some of its terms and it being a battle between the dealer (the house) and the players. Unlike in real Poker, bluffing doesn't work for either side.

The Table
The table used is the same dimensions as a standard Blackjack table and, indeed, some casinos have tables with surfaces that are reversible: one side has a Blackjack layout, the other a Three-Card Poker layout. As with Blackjack,

there are a number of seats and betting positions, usually between six and eight.

As with all Table Games, you lay down your cash to be changed into chips, and take the seat of your choice. Since it is a small table, there are no sightline problems with any position and there is no advantage of taking one seat over another.

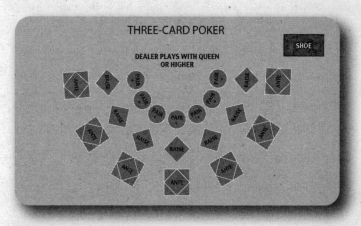

How the Game Works

There are three betting boxes on the layout in front of each player: a circle or box marked "Ante", a circle or box marked "Raise", and a circle or box marked "Pair Plus". The Pair Plus is a completely separate bet from the main game, and we will look at it in a moment.

Place your bet (table minimums vary, usually from $5 upwards) in the Ante box. Once everyone at the table has placed their bets, the dealer (nearly always using a dealing machine) will lay three cards face down in front of each player, and then deal three cards to himself, also face down. Once those cards have been dealt, players may look at their cards.

If you think your "Poker" hand will beat the dealer's hand, you place a bet precisely equal to your Ante Bet in the Raise box. If you do not think that your hand will beat the dealer's hand, you fold your cards (in effect, dropping out of the hand), surrendering your Ante Bet, which will be collected by the dealer.

When all players at the table have made their decisions, the dealer turns over his three cards and arranges them into the best hand possible.

This is the order of value of hands at Three-Card Poker:

Straight Flush	K♠ Q♠ J♠
Three-of-a-Kind	8♥ 8♣ 8♠
Straight	7♣ 6♦ 5♥
Flush	K♥ 7♥ 4♥
Pair	J♠ J♥ 4♣
Queen High Highest card lower than Queen	Q♣ 6♦ 3♦

Poker players will immediately observe that, unlike in the real game, a Straight is a more valuable hand than a Flush. This is simply because with only three cards in your hand you are more likely to make a Flush than a Straight.

For the dealer to "qualify" (compete with the players' hands), he must hold a hand which contains at least one queen. If he holds a hand which contains no Poker hand, and no card higher than a queen, he does not qualify. In that situation, all players get paid at even money (1–1) on their Ante Bets; their Raise Bets are a stand-off, or "push", and their bets are returned to them.

If the dealer does qualify, and if you have a hand that is higher-ranking than the dealer's hand, then you will be paid even money on your Ante Bet, plus even money on your Raise Bet.

If the dealer's hand qualifies and he holds a hand higher-ranking than your hand, then you lose both your Ante Bet and your Raise Bet.

Splitting a Tie

In the unlikely event that both you and the dealer hold a similar hand, a tie can be split by the second or third cards – or "kickers", as they are known. For example:

If you hold	J♠ J♥ 7♣
and the dealer holds	J♦ J♣ 6♦

You would win, because your third card is higher than the dealer's third card.

If you hold	A♠ J♦ 4♣
and the dealer holds	A♥ 9♥ 8♠

You would win because, although you both hold ace-high hands, your second card is higher than the dealer's second card.

In the extremely unlikely event of a complete tie:

If you hold	9♥ 8♦ 7♣
and the dealer holds	9♦ 8♣ 7♥

then, in most casinos, both the Ante and the Raise bets are stand-offs, but you would still get paid the Ante Bonus at 1–1.

There have been occasions where casinos offer a win to the player in the case of a tie, but this is uncommon and gives only a small advantage to the player since perfect ties are very rare.

Ante Bonus Payouts

If you hold a premium hand – a Straight or better – then, whether or not the dealer qualifies, you will receive an Ante Bonus payout. The scale of these payouts may vary from casino to casino, but, generally, the Ante Bonus payouts are as follows:

Straight	pays	even money	1–1
Three-of-a-Kind	pays		4–1
Straight Flush	pays		5–1

If you find that at the casino in which you are playing, these Ante Bonus payouts are reduced from the scale above – from 5, 4, 1 to, say, 3, 2, 1 – then the casino is being unduly greedy and may be affecting their advantage over you by as much as 1 per cent.

The scale of 1–1 for a Straight, 4–1 for Three-of-a-Kind, and 5–1 for a Straight Flush are the industry standard levels and it is recommended to reject any casino offering poorer payouts than this.

If you find anyone offering superior Ante Bonus payouts, this will benefit you. These payouts are usually listed on the baize in front of every betting position.

Playing Strategy

To mimic the house strategy of playing any hand containing a queen or better is almost the best option available to you. On this basis, any hand containing Q6 or better is worth playing, while hands containing no queen, or Q5 or worse, should be folded without placing a Raise Bet. Following this strategy yields the house an edge of 3.38 per cent.

With this house advantage, Three-Card Poker is not a very attractive game to play, and there are certainly other Table Games which offer the player a far better chance to take money off the casino. However, considering that the best strategy is so simple to implement, and the game can be a sociable and moderately slow-moving one (when there are plenty of players at the table), it can be an enjoyable way of gambling for low stakes.

The Pair Plus Bet

This additional bet is a completely separate bet from the Ante and Raise game played at the Three-Card Poker table. It appears to be the more dynamic and exciting element of the game, and dealers and your fellow players will encourage you to play it. It seems to have higher payoffs and a greater chance of winning big. However, it is not a particularly good bet, and certainly less so than many other Table Game bets.

A bet in the Pair Plus box will yield impressive payouts if your hand contains a Poker hand of a Pair or better. If your hand does not contain a Pair or better, you lose your Pair Plus Bet. It does not matter whether the dealer qualifies or not; if you have a winning hand, you will paid; if you have a losing hand, you will lose your bet.

This should be the standard scale at which you will be paid on a Pair Plus Bet:

Pair	pays	even money	1–1
Flush	**pays**		**4–1**
Straight	**pays**		**6–1**
Three-of-a-Kind	pays		30–1
Straight Flush	pays		40–1

At this scale, the house edge against you is a little over 2.3 per cent, which is just about acceptable. However, before playing you must look carefully at the payouts offered, since many casinos offer poorer payouts than those indicated above.

Some, for example, offer only 35–1 and 25–1 for the Straight Flush and "Trips" (Three-of-a-Kind) respectively, and this gives the house double its edge, coming in at close on 4.6 per cent.

The real figures to focus on, however, are the payouts for Flushes and Straights (marked in bold in the table opposite). This is because these hands will occur far more frequently than the rarest hands. Any reduction in the payout on these hands will hugely affect the value of the Pair Plus Bet.

Many casinos are currently offering only 5–1 for the Straight (adding another 1 per cent to the house edge), and some offer a still worse proposition, paying only 3–1 for a Flush. Even if the casino is paying 6–1 for a Straight, the reduction to 3–1 for the Flush gives the house an edge almost three times bigger than the original industry standard, at just short of 7.3 per cent!

So, if you are considering making a Pair Plus Bet, ensure that the casino in which you are playing is offering you the best scale, as shown in the figures opposite. If they are not, then reject the Pair Plus option.

These payouts will be listed either on the baize in front of each player, or on a sign which should be facing all the players.

Mini-Royal Bonus

To add to the excitement, a Mini-Royal is now offered as the best hand of all in some casinos. This is a Straight Flush headed by ace-king-queen – AKQ.

If the casino offers a superior payout for this hand, say 50–1 or even 100–1, then this benefits the player. However, be warned! Some casinos offer a high payout for the Mini-Royal, but a lower payout for hands such as Flushes and Straights. This has a major impact on the house edge – and your chances of winning – since you will see Flushes and Straights galore, but only very, very rarely, a Mini-Royal.

Mini-Royal Progressives

Word comes to me that this innovation is beginning to be seen in some casinos in Las Vegas and London. An additional bet of $1 is required to be part of this, and there are fixed bonus payouts for hitting Three-of-a-Kind, Straight Flush and a Mini-Royal Flush, plus the full value of the Progressive total if you hit a specified Mini-Royal (in one case, a Mini-Royal in spades; in another, a Mini-Royal in diamonds).

Generally, Progressives are not worth playing unless they have built up a good head of steam. You are looking for something in the region of 12,000 times the Progressive stake – so, Progressives at $12,000 or more look worth playing. If the Progressive total is less than this, you will be playing well against the odds.

Finally, take note that when casinos offer deals like Progressives, they often contribute to those Progressives by making other elements of the game less attractive. Since the chances of you hitting the Progressive Jackpot are very small, it is far more important for you to check on the payouts for the Ante Bonuses and the Pair Plus payout scale, particularly for the Straight and Flush hands.

Betting Strategy

As with all games with a negative expectation for the player, betting strategy in itself will not lead to greater winnings or losses. However, resist the temptation to press the size of your bets when you are losing and, instead, keep betting at a minimum level until you win a hand or a combination of hands. Then, raise your bet size slowly, so that if your winning streak develops, you are increasing your stake into it. If you suffer a run of poor luck, all your lost bets will be minimums.

Bankroll

For a full session of Three-Card Poker, bring 40 times your base stake to the table. This means that if you are planning to bet on the Ante, and then the Raise, boxes, as well as taking $5 on the Pair Plus box, you must bring 40 x $15 = $600 to the table. For a short session, bring 20 times your base stake. On the above basis, this would mean a short-session bankroll of $300.

Since Three-Card Poker is weighted quite heavily against the player, if, at any time, you have made a 25 per cent profit on your original bankroll, leave the table immediately with your profit. You have done very well to make it and the likelihood is that you will lose your profit back to the casino if you continue to play.

Summary

Three-Card Poker is a simple, reasonably entertaining Table Game offering poor, but not terrible, odds to the players. The key to having any hope of success at this game is to check the payout schedules, both for the Ante bonuses, and for the Pair Plus awards. If these payouts are not as recommended, walk away from the Three-Card Poker table.

- Note table minimums and then pay special attention to the payout schedules for your Ante Bonus awards. The scale should be: Straight 1–1; Three-of-a-Kind 4–1; Straight Flush 5–1. If the payout schedule indicates lesser payouts than these, walk away from the game.
- If you plan to play Pair Plus Bets, check the payout schedule carefully, concentrating particularly on the payouts for Flushes and Straights. These should be 3–1 and 6–1 respectively. If they are lower than this, do not play the Pair Plus feature, as the house edge against you will almost certainly ruin you – and ruin you quickly.
- When playing the Ante/Raise Bets, place a Raise Bet when your hand contains a queen and a 6, or a better Poker hand. With a poorer hand than this, fold your cards and wait for a better chance to beat the house.
- Three-Card Poker is a tough game at which to beat the casino. Plan to play it only for a short time and leave immediately you have made a 25 per cent profit on your original stake.

7
Caribbean Stud Poker, or Casino Stud Poker

CARIBBEAN Stud Poker is another casino Table Game loosely based on proper Poker, but lacking all the key elements of the real game. It is also a hugely frustrating game – as you will see – but it can lead to short-term profits and offers a long-shot chance at hitting it big.

Known in the UK as Casino Stud Poker, this game has proven very popular, despite it offering the house a pretty substantial edge.

The Table

Caribbean Stud Poker is played on a standard size table, similar to a Blackjack table. There are usually seven seats and betting positions, which feature boxes marked "Ante" and "Raise". In most casinos there is also a Progressive Jackpot to which you can contribute $1 if you wish to be included in that element of the game.

As with all Table Games, you lay down your cash to be changed into chips, and take the seat of your choice. Since it is a small table, there are no sightline problems with any position and there is virtually no advantage to taking one seat over another. The one time your seating choice might matter is in the extremely unlikely event of two players holding major winning hands in the Progressive game. The odds against this happening are so astronomical it really isn't worth worrying about.

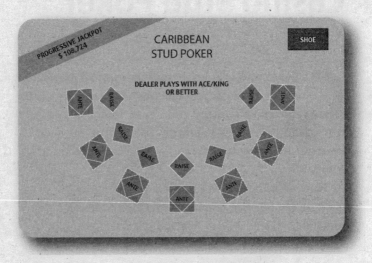

How the Game Works

There are two betting boxes on the layout in front of each player: a circle or box marked "Ante" and a circle or box marked "Raise". The Progressive Jackpot game is separate from the main game, and we will look at it in a moment.

Place your bet (table minimums vary, usually from $5 upwards) in the Ante box. Once everyone at the table has placed their bets, the dealer (nearly always using a dealing machine) will lay five cards face down in front of each player, and then deal five cards to himself, turning one face up for everyone to see. The players may then look at their cards.

Casinos are generally very strict on players not comparing their hands, or discussing what they hold. Often there are signs stating that only English may be spoken at the table. This is because if players were to tell each other which cards they held they could, in theory at least, create a situation where the players, working as a group, would have an edge against the house.

If you think your Poker hand will beat the dealer's hand, you place a bet in the Raise circle, or box. This bet must be exactly double your Ante Bet. Some casinos prefer you to place your cards in the Raise box and your bet on top of them; others will ask you to place your cards beside the betting box.

If you do not think that your hand will beat the dealer's hand, you fold your cards, surrendering your Ante Bet, which will be collected by the dealer.

When all players at the table have made their decisions, the dealer turns over his remaining four cards, and arranges them into the best hand possible.

The standard universal value of Poker hands is used:

| Royal Flush | A♣ K♣ Q♣ J♣ 10♣ |
| Straight Flush | 9♦ 8♦ 7♦ 6♦ 5♦ |

Four-of-a-Kind	8♣ 8♦ 8♥ 8♠ 4♥
Full House	Q♠ Q♦ Q♥ 3♥ 3♣
Flush	9♣ 7♣ 5♣ 3♣ 2♣
Straight	J♦ 10♥ 9♥ 8♠ 7♣
Three-of-a-Kind	K♦ K♥ K♣ 7♦ 3♠
Two Pair	J♦ J♥ 7♦ 7♣ 4♦
One Pair	9♦ 9♥ K♠ 5♣ 3♠
Ace High	A♠ 8♣ 7♣ 5♦ 2♠

For the dealer to qualify, and for the hand to be played out in full, he must hold a hand which is headed by a minimum of ace-king. If he holds a hand which contains no Poker hand, nor an Ace High hand containing ace-king, he does not qualify. In that situation, all players get paid at even money (1–1) on their Ante Bets. Their Raise Bets are a stand-off, or push, and their bets are returned to them. On average, the dealer will qualify a little over 55 per cent of the time.

If the dealer's hand qualifies and he holds a hand that is higher ranking than your hand, then you lose both your Ante Bet and your Raise Bet.

If the dealer's hand qualifies, and you have a hand that is higher-ranking than the dealer's hand, you will paid even money on your Ante Bet, plus the following payouts on your Raise Bet:

Royal Flush	100–1
Straight Flush	50–1
Four-of-a-Kind	20–1
Full House	**8–1**
Flush	**6–1**
Straight	4–1
Three-of-a-Kind	3–1
Two Pair	2–1
One Pair	1–1
Ace-King High	1–1

Not all casinos worldwide pay the same bonuses for the premium hands, and you should always check the pay-table carefully before deciding whether or not to play at any particular casino, land-based or online. As so often is the case, it is the payouts for Full House and Flush that vary most frequently and make a big difference in terms of house edge.

Look out for casinos which offer only 7–1 for a Full House and 5–1 for a Flush, as these hands, though rare, make up a good chunk of the player bonus.

The crucial element of Caribbean Stud Poker is this: if you make a great hand – say, a Full House – and the dealer does not qualify, you do *not* get paid the Raise bonus. You simply win even money on your original Ante Bet. This can be unbelievably frustrating, since the chances of hitting a Full House, Four-of-a-Kind or better are extremely low; to hit one and not be rewarded is almost a form of intentional cruelty!

Splitting a Tie

Ties are rare, but if one occurs then it is split – as in the real game of Poker – by using the kickers (the lower cards not involved in the formation of the qualifying Poker hand). So, if both the player and the dealer have a pair of 9s, the next card in each hand comes into play:

If you hold	9♠ 9♥ K♥ J♦ 4♣
and the dealer holds	9♦ 9♣ Q♦ 7♥ 6♥

You would win, because your third card is higher than the dealer's third card.

If you hold	A♠ K♦ J♣ 8♥ 5♥
and the dealer holds	A♥ K♥ 9♠ 8♦ 2♠

You would win because, after the qualifying ace-king, your third card is higher than the dealer's third card.

If the third card does not decide it, then the fourth card comes into play and, if the fourth card doesn't split the tie, the fifth card becomes live.

If you hold	J♠ J♥ K♣ 7♦ 4♣
and the dealer holds	J♦ J♣ K♦ 7♥ 3♥

Yes! You win again, courtesy of holding a 4 as your fifth card, opposed to the dealer's 3. This kind of win is particularly satisfying.

If there is a complete tie, over all five cards, all bets would be a stand-off.

Playing Strategy

The game requires only a basic understanding to achieve almost the best playing strategy. Analysts have come up with complex rules to eke every last drop from a game with a high house edge. Depending on the pay schedule – and your play strategy – the edge to the casino varies from between 2.5 per cent and 5.5 per cent, making this game a poor one to spend much time playing. You can certainly reduce the advantage the house holds over you by playing correctly, but it still represents a poor game to play for anything but minimum stakes for a short while.

When to Raise
- **Never raise** if you hold less than ace-king. Bluffing does not work in this game since the dealer must always study his hand and compare it to yours.
- **Always raise** if your hand contains a Pair or better. Even if you have a modest pair of 2s, it will benefit you in the long run to raise and play out the hand. If the dealer qualifies, you may lose (unless he holds ace-king, or a Two Pair with a lower kicker); if the dealer does not qualify, you simply win even money on your Ante Bet.

When you hold ace-king yourself, two further strategies are required to play correctly:
- **Raise** if you hold AKQ or AKJ and the dealer's up card is an ace or a king.

Here, you are hoping that the dealer will also make ace-king and qualify, but that your high kicker (queen or jack) will split the tie in your favour. Since you already hold ace and king, the chances of the dealer pairing his ace or king are greatly reduced.

- **Raise** if you hold ace-king and one of your remaining three cards matches the dealer's up card.

Here, you are hoping that the fact that you hold one of the cards with which the dealer could make a pair reduces his chances of doing so, and moves the Raise option into positive expectation over the long term.

Even if you forget the second of these two rules, you would be playing close to the optimal strategy and you would lose a little less quickly than uninformed players. Personally, I don't like this game and nor, it seems, do increasing numbers of players in the United States. I guess, after losing session after session, eventually it doesn't seem worth the effort.

Progressive Jackpot Play

The one element that keeps players rolling up to the Caribbean Stud Poker tables is the Progressive Jackpot element. There is nothing like a neon or LED sign displaying a five or six figure payout to attract the punters. Like most huge payouts on offer, the chances of hitting them are minuscule. However, you never know when Lady Luck will be smiling on you, and there is always a chance that this will be your day.

Most Caribbean Stud Poker tables now offer players a chance to bet $1 on the Progressive Jackpot game on every hand. Good dealers (from the point of view of the casino) will encourage you to make this bet and, if you want to try to hit the long-shot prize, you could have a go. Most of the time, this bet is a terrible one – truly terrible – offering the house in many cases in excess of a 20 per cent edge.

The advantage of the bet is that you get paid regardless of whether or not the dealer qualifies in the main game. So, if you do manage to hit your Full House, or Four-of-a-Kind, or even a Straight or Royal Flush, you will get paid, whatever the dealer holds.

This is the standard pay-table you will find in many casinos:

Royal Flush	Progressive Jackpot
Straight Flush	10 per cent of Progressive Jackpot
Four-of-a-Kind	$500
Full House	$150
Flush	$50

The chances of making any of these hands is very small, but at least when you do hit them you get something. As usual, it is very important to note the payouts for the Flush and Full House (they are sometimes less than this), since these are the hands you are most likely to see.

Depending upon the other payouts offered by a particular casino, you are looking for a Progressive Jackpot close to $200,000 in order to make the bet a decent one. In my experience, it is rare to see Progressives that high on Caribbean Stud Poker, although I have certainly seen them and heard of them. If you are serious about playing this game, and think that it is your time to hit the nigh-on impossible Royal Flush (only one is likely to be seen every 650,000 hands!), then at least do it at a casino where the Progressive is high.

Most casinos start their Progressive Jackpots at $10,000 and then donate a proportion of the $1 you bet into the jackpot. Usually, this is at a rate of between 50c and 75c. The Progressive Jackpot is usually linked to all tables in the pit or casino, and sometimes state-wide or nationwide. If you see a total that is not impressive, check the payouts for the lower prizes (since these are far more likely to occur) and, if they do not impress you, walk away.

My own experience of the Progressive Jackpot at Caribbean Stud Poker is uncharacteristically good. I've hit a Straight Flush online and received 10 per cent of a hefty jackpot, and then, guiding a friend around the tables in Las Vegas, I hit a Full House on the very first deal and collected $250. Considering how little I ever play this game – usually just as a demonstration or to test online rules and procedures – this is nothing short of gobsmacking.

My guess is that, if you are going to play a game pretty heavily weighted against you, you might as well invest the $1 on the Progressive Jackpot just in case. But, remember, those $1 bets all add up.

Betting Strategy

There is no betting strategy that will increase your chances of beating Caribbean Stud Poker and the more you bet, the more you will lose. Generally, I recommend minimum bets, perhaps with a gentle parlay when the dealer qualifies and you win a hand. For example, if you started out with a $10 Ante Bet and you made Two Pair and the dealer qualified, you might increase your bet to make a $15 Ante Bet the next time. Win again, and you might raise it to $20. However, if you lose, or you fold, you should return to your base bet once again. And, remember, if you raise your Ante Bet, your Raise Bet must always be exactly double that amount, so a modest-sounding $5 increase actually equates to a $15 increase when you make your Raise Bet.

Bankroll

Since this is a poor-expectation game for the player, I recommend a small bankroll, or 20 times the base bet you plan to make, including the raises. This means that for a base bet of $5, you actually need $15 per hand, making your bankroll $300.

If you are lucky enough to make a 25 per cent profit on your original bankroll at any time, my advice would be to stop playing, cash in your winnings and congratulate yourself on bucking the odds and beating the house. Just remember, the longer you play, the more likely you are to lose.

Summary

Caribbean Stud Poker (or Casino Stud Poker) is a frustrating Poker-based game, offering poor odds to the player. Check that the payouts for Flushes and Full Houses are decent (ideally, 6–1 and 8–1 respectively).

If you want to play the Progressive Jackpot, check the pay scales (particularly Flushes and Full Houses, where you are looking for 50 times the stake and 150 times respectively, as a minimum), and also the jackpot total. For a $1 bet, the Progressive Jackpot should be approaching $200,000 before your bet becomes a decent gamble.

- Place a Raise Bet every time you hold a Pair or better.
- Place a Raise Bet when you hold AKQ or AKJ, and the dealer's up card is an ace or a king.
- Place a Raise Bet if you hold AK and the dealer's up card matches one of your other cards.
- Do not discuss what you have in your hand with other players. Casinos are very strict about enforcing the rule of no shared knowledge between players.
- Caribbean Stud Poker is a very tough game at which to beat the casino. Plan to play it only for a short time and leave immediately you have made a 25 per cent profit on your original stake.

8
Let It Ride

L ET IT RIDE was one of the first Poker-based casino Table
Games to hit the global scene and it remains popular
because there appears to be a high level of player
input. Indeed, there are actions the player can take to reduce
the substantial house edge on this game, and it can be a
sociable and relaxed-pace game. However, as a gambling
investment it offers poor odds and, perhaps more
importantly, rare occasions when you, the player, are raking
chips in your direction.

The renewed attraction of Let It Ride is that, in a small way,
it mimics Texas Hold 'Em, the most popular version of Poker
being played. Following its television appearance, everyone
thinks they are now a Poker player, and the Poker rooms are
packed with punters, both skilled and totally hopeless. For those
who dare not play against live opponents, this watered-down
version allows them to play, at poor odds, against the house.

Apparently, this game was invented by the same people who invented the automated dealing machine (now, a company called Shuffle Master). This was a fine piece of commercial synergy, since the machines originally dealt only one deck, and this game requires the use of one newly shuffled deck at the start of each round. Incidentally, most casinos use two decks; while one is in play, the other is being shuffled. This speeds up the game for both the casino (the more bets, the more profits) and also for the players.

I have also seen this game called "Let 'Em Ride" and "Triple Chance Poker".

The Table

Approach the table and take the seat of your choice. Since it is a small table, there are no sightline problems with any position and there is no advantage in taking one seat over another.

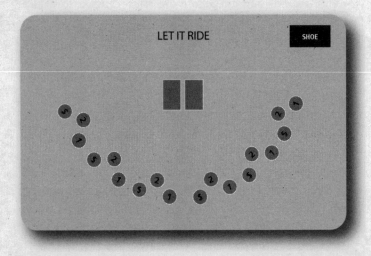

Let It Ride is played on a standard Blackjack-style table, with six or seven seats and betting positions. Each betting position consists of three betting spots, or circles. Some Let It Ride tables offer bonus, or even Progressive Jackpot, bets. These, however, are separate from the main game.

Look out for a Maximum Payout notice. Some casinos announce that if there is a very big win, they may not pay it out! Outrageous? Of course it is. These casinos only want to win big themselves; they'd hate you to win big. So, bet small, and ensure that such a limit can never affect you. Usually, the limits start kicking in when you are betting more than $25 per betting circle. I advise you always to play this game for minimum stakes, and save your high-rolling ambitions for games where the player stands a much better chance of winning.

How the Game Works

Having changed your cash with the dealer, to start the game each player places a bet of the same size in each of his three betting boxes. The dealer takes three cards from the dealing machine and places them face down in front of each player. He then takes three cards for himself and discards one of them, leaving two cards face down in front of him. These will become "community cards" which, when they are shown face up on the table, will be used by each player to complete a five-card Poker hand.

The players study their cards at this point. If you have a very poor hand, you can remove the bet from the first betting spot. If you wish to remain in the hand, you leave all your bets in play and... "Let It Ride!"

Next, the dealer turns over the first of his two cards. If the knowledge of the first community card has not improved your hand, you now have the option of removing the bet from the second betting spot, leaving you with just your original $5 bet in play. This bet can never be removed.

Alternatively, if this fourth card has improved your hand, you can opt to leave the second bet in play (regardless of whether or not you removed the third bet earlier) and see the final card.

Finally, the dealer turns over the second community card, and all players use those two cards, plus the three in their hand, to make the best Poker hand possible according to the standard scale of Poker hands, as illustrated in the payout schedule below.

Payout Schedule

Royal Flush	1,000–1
Straight Flush	200–1
Four-of-a-Kind	50–1
Full House	11–1
Flush	8–1
Straight	5–1
Three-of-a-Kind	3–1
Two Pair	2–1
One Pair (10s or higher)	1–1

If you have let all three original bets ride, then you will be paid at this schedule on all three hands. If you have let two bets stand, you get paid on two bets and, if you took back your third and second bet, then you get paid on only one bet.

Clearly, if you are lucky enough to hit a Full House or better, and you have all three betting circles in action, you can expect a good payout.

However, making a hand of a Pair of 10s or higher is quite hard to do and, unless you hit that hand in your first three cards, you are likely to have rejected the chance to leave on your bets until the end, so you may get paid on only one bet.

The dealer has no hand in this game; you play against the house payouts only. The dealer's two cards are really your cards – shared with any other players at the table to make the best hand possible. Even if your three cards contain no useful cards, the dealer's two cards can form a pair of 10s or jacks, queens, kings or aces, and then all bets will be paid off at even money (unless someone has a third card, making Three-of-a-Kind, or even Four-of-a-Kind, also known as "Quads").

Just before the dealer turns over his second card, you will often hear players calling out: "Pair for the table!" – meaning that if the dealer makes a pair of 10s or better, everyone gets paid.

Be aware that you will encounter many variations on this payout schedule, although this one is the most common in Las Vegas at the moment. Online casinos, in particular, tend to offer poorer payouts on the really long-shot hands, such as Royal or Straight Flushes, but superior payouts for the more common hands, such as Straights and Flushes. Frankly, the online payment schedules are much more likely to suit you, since it is very rare to see a Straight Flush or Royal Flush. However, all variations seem to end up offering the house an unduly healthy edge of about 3.5 per cent. This kind of edge against the player is enough to cripple anyone, and quickly – unless you run into a series of lucky hands, and then get out while you are still on top.

Playing Strategy

Although the inbuilt house edge is around 3.5 per cent, many players offer the casino a far higher percentage by playing recklessly, gambling to hit perfect cards at odds that are massively against them. However, if you follow a key Basic Strategy, you will at least optimize your chances of winning and keep the house edge to a minimum. Most important are the decisions you make on whether to let your bets ride, or whether to take them back and out of play.

First Decision (based on your three cards alone)

Leave all bets on to play if you have:

- A made hand: a Pair of 10s or better.
- Three Royal Flush cards.
- Three suited cards to a Straight Flush, either consecutive (5, 6, 7) or with a one-stop gap only (5, 7, 8).
- Three suited cards to a Straight Flush, including at least two cards, 10 or higher, with a one-stop gap or two-stop gap only (8, 10, J or 7, 10, J).

With none of the above, take back bet number three.

Second Decision (based on your three cards, plus the first of the dealer's community cards)

Leave all bets on to play if you have:

- A made hand of a Pair (10s or higher), Two Pair, or Three-of-a-Kind.
- Any four cards to a Royal Flush, a Straight Flush, or a Flush.
- Any four cards to an Open-ended Straight.*
- Any four cards to a Gutshot Straight if all four cards are 10 or higher.**

* An Open-ended Straight is one which can be made if one of two different value cards appears. For example, if you hold 9, 8, 7, 6, then either a 10 or a 5 will make your Straight – i.e. there are eight cards in the deck which can make you an Open-ended Straight.

** A Gutshot Straight is one which can only be made by the appearance of a card of one value. For example, if you hold 9, 8, 6, 5, then only a 7 will complete your Straight – only four cards in the deck can make you a Gutshot Straight.

So, an Open-ended Straight draw is twice as likely to hit as a Gutshot Straight draw.

If you note these decisions down, most casinos will be quite happy for you to consult your crib sheet when you play. The house has a big enough edge built in not to worry if you play the best strategy available. Players who let their bets ride on hands that are worse than those shown above are only adding to the house edge. If they want to give their money to the casino, that's their business, but you should aim to avoid this at all costs.

Three-Card Bonus Bet

Some casinos offer an additional wager on top of the three
bets placed in the standard version of Let It Ride. This bet is
very similar to the Pair Plus Bet in Three-Card Poker
discussed earlier. Indeed, this option is often offered at casinos
where they do not offer Three-Card Poker, other than as part
of the Let It Ride main game. The payout schedule is similar
to the Three-Card Poker Pair Plus, but take note of one small
variation, which means quite a lot to you, the player:

Payout Schedule for Three-Card Bonus Bet

Mini Royal	50–1
Straight Flush	40–1
Three-of-a-Kind	30–1
Straight	6–1
Flush	**3–1**
Pair	1–1

The low payout for a Flush (3–1) cripples the player because
Pairs and Flushes are the most common hands to occur.
Remember that a Straight is less likely with three cards, than
a Flush. The 3–1 payout, assuming that all the other payouts
are the same, increases the house edge to just over 7 per cent,
and makes this bet a very poor proposition.

If you can find a casino online, or land-based, which
offers the more usual 4–1 for a Flush, then the edge is
reduced to just under 2.2 per cent, which makes this bet
bearable in the short-term. As always with these schedules,

the really important figures to you are not the jackpot and major prize payouts – since these occur so rarely – but the bread and butter, everyday payouts, towards the bottom of the payout schedule. The meaner they are, the meaner the casino you are in. Beware!

Some casinos offer other payouts from special side bets. Without exception, I have found these to offer even poorer odds than the Three-Card Bonus wager and the main Let It Ride game, which, as it is, provides only a slim, short-term chance for the player to beat the house. Ignore all other bets offered at the Let It Ride table.

Bankroll

Let It Ride is not a game I recommend to you. At a 3.5 per cent edge, it will wear you down. At a busy table, it can be a very slow, laborious game, with people taking their time to make decisions. However, it can create an amiable atmosphere, since everyone is playing against the house payouts, and not against a dealer's hand.

If you want to try the game, or it is one you particularly enjoy, I recommend a small bankroll of 30 times your base bet. This means that if your base stake is $5, you must have $15 per round in case you wish to let your bets ride until the end. This means a bankroll of $300.

Betting Strategy

As with all negative-expectation casino games, no betting strategy will increase your chances of winning. However, in terms of trying to build up a profit, a modest increase of bets when you are winning may lead to you being able to leave the table a winner. Be aware that if you increase your base stake even by $5, this actually increases your exposure by a further $15 per hand, since you have to place three bets originally and, without doubt, you should be assuming that you are going to be leaving those bets on to play. (If you are assuming that you will not be leaving them on, then you are approaching the game with a negative attitude.) Of course, there will be many hands where you decide to take back bets, and this will prolong your bankroll.

Because the house has such a convincing edge over you, I strongly recommend that if you find you have a 25 per cent profit from your original bankroll you stop playing immediately and leave the table.

Summary

Let It Ride is a leisurely, but punitive version of casino-based Texas Hold 'Em Poker, offering poor odds to the player. Check that the payouts for Flushes and Full Houses are decent (ideally, 8–1 and 11–1 respectively).

- Place a bet on each of the three betting circles before receiving your cards. Following the recommended strategy, remove or retain each bet as the dealer offers you it. Do not be tempted to try for a perfect outcome. Follow the odds correctly to reduce the house edge.
- Resist the urge to make side bets; these are almost always a very poor option.
- Play for low stakes, for a short time only, or the house edge will grind you down and leave you with nothing.
- Do not be surprised if you see no paying hands for long periods. Let It Ride can be a very streaky game with small runs of good and, more likely, bad luck for the player.
- If there is a Maximum Payout limit in force, do not bet more than the table will pay out if you hit the jackpot (usually $25 per betting circle).

9
Spanish 21, or Casino Pontoon

I FIRST ENCOUNTERED Casino Pontoon in Australia and while watching a game felt that it might offer decent odds to the player, despite some strange variations from the usual game of Blackjack. Researching further, Spanish 21 – as it is called in most countries – seems to offer a superior game to Blackjack in terms of house edge, especially when combined with an efficient counting system. If you are tiring of Blackjack, look for Spanish 21, because it is an exciting game with multiple betting opportunities.

A company called Masque Publishing owns the rights to the game, both in land-based and online casinos. They offer players a breakdown of the rules and advertise where the best games of Spanish 21 are available, as well as promoting which casinos offer the most favourable playing conditions. Search online for their latest information.

The key difference between Blackjack and Spanish 21 is that the latter game utilizes a so-called Spanish deck, which contains only 48 cards, the four 10s having been removed from each deck. Dealt either from a six- or an eight-deck shoe, or from a continuous shuffle and dealing machine, the removal of 10 cards is detrimental to the player's prospects. For that reason, a myriad of beneficial bonus options and rules are brought into effect. It is these which make Spanish 21 such an entertaining prospect compared to normal Blackjack.

There is a large variance in house rules depending on where you find a Spanish 21 table. As you become familiar with the game, you will be able to determine whether a particular casino is offering the best rules for you. Primarily, however, you should look for a key rule in both Blackjack and Spanish 21 – does the dealer stand on soft 17, or hit soft 17? The former will prove advantageous to the player in the long run.

The Table

Spanish 21 is usually played on a standard casino Blackjack table with a slightly different printed baize layout. There will be six or seven seats and betting positions. Many tables offer subsidiary bets and some even offer Progressive Jackpot bets. Take the seat of your choice. Since it is a small table, there are no sightline problems with any position and there is no advantage to taking one seat over another.

How the Game Works

As with Blackjack, your intention is to make a hand as close to 21 as possible, without exceeding that total.

You place your bet in the betting box and receive your first two cards. Working from the dealer's left to right, players will be offered the opportunity to stand, hit, split, double, or surrender, as in Blackjack.

The dealer will always take a hole card, and check for Blackjack before playing out the players' hands.

The house rules will vary from casino to casino, and certainly from country to country, as will the payout schedule. However, you should be able to see the rules displayed at the table, or ask casino staff what the local rules are. Bonus payouts will always be described at the table, and the main elements printed on the green baize in front of you.

The house edge is hugely dependent upon the rules and bonus payouts that are offered:

- Where the dealer stands on soft 17, the house edge is approximately 0.4 per cent.
- Where the dealer hits soft 17, the house edge is approximately 0.8 per cent.

- Where the dealer hits soft 17, and double-doubles (re-doubles) are permitted, the edge falls once more to just over 0.4 per cent.

These are refreshingly low percentages but, as with standard Blackjack, these percentages are reliant upon you playing correct Basic Strategy. If you are familiar with standard Blackjack Basic Strategy, you should find Spanish 21 reasonably easy, entertaining and quite stimulating.

Spanish 21 Payout Schedule

Let's take a look at the most common rules for Spanish 21 and see how they affect the game:

- **Player's 21 beats any 21 by the dealer, except for a natural Blackjack.**
- **Player's Blackjack beats dealer's Blackjack.**
  Although it occurs only infrequently, not being paid for a Blackjack is very frustrating. In this game, you always get paid for a Blackjack. However, note that seeing a Blackjack is a little more unlikely since 25 per cent of the ten cards have been removed from the shoe/dealing machine.
- **Double after split.**
  All good Blackjack games should allow you to do this, but in Spanish 21 it is an integral rule, allowing you to make money when, for example, you split 33 against a dealer 6, and receive a 7 on one hand and an 8 on the other. Both these hands can now be doubled, putting you, the player, in a very advantageous position.

- **Re-splitting of aces.**
  Most casinos allow re-splitting of aces up to four times. (A few casinos offer a 3–2 payout on Blackjacks formed after splitting. This is a very advantageous rule for the player.)
- **Players may double down after any number of cards.**
  For example, the dealer shows 8, you are dealt 6, 3, and you opt to hit your hand. If you then receive 2, you have a total of 11 and you want to double down. If you then receive K, you have 21 with double the money in your betting position.
- **Players may double-double down.**
  For example, if the dealer shows 4, you are dealt 5, 4, and you opt to double down. If you then receive 2, you have a total of 11. Now you can double down again, multiplying your original bet four times at the most advantageous moment. If you then receive J, you have 21 with a maximum money bet.

  Some casinos may permit you to double-double down more than once. However, this may encourage you to start doubling on hands such as 3, 2, when the dealer's card is good for you (a 5 or 6). This can lead to poor decisions and a marked increase in the house edge against you.
- **Players may surrender after doubling down.**
  If you hold 6, 4 against the dealer's up card of 7 and decide to double down, this is correct strategy. However, if you are then dealt a 3, and it looks as if you will lose both your bets, "Double down Rescue" (as it is sometimes called) allows you to surrender half your bets and exit the hand before the dealer makes his hand.

In addition to these very favourable and exciting variations on standard Blackjack rules, Spanish 21 also offers bonus payouts for specific hands.

Spanish 21 Bonus Payouts

These payments apply even after hands have been split, but not if doubles have been used:

Five-card 21 pays 3–2. A five-card trick totalling 21.

Six-card 21 pays 2–1.

Seven-card 21 pays 3–1.

21 composed of mixed suits 7, 7, 7 or 8, 7, 6 pays 3–2.

21 composed of same suit 7, 7, 7 or 8, 7, 6 pays 2–1.

21 composed of 7♠, 7♠, 7♠ or 8♠, 7♠, 6♠ pays 3–1.

A Super Bonus is paid if you make a same suit 7, 7, 7 and the dealer's up card is also a 7, of any suit. This is not paid when hands have been split or doubled.

Bettors staking below $25 are usually paid $1,000.

Bettors staking $25 or above are usually paid $5,000.

All other players in the hand are paid $50 for what is called an "Envy Bonus".

Playing Strategy

The strategies are similar for games where the dealer hits soft 17, and for those (more favourable for the player) where the dealer stands on any 17. For simplicity and ease of learning, the Basic Strategy discussed below is for games where the dealer stands on all 17s. Even if your local casino plays for the dealer to hit soft 17, this version will ensure that you are still playing at near optimum odds.

The easiest method of displaying the Basic Strategy is in a chart. Although this may look complicated at first glance, if you study each section you will see that almost all the suggested decisions are quite logical and intuitive.

There are many playing strategies available, with minor discrepancies between each. Where discrepancies have been noted – and they are always very small – I have used the more conservative option for this strategy.

Hard Totals Hit/Stand/Double Strategy

Player	Dealer's Up Card									
	2	3	4	5	6	7	8	9	10	A
4–8	H	H	H	H	H	H	H	H	H	H
9	H	H	H	H	D4	H	H	H	H	H
10	D	D	D	D	D	D4	D3	H	H	H
11	D	D	D	D	D	D4	D4	D4	D3	D3
12	H	H	H	H	H	H	H	H	H	
13	H	H	H	H	H	H	H	H	H	
14	H	H	S4*	S5*	S4*	H	H	H	H	

15	S4*	S5*	S5**	S	S	H	H	H	H	H
16	S5	S	S	S	S	H	H	H	H	H
17	S	S	S	S	S	S	S	S	S	S
18	S	S	S	S	S	S	S	S	S	S
19	S	S	S	S	S	S	S	S	S	S
20	S	S	S	S	S	S	S	S	S	S

H = Hit S = Stand D = Double down S4/S5 = Stand, but hit if your hand contains 4 cards or 5 cards. * Hit if you hold any two cards from any 6, 7, 8 (mixed suits). ** Hit if you hold any two out of 6♠, 7♠, 8♠.

Soft Totals Hit/Stand/Double Strategy

Player	Dealer's Up Card									
	2	3	4	5	6	7	8	9	10	A
<16	H	H	H	H	H	H	H	H	H	H
16	H	H	H	H	D4	H	H	H	H	H
17	H	H	D3	D4	D5	H	H	H	H	H
18	S4	S4	D4	D5	D5	S	S4	H	H	H
>18	S	S	S	S	S	S	S	S	S	

H = Hit S = Stand D = Double down D3, D4, D5 = Double, but Hit if you hold 3 cards, 4 cards, or 5 cards. S3, S4 – Stand, but Hit if you hold 3 cards or 4 cards.

Splitting Strategy

Player	Dealer's Up Card									
	2	3	4	5	6	7	8	9	10	A
22	SP	SP	SP	SP	SP	SP	SP	H	H	H
33	SP	SP	SP	SP	SP	SP	SP	H	H	H
44	H	H	H	H	H	H	H	H	H	H
55	H	H	H	H	H	H	H	H	H	H
66	H	H	SP	SP	SP	H	H	H	H	H
77	SP	SP	SP	SP	SP	SP*	H	H	H	H
88	SP	SP	SP	SP	SP	SP	SP	SP	SP	SP
99	S	SP	SP	SP	SP	S	SP	SP	S	S
1010	S	S	S	S	S	S	S	S	S	S
AA	SP	SP	SP	SP	SP	SP	SP	SP	SP	SP

Hit = Hit SP = Split S = Stand * = Do not Split if your two 7s are suited. Hit instead.

Notice that much of the strategy is similar to Blackjack Basic Strategy (see pages 77–78), although "slim doubles" (doubles where the statistical edge to the player is very small) are not included since there are 25 per cent fewer tens in the shoe/machine than usual.

Notice also that the strangest plays are made when:

- attempting to make five-, six- or seven-card hands totalling 21 for bonus payouts.
- a 7, 7, 7 is possible, especially when suited, since this bonus payout is not made when hands have been split.

Match the Dealer

Match the Dealer is a side bet which has now become almost standard on all Spanish 21 tables. Like the Proposition Bets at the Blackjack table, these side bets offer far poorer odds than the main game and generally should be resisted. Here, you place a bet in a side circle, or a box attached to the top of the standard betting circle.

If your initial first card, and/or first and second cards, match the suit rank of the dealer's card, you receive a payout. The rate of payout will vary from casino to casino. The payout schedule below represents an average taken from a number of Spanish 21 tables, both land-based and online, offering the Match the Dealer side bet. If your casino offers poorer odds, then reject this bet; if the odds are superior, then consider making small wagers only.

One-card non-suited match	4–1
Two-card non-suited match	8–1
One-card suited match	9–1
Two-card suited match	18–1

The house edge on this payout schedule, assuming six decks or more, or a continuous shuffling-dealing machine, is a little over 3 per cent. Compared to the main game of Spanish 21, this is not a sensible wager.

Card Counting at Spanish 21

It is clear from a wide variety of articles and published research that card counting at Spanish 21 is, if anything, more profitable than at Blackjack – at least while the game is still dealt out of a shoe. When continuous shuffle-dealing machines become widespread, counters will suffer.

In the meantime, casinos still seem quite relaxed about counters at Spanish 21. I have spoken to one professional player who has now given up Blackjack – since he received so much scrutiny – to turn his attention instead to Spanish 21.

Because 25 per cent of the ten cards have been removed from the deck, aces become even more valuable in Spanish 21. It is also true that the player is less likely to receive a ten card on double down opportunities and, for this reason, the doubling strategy is significantly different from that used for Blackjack.

It is also the case that, as cards are removed from the shoe, players' strategies will change far more radically than at Blackjack, so the counting and playing strategy will be even more complex. However, since casinos are, at the time of writing, permitting huge betting spreads, and allowing players to duck in and out of the game throughout the shoe, expert counters will certainly be able to ensure an advantage.

The downside is that, despite it's growing popularity, Spanish 21 is usually represented by only one or two tables, even in the biggest casinos. Casino staff who see counters consistently beating the game will not take long to notify management and the counters may once again become a hunted breed.

Online there are several recommended counting systems, but only players serious about many months of study, practice and hard work should even consider taking on one of these methods.

Bankroll

Use a similar bankroll to Blackjack. Ideally, this should contain 40 base bets to allow for natural variations and the possibility of a sustained poor period. If you plan to place side bets, such as the Match the Dealer wager, make sure that this is included in addition to your main-game bankroll.

I like to separate the bankrolls which I use for the main game from those I might decide to use for side bets. When you do this, you often find that the side bets have cost you far more than you expected. You realize that, by including those bets in your main bankroll, you are reducing your overall chances of recording a profit, since you don't notice the drain on your main bankroll.

Betting Strategy

Despite Spanish 21 being a good-value game for the gambler, it is still a negative-expectation game, i.e. the more you bet, for the longer term, the more you will inevitably lose. However, for occasional sessions, this game offers the player a really good chance to beat the casino – and to beat it well.

Small increases in bet size to take advantage of hot streaks is the best way to accumulate profits. Returning to your base stake after a loss, and then maintaining that even base stake when the going is not good, will keep losses to a minimum.

Because Spanish 21 is almost an even-money game, you can operate a liberal profit retention system. I recommend that when you have doubled your money you should remove half of the profit, plus the original bankroll, and put it aside. Do not touch this money: this ensures that you will leave the table with at least a 50 per cent profit.

Play out the remaining 50 per cent profit (or stop and bank more of it) and, if you double this again, once more remove 50 per cent and continue playing with the remaining 50 per cent.

Even if you think you are "due" a change of luck, do *not* dip into the profit that you have put aside. That discipline alone will save you hundreds, even thousands, of dollars whenever you play in a casino.

Summary

Spanish 21 is an exciting variation of Blackjack, with liberal rules and opportunities to double, and sometimes re-double, your initial wager in profitable situations. The overall house edge for almost any version of this game is lower than 1 per cent, making it a good game to try to beat the house. However, regular Blackjack players should be aware of some major Basic Strategy changes and should study the strategy in detail as outlined in this chapter.

Side bets, such as Match the Dealer, should generally be avoided or played only for low stakes. These side bets almost always offer far poorer odds than those proffered by the main game.

- At a house edge of between 0.4 and 0.8 per cent, played with correct Basic Strategy, Spanish 21 is one of the most attractive bets available to the gambler in a casino.
- The increasing popularity of the game ensures that it will be seen in more and more casinos.
- Check payouts and rule variations at the table. "Dealer Stands on All 17s" emblazoned on the baize in a semicircle near the dealer gives you, the player, a further 0.4 per cent advantage over tables where "Dealer Hits Soft 17s and Stands on Hard 17".

10
Blackjack Switch

I**N THE SEARCH** for ever-more exciting Table Games, where the player appears to have more of an input, the game inventors have come up with yet another version of Blackjack. Blackjack Switch is a clever design, since it gets you to play two hands, hence doubling your minimum stake, and gives the impression that your fate is in your hands. In fact, the advantages of the switch are almost entirely wiped out by the strange variations on the rules. However, Blackjack Switch played properly allows you to play another Table Game against the house where the inbuilt edge against you is below 1 per cent. This provides you with a genuine opportunity to beat the house over the medium term and record some handsome profits.

The Table

Blackjack Switch is played at a standard-size Blackjack table with a slightly different printed baize layout. You will usually find six seats and betting positions. Many tables offer subsidiary bets. Take the seat of your choice; since it is a small table there are no sightline problems with any position and there is no advantage of taking one seat over another.

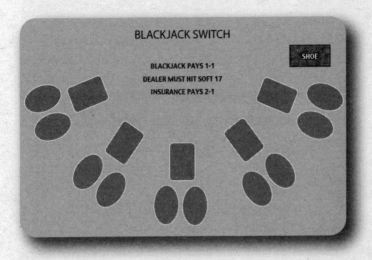

How the Game Works

The game is usually played with six decks. In many casinos, it is dealt out of a continuous shuffle-dealing machine (many of these machines hold only five decks).

The player places two bets of equal size in each of his two betting circles. There may be opportunities to place side bets but, as usual, these do not offer as favourable odds as the main game.

The dealer distributes one card to each of your hands, and one to himself. He deals a second round to complete your two-card Blackjack hands. The dealer then checks for Blackjack in his own hand – if he holds it, you lose all bets (except for "natural" Blackjack hands – see page 199 – which are a stand-off). Then the big player excitement kicks in: you may switch your second card between your two hands. For example:

> The dealer shows: 7
> Your hands are: 10, 5   and   6, Q

You should switch your second cards between hands, making:

>   10, Q   and   6, 5

This gives you one solid hand (20) and one hand perfect for a double down (11).

As you can see, the opportunity of switching gives you great flexibility; in this example it turns two terrible hands into two wonderful hands with the potential, if you double down and win, to win three times your base stake.

To compensate for this huge player advantage, the house has to adjust the rules to provide itself with an edge. These are the three rule changes in Blackjack Switch that are highly significant for the house:

- Dealer always hits soft 17.
- Blackjack pays even money (1–1) and not at the usual 3–2.
- If the dealer makes a total of 22, this becomes a magic score for him, since it will *tie* with any hand you have still in play, unless it is a natural Blackjack (a Blackjack that you have been dealt, and not created via a switch).

Otherwise, standard Blackjack rules are usually in play:

- Double down available on any two-card hand.
- Multiple splits (re-splitting) permitted.
- Double after split should be available.

Pay careful attention to the House Rules as they will affect your overall chances of winning quite considerably. Some casinos are now offering early surrender, which includes surrender against the dealer's ace (providing he does not hold Blackjack). This rule offers the player a great extra edge against the house. Providing its inclusion does not result in other favourable rules being removed or compromised, this is definitely one that players should seek out.

Playing Strategy

To keep the house edge against you to a minimum, you will need to know not only the key elements of Basic Strategy for Blackjack Switch but also the correct times to make switches. There are plenty of occasions when it might be tempting to switch, but to do so would seriously harm your chances, and vice versa.

To work out when it is correct to switch, you need to know the edge any given hand has over the dealer's up card. You must then compare the combined expectation for your two current hands with the combined expectation of the two hands formed by switching. In some cases, one will show expected profit, while the other shows expected loss. Sometimes, your original hands will show expected loss, and switched hands a bigger expected loss, or the same with expected profit. It is almost impossible to work out the correct strategy accurately without the use of a computer or huge sheets of tables and numbers. Since most casinos will bar you from bringing in any kind of computer to aid you at the gaming tables (in Las Vegas you may be arrested and end up in jail) the game is very tough to play perfectly and therefore to realize the calculated house edge. As you become less accurate in your play, so the house edge against you rises and it is, I expect, for this reason that the casinos are as happy with this new game as the players. One casino executive suggested to me that Blackjack Switch probably takes, on average, 3–5 per cent from players every hand. For this reason, Blackjack Switch is one of the few games where you will stand a much better chance playing online, rather than in a casino.

At home, playing online, you can consult your notes, take as much time as you like, look at online information regarding the correct plays, and visit websites which show you all the facts and figures. There is even one site with a link to a Blackjack Switch calculator. You just feed in your two hands and the dealer's up card, and click. Immediately, it tells you whether or not it is correct to switch cards. No errors, resulting in perfect play of the best strategy. How easy is that?

In a casino setting, you need to ensure that you have the basic concepts of when it is right to switch and when not to switch (which I will show you below), as well as following the correct Basic Strategy for standing, hitting, splitting and doubling your Blackjack hands.

Hit/Stand/Double Basic Strategy – Hard Totals

The rules for hit/stand with hard totals (a hard hand is one that contains an ace) are almost identical to the standard Blackjack Basic Strategy. Note however:

- You are more keen to hit with hands totalling 12.
- You are less keen to double down, especially with 9.

Player	Dealer's Up Card									
	2	3	4	5	6	7	8	9	10	A
5-8	H	H	H	H	H	H	H	H	H	H
9	H	H	H	H	D	H	H	H	H	H
10	D	D	D	D	D	D	D	H	H	H
11	D	D	D	D	D	D	D	D	H	H
12	H	H	H	S	S	H	H	H	H	H
13	H	S	S	S	S	H	H	H	H	H
14	S	S	S	S	S	H	H	H	H	H
15	S	S	S	S	S	H	H	H	H	H
16	S	S	S	S	S	H	H	H	H	H
17+	S	S	S	S	S	S	S	S	S	S

H = Hit S = Stand D = Double down

Hit/Stand/Double Basic Strategy – Soft Totals

A "soft" total is one where you hold an ace in your hand which, as always in Blackjack, counts as one or eleven.

Most casinos and online games offer soft doubling. However, in all forms of the game, soft doubles only offer the player a very small percentage improvement. In Blackjack Switch, there is even less need to double on soft totals and, if you have trouble remembering the correct strategy, it would cost almost nothing in terms of lost edge to resolve to make no soft doubles at all. Note:

- Soft doubling is greatly reduced.
- Hit/Stand rules for soft hands are very close to standard Blackjack Basic Strategy.

Player	Dealer's Up Card									
	2	3	4	5	6	7	8	9	10	A
A2	H	H	H	H	H	H	H	H	H	H
A3	H	H	H	H	H	H	H	H	H	H
A4	H	H	H	H	H	H	H	H	H	H
A5	H	H	H	H	D	H	H	H	H	H
A6	H	H	H	D	D	H	H	H	H	H
A7	S	S	S	D	D	S	S	S	S	S
A8	S	S	S	S	S	S	S	S	S	S
A9	S	S	S	S	S	S	S	S	S	S

H = Hit S = Stand D = Double down

Splitting Basic Strategy

Again, the "Stand-off if Dealer Makes 22" rule affects the way you play some of your hands in Blackjack Switch rather than in the standard "pure" game.

Notice that with splitting:

- There are fewer occasions in which it is correct to split pairs.
- You do not split 88 if the dealer shows 10 or Ace.
- If it is correct to split the first time, you should split again if the split results in a pair.

Player	Dealer's Up Card									
	2	3	4	5	6	7	8	9	10	A
22	H	H	H	SP	SP	SP	H	H	H	H
33	H	H	H	SP	SP	SP	H	H	H	H
44	H	H	H	H	H	H	H	H	H	H
55	D	D	D	D	D	D	D	H	H	H
66	H	H	SP	SP	SP	H	H	H	H	H
77	SP	SP	SP	SP	SP	SP	H	H	H	H
88	SP	SP	SP	SP	SP	SP	SP	SP	H	H
99	S	S	SP	SP	SP	S	SP	SP	S	S
1010	S	S	S	S	S	S	S	S	S	S
AA	SP	SP	SP	SP	SP	SP	SP	SP	SP	SP

H = Hit S = Stand D = Double SP = Split

Most casinos will allow you to take in an aide-memoire written on a small card or sheet of paper in order to follow Basic Strategy at Blackjack games. If in doubt, when you arrive at the table check with a supervisor or pit boss that this is permitted. If you can't remember the Basic Strategy, it may cost you many dollars if you make the wrong plays.

When To Switch – Broad Guidelines

In order to keep Blackjack Switch to its minimum house advantage, you need to make the correct decisions when deciding whether or not to switch your second cards between your two hands. To do this accurately, you require a computer, or the statistics, in front of you. Since the information you need is almost impossible to learn in your head, and taking electronic devices of any kind into casinos is a really bad idea, let's see if we can come up with some general guidelines to help you make the right decisions.

- **If you have two intermediate hands, it is better to create one strong hand and try to improve one weak hand. For example:**

The dealer shows:	8		
You are dealt:	K, 3	and	4, Q

If you do not switch, both your hands have negative expectations to win. If, however, you do switch, your hand of 20 has a strong positive expectation of winning, and your hand of 7 has a smaller negative expectation than either 13 or 14 (your totals prior to switching).

So, switch and play:

K, Q	and	4, 3

- **Switch if you can create really favourable double down, or splitting, situations. For example:**

> The dealer shows: 6
> You are dealt: 5, 9   and   9, 6

You definitely want to switch here since hands of 14 and 15, although they may win if the dealer breaks from his 6, will both lose even if he makes 17. However, if you switch, you gain maximum betting potential by forming two "action hands" (an action hand is one where action can be taken by the player in the form of splitting and doubling down, rather than the simple hit/stand decisions which are usually faced). When the dealer is showing a 5 or a 6, these are the times to create action and get more money onto the layout. So, switch to:

> 5, 6   and   9, 9

You now have a perfect double down on 11 versus the dealer's 6, and a smart split of 9, 9 versus the dealer's 6.

Assuming that you are lucky, and the dealer does not score 22 – and therefore turn all your great hands into stand-offs – you may well win four times your base stake on this one hand.

- **Switch if, by doing so, you create one adequate hand and one hand with strong hitting potential. For example:**

| The dealer shows: | 7 | |
| You are dealt: | 6, 10 | 7, 2 |

Here, you have one hand which is very likely to lose (16) and another with decent hitting potential (9). However, if you switch, you will have 8 on your first hand, which offers good hitting potential (if you can score a ten on it), and a second hand of 17, which may well tie with the dealer. It's close, but it is better to switch.

There are many more subtleties. One word of warning: as with normal Blackjack, dealers, supervisors and pit bosses know very little about the game. Unless you are lucky and encounter one who has genuine knowledge of the game, they will almost certainly know less than you if you have a decent basic knowledge (as contained in these pages). You would think that someone dealing these games all day would know all the best plays, but they don't; often their advice is completely wrong. This is why it should be treated with great care.

Once you have read this chapter, try to research the correct strategies further, and then trust your instincts.

Bankroll

Since this is a favourable game for the player, despite still being a negative expectation game in the long run, you can afford to play for a decent period of time and try to hit a hot streak. Your session bankroll should consist of 40 times your base stake. Remember, however, that each bet is actually two bets. So, even if you were to play a minimum stake of

$5 per betting box, that is still $10 per round, requiring a minimum bankroll of $400.

You can afford to be ambitious with this game as, played well, it is almost an even-money proposition. Aim to double your money. If you achieve this and wish to continue playing, put aside your original stake, plus 50 per cent of your profit. Do not touch this money, as this ensures that you will leave the table a winner with a 50 per cent profit.

Continue to play the remaining 50 per cent profit, until you choose to stop, or you lose it. If you succeed in doubling this stake, continue to take out 50 per cent of your remaining bankroll and lock it away together with your original bankroll, the first 50 per cent profit you made, and now these additional profits. Never dip back into these profits while you are at the table.

Betting Strategy

Keep it simple: raise your bets slightly when you are winning; return to the base stake and remain there while you are losing. This strategy allows you to make the most of a hot streak, and to lose the minimum during a prolonged bad spell.

Remember that when you raise the bet in one box, you must also raise it to the identical amount in the second box, so the actual quantity of risk is twice as great as playing a single box on a standard Blackjack table.

Super-Match Side Bet

Many online sites which carry Blackjack Switch, as well as an increasing number of land-based casinos, now offer a side-bet

proposition which, as ever, offers poorer odds to the player
and a better edge to the house. However, all casino operators
know that most gamblers want as much action as possible and
so they find that these side bets are frequently taken up.

In the case of this bet, the odds are not too bad for the
player: roughly a 2.5 per cent long-term edge to the house.
However, what is a little odd is that the side bet has far more
to do with Poker than with Blackjack.

Your first four cards – your two 2-card Blackjack hands –
are considered a Poker hand. If you place a bet in the Super-
Match betting circle at the same time as your Blackjack
Switch bets, then if your hand contains one of the following
Poker-hand features you receive the payouts as illustrated
below:

Any Pair	even money	1–1
Three-of-a-Kind		5–1
Two Pair		8–1
Four-of-a-Kind		40–1

Notice that Two Pair pays more than Three-of-a-Kind
because, with only four cards forming the hand, the chances
of Two Pair is less than for "trips" (Three-of-a-Kind). The
chances of seeing two identical pairs – forming Four-of-a-
Kind – are very small (about 1/3000), so you are really
playing for the other awards. This is the kind of side bet that
usually drains your bankroll, and does not contribute much

fun to the overall game. You would do much better to concentrate on trying to make the correct switch decisions than worry about placing and watching for the Super-Match Side Bet.

Summary

Blackjack Switch is an interesting and challenging variation on the standard game, which offers the player as good odds as the original version. At a house edge of approximately 0.6 per cent, you can play Blackjack Switch, following the correct Basic Strategy and switch decisions, for a long period on a modest bankroll, and still have a good chance of beating the house.

- Check playing conditions, table minimums and house rules. If they are more restrictive than those outlined in this chapter, consider playing elsewhere or switching to a different game.
- Take your time deciding whether you wish to switch and how you should play your hands. Unless you are heartbreakingly slow, no one should rush you.
- Stick to a sensible size of bankroll (at least 40 times your base stake) and lock away any profits. Do not take more money from your pocket/wallet if the session fails from the start, or once you have stored away some profits. Walk away, decide on your next moves and return to the tables later when refreshed.

- Avoid the Super-Match Side Bet. If you must play it, consider it separate from your main bankroll and ensure that you bring extra money with which to play it (you will probably lose that money).
- Consider playing Blackjack Switch online rather than in a live casino. There, from the comfort of your own home, you can consult the charts, assess when it is statistically correct to switch, and when it is not, and consult your notes on the correct Basic Strategy for the playing of each hand in every situation.

11
Pai Gow Poker

PAI GOW POKER is an intriguing and challenging casino Table Game. Based on Poker hands, but with elements of many other casino games, Pai Gow Poker involves the player in hand formation decisions, banking decisions and skills applying sound Basic Strategy.

Invented by Fred Wolf – a former casino manager – and Sam Torosian, Pai Gow Poker has taken both land-based and online casinos by storm, cashing in on the vast new Poker market. From the point of view of the casino, the game increases in popularity yearly; from the player's angle, it is a game which, with a little luck, can yield substantial winnings.

Incidentally, research reveals that the inventors were misadvised as to the possibilities of patenting their invention. They were told it could not be protected although, later, it seems that this was incorrect. As a result, they have missed out on a fortune which this game would have brought them.

Played globally, its combination of Asian influences and Poker-style action has proved to be a huge hit, and more and more casinos offer this game.

Many casinos advertise "Pai Gow". Be aware that this might refer to a dominos-based game called Pai Gow, an ancient Chinese game which requires quite a bit of study to master. Pai Gow Poker is played with a single deck of playing cards, including one joker. You might find some casinos referring to Pai Gow, even though they are really offering Pai Gow Poker.

The Table

The style of table will depend upon the casino and the setting in which it is placed. It is certainly playable on a standard-size Blackjack-style table, but often a larger table is used, since you require more space to display your Poker hands.

Where you sit is irrelevant, since the hands you are dealt will be decided at random (either using three dice in the traditional style, or via an electronic randomizer and a dealing machine).

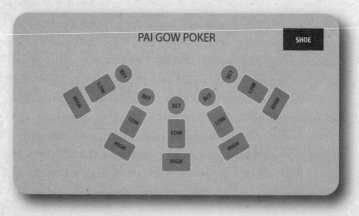

The table holds a maximum of six seating and betting positions, plus the dealer's position, and the empty betting positions are dealt out and then discarded to ensure that the game uses all but four cards for each deal.

How the Game Works

Each player places a bet. The throw of three dice, or a randomly generated number, is then used to decide who will receive the first hand. The deal starts with the chosen seat and then proceeds anti-clockwise, distributing the hands to each betting position, regardless of whether there is a bettor present or not. Where there is no bettor present, those hands are then immediately added to the discard pile.

Each hand dealt consists of seven cards. The player must then use those seven cards to create two Poker hands. The first, usually known as the "High" or "Big" hand, consists of five cards; the second, usually known as the "Low" or "Small" hand, consists of two cards.

The High hand must contain the stronger Poker hand; the Low hand must contain the weaker of the Poker hands. The joker in the pack is a semi-wild card. It can be used to complete a Straight or a Flush in the five-card Poker hand, or it can be used as an ace.

In most Nevada casinos, "the wheel", A, 2, 3, 4, 5, is played as the second-highest Straight, losing only to A, K, Q, J, 10. However, this is not the case in all casinos, and you should check the house rules (which are usually clearly displayed) to ensure that you do not make a mistake.

When you have decided how you are going to place your seven cards between the two hands, you arrange them in the two boxes. Once this is done, some casinos allow one of the vacant hands to be left in play and offered to players as what is called the "Dragon hand". Players are asked in turn if they would like to play this hand, in addition to their own hand. If a player accepts, he places his wager and plays out the Dragon hand. In effect, this simply allows you to play two hands against the dealer on a particular deal.

Once all hands have been set by the players, the dealer, acting as the Bank, turns over his cards and sets them into two Poker hands, exactly as the players have done. He will set his hands according to a prescribed set of rules, called the "House Way". Although the basis of the House Way is standard globally, there may be variations from casino to casino.

Now, the dealer compares his two Poker hands to each of the players' hands:

- If a player's first and second hands both beat the dealer, the player is paid at even money (1–1), minus a house commission of 5 per cent. (Some card clubs and private games take a flat fee per hand instead of the commission, but most casinos charge the commission on winning hands.)
- If the dealer's two hands both beat the player's two hands, the player loses his wager.
- If one hand wins and one hand loses – whichever hands they may be – the wager is a stand-off, and the bettor receives his wager back.
- In the event of an exact tie, called a "Copy" – a rare occurrence – the tie is awarded to the dealer's hand.

I read that some casinos allow players to place a bet which pre-pays the commission if they win the hand. Hence, on a $50 bet, you would place $52.50 and win $50 if both your hands beat the dealer's two hands. This reduces the house commission by approximately 0.25 per cent. A small amount, but one which soon adds up over time.

Note that, on average, around 40 per cent of hands dealt at Pai Gow Poker result in ties, where your bets stand off against the house. This makes the game leisurely and allows you to retain your bankroll for some period of time. Naturally, there will be spells when the dealer seems to make two strong hands, deal after deal, but also times when the players consistently beat the banker and make substantial profits.

Banker Privileges

One of the exciting elements of Pai Gow Poker – rather like the old-fashioned Chemin de Fer games – is that each of the players is offered the chance to be the Banker. You do not have to accept this role, but it is advantageous to you to do so. However, to be the Banker demands certain responsibilities:

- You must have played at least one hand against the Banker.
- You must have sufficient funds on the table to pay off all winning bets that may be made against you on the next deal, by all the players present.

One of the privileges of banking is that you can set your two Poker hands the way you wish to do so. As you will see from the strategy, there are safe and aggressive ways of doing this, so your gambling personality can come to the fore here.

Some casinos offer you the chance to co-bank with the house. This means that you are responsible for 50 per cent of the bets made, while the house covers the remaining 50 per cent. However, if you take this option, you will have to set your two Poker hands following the "House Way". This reduces your input, but insures you against a multiple losing hand where you have to pay out to everyone.

The general house edge on Pai Gow Poker will vary, depending on player numbers, hand setting skills (see page 218) and how often you get to be Banker. However, to take a general figure, as a player the edge against you is approximately 2.7 per cent; as the Banker the edge reduces considerably, to below 0.3 per cent. Assuming a full table, where you take the option to be Banker, the overall edge will come out to be around 1.5 per cent against you, making Pai Gow Poker a pretty decent bet.

Add to this the opportunity to bank more frequently than one deal in seven (if there are fewer players at the table) and the house edge can be reduced still further – heading towards as little as a 1 per cent edge against you.

The House Way

The casino will have a pre-determined method of setting its two hands, based on key principles which, by and large, are universal. The House Way will be close to the optimal method of setting hands, but will tend to err on the side of optimizing the chances of winning at least one hand and therefore creating a stand-off. Most casinos will allow you the option of letting the house set your hands for you according to the House Way. If you are uncertain of the basic idea behind hand setting, and you are just dipping your toe into Pai Gow Poker, this can be a good decision to make.

Playing Strategy

To produce the optimal playing strategy would require pages of analysis and charts. If you were playing online you could, in theory, follow every last detail to give yourself the very best chance of winning. However, there are easier methods which come close to the very best strategy and it is these which we will look at here.

Firstly, if you are playing online, there is an excellent online Pai Gow decision-maker program, which is free on several websites. See the Online Gambling section (page 352).

If you are playing in a land-based casino, do not attempt to take in any electronic device which might assist you. Not only will you be warned off, you may be thrown out, or arrested, tried and put in prison. Many casinos will allow you to take in a written aide-memoire, but check that you are permitted to do this in the casino where you are playing.

If you have knowledge of Poker, then you will be able to work out the most basic situations; to deviate from the perfect play in more complex positions is unlikely to add more than a tiny amount to the overall house edge against you. So, focus on getting the key decisions right and you will be able to relax, enjoy the game, and give yourself a good chance of winning.

Hand Setting

An average hand at Pai Gow Poker is a medium pair and an ace-high hand. So, if you can see hands better than this, then you are off to a good start; poorer than this and you are likely to be struggling on this particular deal.

You must set your five-card hand (the High hand) as the better of the two Poker hands, and your two-card hand (the Low hand) as the poorer of the two Poker hands. You can always set your hand to the House Way, which will be close to optimal strategy, but may veer slightly towards the stand-off, rather than going in for the kill and winning both hands. Here are the key elements of the Basic Strategy – if you have a grasp of these, you will know enough to play Pai Gow Poker decently:

- 60–70 per cent of your hands will contain only One Pair.
- You must place that pair in your five-card hand and set the two highest cards after the pair in the two-card hand. Then set the remaining cards to sit alongside your pair. For example:

You are dealt:	A, J, J, 8, 6, 5, 4
Set your hands as follows:	J, J, 6, 5, 4 and A, 8

- If your hand contains no Pairs, no Straight or Flush, set your highest card in the five-card hand; set your second highest and third highest cards in your two-card hand. For example:

You are dealt: A, J, 9, 6, 5, 4, 2

Set your hands as follows: A, 6, 5, 4, 2 and   J, 9

- If your hand contains two pairs, this is the most complex decision to make. There are seemingly endless charts and statistics to suggest the best methods. Here are some key points:

  - If your higher pair consists of aces, kings or queens, split the pairs between your five-card and two-card hands, placing the ace/king/queen pair in the five-card hand, and the lower pair in the two-card hand.
  - If you hold two low or medium pairs and you have a high card, such as an ace or a king, you should split the pairs, setting the Two Pair in the five-card hand, and the ace- or king-high in the two-card hand.
  - If you hold two low pairs, but no high card outside, split the pairs between the five-card hand and the two-card hand, using the higher pair for the five-card hand.

- If your hand contains three pairs, this is very strong. There is a hard and fast rule for these hands which is always to set the highest pair in the two-card hand, and leave the remaining Two Pair for the five-card hand. In this situation, the Two Pair will probably win

the five-card hand, and a high pair will surely win the
two-card hand. It is very likely to be a winning deal
for you. For example:

You are dealt:	Q, Q, J, J, 5, 5, 3
Set your hands as follows:	J, J, 5, 5, 3 and Q, Q

- If your hand contains Three-of-a-Kind, you should
  play the trips in the five-card hand, and the two
  highest remaining cards in the two-card hand.
  However, when the trips are A, A, A or K, K, K, you
  should split the hand! That is to say, you should put
  A, A or K, K into the five-card hand, and make the
  two-card hand ace- or king-high. This is because you
  are striving to win both hands, not just one. Trips will
  almost certainly win the five-card hand, but jack-high
  is likely to lose the two-card hand, resulting in a
  stand-off. For example:

You are dealt:	A, A, A, J, 8, 5, 3
Set your hands as follows:	A, A, 8, 5, 3 and A, J

- If your hand contains a Straight and a Flush, use
  whichever hand allows you to form the stronger two-
  card hand. Once again, this is because to win one
  hand and lose the other results in a stand-off, no
  matter by how much you win the one hand.

- If your hand contains a Full House, it is nearly always right to split the Full House and put Three-of-a-Kind into the five-card hand, and the Pair into the two-card hand.
- With two Three-of-a-Kind hands contained in the first seven cards, it is always right to play the lower trips in the five-card hand, and the higher trips broken up to form the high pair in the two-card hand. For example:

> You are dealt: K, K, K, 6, 6, 6, 4
>
> Set your hand as follows: 6, 6, 6, K, 4   and   K, K

- With Four-of-a-Kind, players should split the quads if it is high – say 10, 10, 10, 10 – putting One Pair into each hand; but if the Four-of-a-Kind is low, then the quads should be retained in the five-card hand, and the two highest other cards set in the two-card hand.

There are many other subtleties, mainly occurring only rarely which, as you become used to the game, you might try to learn. Most casinos will allow you to set your hands in the House Way, and it is my experience that Pai Gow Poker dealers are among the most friendly in the casino. Perhaps this is because the game is a reasonable one for the players, with many ties, and requires a little more thought than most casino games, both for the player and for the dealers.

Bankroll

Although the house edge is greater on Pai Gow Poker than on Blackjack, Baccarat or Craps, because the game is played at a leisurely pace you will find that, even during a poor spell, your bankroll will seem much more robust. For this reason, if you are planning to gamble for many long hours in the casino, Pai Gow Poker is one of the most enjoyable games to play.

I recommend a bankroll of 40 times your base bet. This will allow you to weather a poor run of cards and still have chips remaining to take advantage of a hot streak for the players. Seeing the dealer (or Banker) set up a series of weak hands is a great joy.

If you succeed in making a 100 per cent profit at any time, put aside your original stake and half your profit. Play the remaining profit, or lock that away too. Do not touch the money you have set aside.

If you continue to win, once you have doubled the remaining bankroll, divide the profit again in half and lock away one half. Continue this for as long as you can.

Betting Strategy

As with other negative-expectation games where the house holds an edge against you, no betting system will overcome this house edge. However, if you can persuade players to bet big against you when you are the Banker, you have a better chance of winning during this time.

A decent system for retaining your bankroll and benefiting from a hot streak of good fortune is to increase your bets modestly whenever you win, and to continue to do so until you lose, and then return to your base bet.

Remember that, as with virtually all casino games (except for Blackjack), the result of the previous hand has no influence whatsoever over the likely result of the next.

Side Bets

Most Pai Gow tables offer at least one side-bet opportunity. More are being invented all the time. As discussed in previous chapters, side bets are used by casinos to ramp up the action and encourage more betting. Looking at the probability and odds tables for these side bets, I can see that they all offer the house a much bigger edge than the main game. Since the aim of this book is to steer you away from these sucker bets, let's keep this section short. There is plenty of excitement and action in Pai Gow Poker to satisfy even the most hyperactive gambler. If you must take part in side bets at the Pai Gow Poker table, keep all bets to the absolute minimum.

12
Sic Bo

S IC BO IS A DICE game that originated in China. You may also see it called Tai Sai or Dai Siu. It is hard to categorize the game. Some think that it is a pre-cursor to Craps. It has similarities to Grand Hazard, an old English gambling game – Hazard, probably the original game, is also played with dice (but only two of them). In some ways, as you will see, the betting layout resembles Roulette. It seems to have been introduced to the United States by Chinese immigrants and now, wherever there is a significant Chinese community, casinos are being persuaded to offer the game.

In Las Vegas, many casinos offer Sic Bo in their Asian Games rooms, and it is a game I advise you to try, not because it offers the player as good odds as Craps, but because it is something a little different. If you join a busy table, you will get a hint of the fast and furious ways many Asian gamblers play.

For gambling lovers, a visit to Macau, just across the bay from Hong Kong, is a must. Once again, not because the casinos there offer you good games – quite the contrary, the house edge there is far higher than elsewhere in the world – but because to play there is a cultural experience. When you enter a casino in Macau it is truly a different world, and it is wonderful simply to observe and listen.

When it comes to the various odds on offer, the main body of this chapter will be based on the standard odds for each bet, as found in Atlantic City, most Vegas Strip hotels and many online sites. At the end, we'll take a look at some variations.

The Table

The table on which Sic Bo is played is unlike any other in the casino and may look daunting. It is covered in many different, rather unusual, betting patterns. A little larger than a standard table, and often glass- or Perspex-topped, rather than baize covered, it is a little piece of Macau right there on the casino floor. (In Macau some casinos boast vast Sic Bo layouts where a huge number of players can partake in a gamble simultaneously.) Bets are placed on the layout in a similar way to Roulette or Craps. However, when the winning options are decided, all winning betting positions light up, ensuring that both players and dealers can see immediately who has won what. Some tables boast bells and sound effects, adding to the atmosphere of a truly different style of gambling game.

In one corner by the dealer's hand is a glass dome covering three dice. These dice are shaken and the shaker is then turned over to reveal the values through the dome. The dealer programmes the result into the table and the winning bets are illuminated.

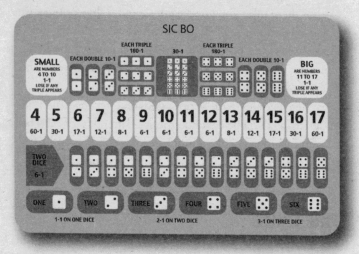

Players all place their bets on the same layout, sometimes using standard casino chips, or sometimes special table-unique Sic Bo value chips to avoid confusion when it comes to the payout.

You can sit or stand at the table and as many people can play as any particular casino will allow. Online, the layout is identical to a land-based casino layout.

Be alert to the payouts being offered. In a moment, we'll see what the industry standard payouts should be. Don't play Sic Bo if the payouts offered are poorer than this. Also, note carefully that some tables express the payouts differently. Paying out at 10–1 means that you receive your original stake back, plus ten times the stake in prize. A prize of "10 for 1" pays out ten times your stake, but it keeps the stake! So, 9–1 is the same as 10 for 1, and you need to watch out for that. Casinos are, you will not be surprised to hear, out to grab every last penny from you.

How the Game Works

There are a number of different bets which you can make, attempting to predict the outcome of each shake of the three dice. These include high/low totals, odd and even totals, specific doubles or triples, specific totals of the spots on the dice, and different number combinations. Let's take a look at each one: how you place the bet, the odds (which are nearly always displayed clearly on the layout itself) and the house edge.

Nearest the dealer is a series of Proposition Bets. These include the Small/Big Bets, Doubles and Triples.

Small/Big Bets

On the far left- and far right-hand sides are the Small and Big Bet boxes. A bet in one of these boxes is betting that the total value of the spots on all three dice will either be high or low.

A bet in the Small betting box covers the totals 4–10; a bet in the Big betting box covers the totals 11–17.

On any occasion that all three dice match – a Triple – then all Big/Small Bets are lost. Hence the absence of totals of 3 and 18 for the betting boxes. Any dice combination of 222, 333, 444 and 555 also loses.

These bets pay even money but, because all Triples lose, the house takes an edge of just under 2.8 per cent.

Odd/Even Total Bets

Some tables offer a bet that the spots on the three dice will add up to an odd number, or an even number. Once again, any Triple thrown and all those bets are lost.

These "even-money" propositions pay 1–1 and carry a house edge of just under 2.8 per cent. Along with the Small/Big Bets, they are the best bets on the table.

Double Bets

Divided into three blocks of three, adjacent to the Big/Small Bets, you can bet on any two dice matching their score and forming a Double.

A bet in any of the following boxes pays 10–1: Double 1, Double 2, Double 3, Double 4, Double 5, Double 6. The house edge on these bets is a massive 18.5 per cent.

Triple Bets

If you believe that the dice might all roll the same number, forming a Triple, there are two ways to back this outcome:

- **Individual Triple Bets**: these betting areas are located next to the Double Bets, towards the centre and back of the layout. You may bet on the roll that the following outcomes may occur: 111, 222, 333, 444, 555, 666. A bet on these boxes attracts a breathtaking payout of 180–1. However, the house edge is a whopping 16.2 per cent.
- **Any Triple**: this betting box is located in the middle of the back section, nearest to the dealer. It shows all six triples possible and a bet here wagers that the next roll will produce one of the six possible triple outcomes. A winning bet on this box will attract a payout of 30–1, but the house edge is still a prohibitive 13.9 per cent.

Dice Totals Bets

Displayed across the middle section of the layout are boxes representing the numbers which the values of three dice might total. You will notice several elements here:

- There is no total of either 3 or 18 – these are covered by the Triple Bets above.
- Working from the outside inwards, the totals – both high and low – match one another in terms of likelihood of appearing and payout odds. This is the same as the two-dice totals at Craps, where 4 and 10, 5 and 9, and 6 and 8 are the same.

4 and 17

Located at the far right and far left of the line, these totals are the rarest, requiring two dice rolling 1 and the third a 2, or two dice rolling 6, and the third a 5. For this reason, if you bet on this outcome and the dealer does indeed roll it, you will be paid at an impressive 60–1. However, the house edge on this bet is 15.3 per cent.

5 and 16

These are still tough totals to roll, requiring all high or all low scores on each dice. If you bet on these boxes and win, the house pays at 30–1. However, the house still holds a 13.9 per cent edge.

6 and 15

Winning bets on these boxes yield a payout at 17–1, and the house has an in-built edge of 12 per cent.

7 and 14

Winning bets on these boxes pay out at 12–1, with a house edge of 9.7 per cent against the player.

8 and 13

Winning bets on these boxes pay out at 8–1, with a house edge of 9.7 per cent.

9 and 12

Coming into the area of totals likely to be rolled (these will occur between 11 and 12 per cent of the time), winning bets will be paid at 6–1, with a house edge of 7.4 per cent.

10 and 11

Located in the centre two positions of the middle betting section, these are the totals most likely to be rolled by three dice (in the same way that 7 is the most likely total with two dice). Bets on these boxes yield a payout of 6–1, with the house holding an edge over the player of 12.5 per cent.

Proposition Bets on Precise Numbers

In a row beneath the Totals Bets appear 15 Proposition Bets, laid out looking a little like dominoes. These bets ask you to predict which numbers might show on two out of the three dice. Every combination is possible, except for the doubles (which can be covered at the top of the layout). All these bets pay the same: 6–1 if you bet on the correct outcome.

This is one of the best bets on the layout, as the house edge is a meagre 2.78 per cent. But beware: many online casinos and some land-based casinos only pay 5–1, which makes it a terrible bet (16.67 per cent house edge). Even worse is that some casinos display all their payouts in standard odds (5–1), and then change that display for this set of bets, offering 6 for 1, which is only 5–1 in normal odds.

Number Appearances

At the front of the layout are located six betting positions representing numbers one, two, three, four, five and six. A bet on one of these boxes predicts that the chosen number will be rolled by at least one of the three dice. You receive higher payouts if the number appears on two or all three dice.

- If your number appears on one dice, you are paid at even money, 1–1.
- If your number appears on two dice, you are paid at 2–1.
- If your number appears on all three dice, you are paid at 3–1.

However, many casinos offer a bonus payout. I have seen the three-dice payout at 7–1 and 12–1, and those extra payouts improve the bet for the player by reducing the house edge.

At the standard 1–1, 2–1, 3–1 schedule, the house edge is 7.9 per cent. At the biggest bonus payout schedule of 1–1, 2–1 and 12–1, the edge is reduced to 3.7 per cent.

Combination Wagers

I have been told that some tables also offer a series of combination wagers, although I have never seen them myself. These include:

- From a selection of numbers – 6543, 6532, 5432 and 4321 – three of those numbers will appear in the next roll.
- The dice will show a specific combination of three numbers chosen in advance by the player.
- Two of the three dice will show a double, plus the third dice will show a specific number chosen in advance.

These bets offer 7–1, 30–1 and 50–1 payouts respectively. The house edges are reported to be 11 per cent, 14 per cent and 15 per cent respectively. They all sound horrible bets to me.

Playing Strategy

Sic Bo is not the game to play if you want to make big profits in the casino. It generally offers very poor odds, but it is different and is worth a try, even if just for a short session.

The key playing strategy, like with Craps, is to avoid the worst bets on the table. Since you are unable to predict the outcome of the next roll of three dice (if you can, contact me immediately!), it is down to simple, dumb luck whether you will generate a winning pattern of bets. However, whether you have any chance of beating the house will almost certainly depend upon steering clear of the wild bets with a huge house edge, and sticking to the simpler, lower-odds bets, where the house edge is just about manageable. This means that you should:

- Bet on Big/Small results (and Odd/Even, if available). These only pay 1–1 but, equally, only offer the house a 2.8 per cent edge – not dissimilar to an "even-money" chance on the European Roulette table.
- For a wilder, more risky bet, try betting on Dice Totals of 9 or 12. These bets pay at 7–1, and offer the house the lowest edge of any of these bets: 7.4 per cent.
- If you are playing in a casino, or online, and the casino offers 7–1 or 12–1 payouts for the same number appearing on all three dice, then try betting on the Number Appearances layout. These pay 1–1 for one

dice, 2–1 for two dice, and, sometimes, 12–1 for three dice. If this is the case, the house edge is 3.7 per cent. If the casino only pays 3–1 for a triple, then the edge rises to 11 per cent and the bet is very poor value.

Avoid all other bets however much other players, dealers or kibitzers try to persuade you to play them.

Bankroll

Use a small bankroll to keep down losses. If you plan to make a couple of bets per round, take a bankroll containing 40 times your base stake. This means for $10 bets you would need a $400 bankroll. If you make a 25 per cent profit at any time, get up, thank everyone, and leave the table. You have done very well.

Betting Strategy

A game with a sizeable negative expectation like this requires great discipline. Stick to minimum bets, increasing only if you find that you are winning. Return to minimum bets as soon as you lose a single bet. No tactics of betting will affect the odds against you on Sic Bo.

Summary

Sic Bo is a game to experience, not to play seriously hoping to make money. Of course, you could be lucky, but the odds dictate that your luck will not last. If you find yourself modestly in profit at any time, leave the table a winner.

- Try the game for its big differences from other casino Table Games, its atmosphere and wide range of bets.
- Play only the bets suggested in this chapter, which offer the house the lowest possible edge.
- Do not be tempted to place bets on the biggest payouts – they carry the greatest edges against the player.
- There is no system that can beat Sic Bo in the long run. If you make a profit, grab it and run from the tables.

13
Casino War

WANT A MINDLESS game with virtually no decisions to make? If so, this is the game for you. I guess that it's not surprising that such a mundane and repetitive game should become so popular. More and more these days, people seem to crave totally undemanding entertainment. Casino War certainly provides that.

It's a game about whether you or the dealer get the higher card. That's it. If there's a tie, you have a little further battle.

The Table
Played on a standard Blackjack-style table, there are usually six to eight seats and betting positions. There is no advantage to sitting in one place over another. Change your cash for chips and prepare to play.

How the Game Works

Casino War is usually played out of a six-deck shoe; sometimes it is dealt from a continuous shuffle/dealing machine. The dealer deals the player one card and he deals himself one card. If the player's card is higher, he wins; if the dealer's card is higher, he wins. Winning bets are paid at even money (1–1).

If the cards dealt are the same, this is a tie and the player faces his single decision of the game. He can surrender half his bet and lose the other, or he can "go to war". This isn't nearly as exciting as it sounds: the player must place a bet exactly equal to his first bet. The dealer "burns" (discards) three cards, and deals a new card to both the player and himself. This time, if the player wins he gets paid even money (1–1) on only his second bet (and has his first bet returned to him); if the dealer wins, he wins both bets.

In the event of a second tie, some casinos make you go to war again; others call a second tie a win for the player;

others pay you on both your original bets (often advertised seductively as 2–1 on the second bet).

You may bet on a tie at the start of the hand, paying 10–1 should it occur, but this is an appalling bet, offering the house at least an 18 per cent edge – and even more if fewer decks of cards are used. Never make this bet.

Then, it starts all over again.

Bankroll

This is a game that I cannot believe will entertain you, but if you are going to play then take a bankroll of 20 times your base stake. If you make a 50 per cent profit, lock at least half of it away. Ideally, leave the table a winner and count yourself lucky that you went to war against the casino at this game and won.

Playing Strategy

The only strategy here is that, in the event of a tie, you must "go to war". To surrender your hand for half your bet offers the house around a 3.5 per cent edge; to "go to war" reduces that edge to about 2.25 per cent.

In addition, you might glance at how many decks are being employed. With the exception of the Tie Bet – which you should never, ever make – the fewer decks in play means the smaller the edge to the casino. So, if you really must play this game, see if you can find a casino, online or land-based, which offers a single-deck game. On a game where the player receives a bonus for a tie during the "war" element, this would, in theory, reduce the house edge to just over 2 per cent.

Betting Strategy

Because the house holds an edge of over 2 per cent against you, the best betting strategy is to make minimum bets and continue to make minimum bets, thus ensuring that you will lose less in the long run. However, to maximize profits you might try a modest increase in bets after each win, to benefit from a winning streak. When the streak ends (if you manage to hit one), return to the minimum once again and, ideally, leave the table with your profit.

Most casinos offer this game at relatively low stakes, although, in a glamorous Strip hotel in Las Vegas, I have seen it being played for very high stakes. A middle-aged couple, dressed as pirates (I never found out why), were betting $1,000 each on every round and over the course of several hours built up what looked to me to be close on $50,000 in high-value chips in front of each of them. When I next passed the table, they were gone, and I only hope that they took their profits and got out while the going was so good. Maybe the best strategy for this game is to dress up as a pirate... I hadn't thought of that before now.

14
Keno

THIS IS ANOTHER brief section on a casino game which I cannot, in any circumstances, recommend. Keno is a form of lottery game where, out of 80 numbers, players can opt to pick anything from one number up to ten numbers (and sometimes more). The Keno machine then picks 20 numbers at random and, depending on the style of game you are playing, you will win prizes for the number of numbers you catch, or hit. Some games pay nothing if you hit the expected percentage of numbers, but offer prizes if you hit less or more and, obviously, the biggest prizes if you hit all your numbers.

Keno used to be a popular low-stake gamble among wives and girlfriends who wanted somewhere to sit down while their menfolk were working away at the coal-face of gambling – the Craps or Blackjack tables (Vegas was very sexist in the old days). In the usually comfortably appointed

Keno lounge, the waitresses would offer drinks, hand out Keno tickets and collect the small stakes. The Keno numbers would be selected, using a bucket of numbered balls, either picked or blown out by machine, and called out by a Keno caller (like a Bingo caller, but without the witty names for various numbers and cheeky banter).

Even in the smart Strip casinos in Vegas these days, you will see long-legged beauties strolling through the buffets and cafes, collecting Keno bets from those who simply can't stay away from a gamble. On the walls are electronic displays showing which Keno game is in play, how long until the next draw, and which numbers have been chosen by the machine. On every table, there is a small container with Keno forms and pencils. The svelte young ladies are a great addition to any high-cholesterol meal, but do not be seduced by their offerings!

Because Keno is usually played for small stakes, players rarely notice that they hardly ever win. This is just as well because, if they knew the odds of the game, they would surely stop playing altogether. The chance of hitting any major prize is tiny – the very worst bet in the entire casino. Depending upon the bets available and house payouts, the house edge will vary between 20 and 35 per cent. Yes – you read that right!

In fact, Keno is such a bad bet that in Las Vegas, there is an old joke about it: Where do you go when there is a thunderstorm and you are worried about lightening? The Keno Lounge – nothing gets hit in there!

Keno Machines

As ever in Vegas, what can be dealt by a human being and, at least, made sociable, can also be played by a machine, where no human interaction is required. The Keno machines are beginning to appear everywhere, since the idea of a lottery game is gaining in popularity all over the world. The good news is that the odds on Keno machines seem markedly better than in the original bingo-style game. The bad news is that you don't have to wait for the next draw – it'll be ready as soon as you are. Together with exciting sounds and flashing lights, the machines will get you playing ever faster, and tempt you to play at higher stakes. Since the machines seem to be taking between 5 per cent and 15 per cent of the player's money in the long run, this is a sure way to go broke quickly – unless you hit the jackpot. It doesn't happen often – not often at all – but it does happen.

Keno Online

We will talk about this more in the online section (page 387). At first glance, these games seem to offer slightly better odds for the player than in the land-based casinos – still terrible, but less terrible.

15
Red Dog

I HAVEN'T SEEN Red Dog – or similar games – in casinos for some while now, but it is offered by a number of online casinos. For this reason, and in case you find it alive and kicking in your local land-based casino, here is a brief run-down on the key elements. Since this is a game which, at times, offers the player a decent bet, it is well worth knowing the correct strategy.

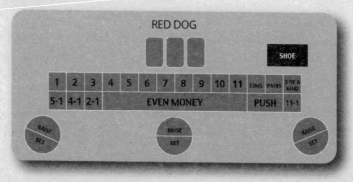

The Table

When I played it last, it was dealt at a standard Blackjack-style table. There is no advantage to any seat position.

How the Game is Played

Using anything from one to eight decks, you place a wager in the betting circle. The dealer places two cards face up in front of him.

Most casinos play that a ten card is worth 10, a Jack is worth 11, a queen 12, a king 13 and an ace 14.

If these two cards are consecutive values (9, 8, or Q, J), the hand is a stand-off.

If these two cards are a pair, the dealer produces a third card. If this card matches the pair (forming Three-of-a-Kind), the player is paid a Trips Bonus at 11–1. If the third card does not match the first two, the hand is a stand-off.

If the two cards do not form a pair and are not consecutive, the dealer then announces the size of "Spread". This figure is the number of cards that fall between the two cards dealt. For example, if the first card dealt is a 3, and the second card dealt is a 10, the "Spread" is six.

At this point, you may choose to make an additional wager, of the same size as your original bet (some casinos allow you to bet a proportion of your original bet if you so wish). You may also simply retain your original bet, but you may not remove it.

A third card is now turned over and, if it falls between the values of the first two cards, you are paid a "Spread Bonus":

- If the spread is just one card, Spread Bonus
  pays 5–1.
- If the spread is two cards, Spread Bonus
  pays 4–1.
- If the spread is three cards, Spread Bonus
  pays 2–1.
- If the spread is four cards or more, Spread Bonus
  pays even money, 1–1.

Playing Strategy

The good news is that there is only one simple playing tip
here. Never increase your bet unless the spread between the
first two cards is **seven or more**. All other spreads offer far
too poor odds to make increasing your bet the correct play.
The more decks used, the lower the house edge, so look for
six- or eight-deck games and avoid one- and two-deck
games. The edge for the house on a six-deck game is
approximately 2.8 per cent.

Bankroll

This is a game with a solid house edge against you, so gamble
only small amounts for a short time. I recommend a bankroll
of 30 times your base stake. Stop playing the moment you
make a 50 per cent profit on your original bankroll.

Betting Strategy

The key strategy here is to increase your bet only when the
"spread" offered is seven cards or more. This gives you an
edge against the house. Unfortunately, you will only rarely

see such a wide spread and so the chances for you to take advantage of this positive expectation bet will be few and far between. Do not be tempted to increase your bet at any other time.

In terms of maximizing profits, you might try increasing your bet a little after a win, and continuing this until you lose a bet, when you should return to your base bet. However, with a 2.8 per cent edge against you, I recommend minimum bets at all times to help you lose less quickly.

Summary

- Play Red Dog rarely, for low stakes.
- Increase your bet when the spread offered is seven cards or more; otherwise retain minimum bets at all time.
- Grab any profit you make and run for the hills!

16
Bingo

WHO WOULD GUESS THAT the UK's most popular low-stake gamble would gain a foothold even in the great Las Vegas? Unlike Keno, the odds actually give the player a chance of winning, even though, on average, you are probably fighting an approximate house edge of about 5 per cent.

Bingo is usually only offered in the casinos off the Strip (which tend to offer better odds, a more friendly welcome to locals and low-bettors, and a more modest level of comfort and service than the large casinos on the Strip). The key is to make the most of your opportunities: if you are a regular – as many Bingo players are – look out for the following:

- Multiple buys of Bingo cards – find the cards that you like and buy them in bulk. Avoid deals which feature a wide selection of cards since, inevitably, they will contain cards offering the very worst selections.

- Cheap cards offering best odds, but not necessarily the highest payouts.
- Times when fewer people are playing – simply because this increases your chances of winning.
- Progressive Jackpot games, but only when the jackpots are high.

I have never played Bingo in a casino and therefore I won't presume to offer any further advice. Clearly, Bingo is not the best game in the house. There are many games which offer far better odds to the player and which require more skill and judgment, and far more player input towards the result.

My friends tell me that, here in the UK, Bingo remains a very popular and social night out – mainly, but certainly not exclusively, played by the ladies. It is a sociable way to spend an evening, with a few drinks, a lot of laughs and the chance to win small prizes, with an outside chance of something rather bigger.

One last point: Bingo is now extremely popular online. This worries me. Gone is the social element (one online casino told me that they have an active Bingo chat room but, in my view, that doesn't count); gone is the interaction with the Bingo caller; gone is the safety-net of having friends around to say that you have lost enough, or it is time to stop and take home your winnings. Either Bingo is a social occasion including a modest gamble, or it is a very poor betting opportunity: one or the other. Online, it seems to fall squarely into the latter category, and that seems a shame.

17
Wheel of Fortune

A T THE FRONT OF many America casinos, especially those in Nevada and Atlantic City, you will find a classic gambling game in pride of place: the Wheel of Fortune. These days, the game is often renamed "Money Wheel" or "Big Six". This is not least because there is now a famous range of Slot machines based on the eponymous television game show. Often manned by an old-timer, the wheel is usually an ornate version of a giant Roulette wheel – except with 54 "pockets" – about 2 metres across and mounted upright. Each pocket is divided by nails and, at the apex of the wheel's mounting, a leather pointer snaps against the pockets as the wheel is spun. When the wheel comes to a stop, the strap ends up falling into one of the pockets, indicating which position is the winner.

The Table

The table is typically a long, fairly narrow flat table with the various denominations, or pocket markings, displayed under glass. These days, the denominations are usually marked with dollar bills: $1, $2, $5, $10 and $20. There are two jackpot symbols: perhaps the casino's logo, a joker or an American Eagle.

Often there are no seats at the table at all, since this is usually a game you play for a couple of spins on your way in or out of the casino. In theory, you can sit down and play Wheel of Fortune all day long – but I would strongly advise against it.

How the Game Works

To place a bet, you put your stake – usually starting at $1 upwards – on the dollar note, or symbol, you hope the wheel will stop on.

If you place a $1 bet on the $1 position, this is what you will win if the wheel stops there. This is true of all the notes/symbols showing. On the two jackpot positions, the payout is 40–1.

If you bet more than $1, you will get paid at the odds indicated by the dollar note. So, a $5 bet on the $10 note symbol would yield a payout of $50 if the wheel stopped there.

The Wheel of Fortune is a truly awful game for the player, a remnant of the bad old days of the Wild West. While the layout of wheels varies from casino to casino, the odds are generally all terrible. These are typical examples:

- Bets on $1 symbol   house edge 11 per cent
- Bets on $2 symbol   house edge 17 per cent

- Bets on $5 symbol   house edge 26 per cent
- Bets on $10 symbol   house edge 18.5 per cent
- Bets on $20 symbol   house edge 22 per cent
- Bets on jackpot symbols house edge 24 per cent

They are probably the worst odds in the entire casino (you might be able find some Keno bets nearly as bad). So, the simple advice is to steer clear. Watch it for a moment if you want to revel in some casino history, but don't waste a dime on playing the game yourself.

Playing Strategy
Don't play it.

Betting Strategy
Don't bet.

Bankroll
Not a penny.

Summary
Strictly a novelty only, the Wheel of Fortune could make a fortune only for the casino. Thankfully, for wise gamblers it doesn't even come onto their radar.

18
The Rise of The Machines

TABLE GAMES, especially Craps and Blackjack, were for decades the mainstay of casino revenues. In turn, gambling was the main source of income for casino resorts and complexes. In the modern world, the emphasis is changing dramatically. Firstly, casino resorts are making almost half their money from their hotel, conference and catering operations and, secondly, their main gaming revenues accrue, not from the traditional Table Games, but from the vast banks of Slot machines which most large casinos now boast.

Originally, Slot machines were introduced as a way to keep the ladies happy while their menfolk did battle at the tables. The stakes were low and the house edge modest. The ladies could lose a little money in an unthreatening environment and feel that the casino was, in some way, also geared to their needs. Even today, the majority of Slots players are women who, in some cases, find the idea of playing at the tables daunting.

Slots have major advantages over Table Games: they require very few staff; the games themselves are almost impossible to cheat, either by players or by casino personnel; the machines require little maintenance; players generally demand fewer perks; percentage holds on Slot machines can be extremely high; and last but by no means least, they flash their hypnotic welcome to players 24 hours a day, 365 days a year.

However, Slots players have begun to demand more value for their money and Slots Clubs and loyalty cards abound, offering complimentary benefits even to modest players. The casinos can well afford these quite generous benefits, because the machines are making such a massive income for them.

Personally, I have problems with Slot machines. It is certainly not that I don't enjoy playing them myself on occasion, and I fully understand the pleasure to be derived from immersing oneself in the all-consuming world of spinning reels, electronic Poker and multi-reel, multi-payout action: it is an escape from the weight of the world on one's shoulders. But, there is something massively anti-social and intrinsically lonely about Slots play, which undermines the fun one can have, in a social way, in a casino.

I also believe that Slots addiction is the most serious form of gambling addiction there is, not only because of the speed at which your money can be taken from you, but also because there is rarely any other human being around to help you realize your errors. This lack of human contact, of someone able to say to you: "Hang on a moment; take a break just for a short while..." can lead to isolation and an inability to face up to a gambling problem.

A quick example: in Cape Town, South Africa, the big casino just out of town suffered a major power outage when the country was hit by power cuts and the casino's own generator broke down. The Salon Privé was plunged into semi-darkness. Slots players who had seen each other day after day, month after month, but who had never spoken to one another, slowly began to converse. After about 20 minutes, there was quite a hubbub, as players sat with drinks and snacks waiting for the machines to sputter back to life. I am often the only player chatting to other gamblers in a casino, so it was a strange experience for me to see all these otherwise pretty silent folks suddenly seem so sociable and friendly. An hour later, the machines came back on; within 20 seconds, no one was talking anymore – everyone was back at their station, in their own worlds, recommencing the lonely battle with the machines.

Slots manufacturers – and the casinos which hire or purchase them – are well aware of the need to attract punters to put in their coins (or notes, or credit cards). Lights are scientifically programmed to flash in an hypnotic, attention-seeking pattern; noises are designed to feed the desire to hear a certain combination of notes. In the past, via the air-conditioning system, casinos have even pumped into Slots areas different additives: more oxygen, for prolonged playing; pheromones to attract and retain players; soothing, or stimulating, scents which seem more attractive than the ambient air.

Furthermore, there is an ingrained belief that if you are not winning now there is a greater chance that you will win later. This is blindingly obviously not correct in the case of Dice or Roulette – or just about any other game (Blackjack, if you are counting, can promise more success later on in a shoe) – and it isn't true for Slots either. But for Slots players, a prolonged session with few wins seems, in their minds, to suggest happier times along the way. The result is that credit cards come out of wallets and purses and the casino cage hands over more cash in exchange for money as yet unearned. Debts mount with frightening ease and no pain – until the final demands appear from lawyers.

For all these reasons, governments should take the moral high ground and limit the stakes and prizes for Slot machines. They should ban the use of credit cards at casinos, and they should effectively regulate online gaming. However, a misplaced debate of civil liberties inevitably begins, and money talks: the tax revenues are just far too great for any legislative body to show any moral backbone whatsoever.

So, with the massive dangers of the hyper-addictive nature of Slots on board, it's time to see if we can fight back against this faceless enemy and enjoy our gaming for longer, indeed even leave the machines with their money, and not vice versa. The good news is that there *are* ways to beat the machines. To do so will require a little time and effort, some gentle study, and a big bundle of discipline and self-control, but it can be done and, right now, is being done by sensible, winning players.

19
Video Poker

O F ALL THE SLOTS available, Video Poker is certainly the best option for players. Many Poker machines retain only a small percentage of money wagered and some, played with the correct strategy, offer the house virtually no edge whatsoever. Indeed – and here is the big news – some will even offer the player an edge! That is the kind of casino deal worth taking advantage of.

The basic Video Poker machine is based around the game of Five-Card Draw. You are dealt five cards at random. You are permitted to hold between none and all five of those cards, and replace those you discard with new random cards. The hand that you make as a result will pay according to the universal value of Poker hands:

Royal Flush   Five cards of the same suit, in
                       consecutive order, from the ace to
                       the ten
                       A K Q J 10

Straight Flush   Five cards of the same suit, in
                       consecutive order
                       8 7 6 5 4

Four-of-a-Kind   Four cards of the same value
                       J J J J 5

Full House   Three-of-a-Kind, plus a Pair
                       K K K 8 8

Flush   Five cards of the same suit
                       J 8 6 5 2

Straight   Five cards, of different suits, in
                       consecutive order
                       Q J 10 9 8

Three-of-a-Kind   Three cards of the same value
                       A A A 7 4

Two Pair   Two pairs
                       K K 7 7 5

Pair   One pair
                       8 8 6 5 4

The machines, although varying in design all over the world,
will basically all resemble the following layout:

The Screen

You will see that the screen shows the payout schedule, the number of credits you have available, what win (if any) has been paid, and the cards that have been dealt. Modern machines offer touch-screen control for almost all functions, while old-style machines have buttons.

The Buttons

Some machines have touch-screens as well as buttons. Most machines still have buttons to select how many coins you wish to bet per play, which cards you wish to hold, and the button which instructs the machine to deal or draw cards.

If you wish to play maximum credits (which, we will see, is usually desirable), there will be a button with "Bet Max" or "Bet 5 Coins" clearly indicated. Once you push this button, the cards are dealt immediately.

If you wish to bet one, two, three or four coins or credits, press the button marked "Bet One". If you push it a second time, it will bet two credits, a third time three, and so on. Unless you bet five credits, the cards will not be dealt until you push the button marked "Deal/Draw". This will activate the game.

Some machines also offer you a double or nothing gamble option on any wins you may hit, and this is also controlled through the buttons beneath the screen.

The Loyalty Card Reader

Most Poker machines found in casinos or resorts have a slot in which to place your Slots Club card or loyalty card. This registers how much action you are giving the machine and allows the casino to calculate how many benefits and complimentary bonuses to offer you. Incidentally, this also allows the casino to see for how long you play, at which stakes, and which machines you prefer. This, in turn, results in you being contacted for specific offers and competitions. It is a bonus for you, and a powerful marketing tool for the casino. You don't have to become a member of a Slots Club, but I advise that you do. It is a free reward for playing at your chosen casino.

Many regular players attach this card to themselves via a string or cord. This is because it is so easy to leave your card behind, and then risk either losing your benefits, or having to re-register and search the computer records for your previous play.

Some casinos now promote cashless gaming, whereby you charge your loyalty card up with credits at the casino cage and play these in the machines. No cash is needed. No dirty coins need collecting, the machines don't need filling, there is no need for change personnel. Even casino security is easier. It takes a little getting used to, but it works effectively and it is here to stay.

By the way, there is another reason the casinos like cashless gaming. It is much easier for you, the player, to press a button and use up five more units from your card, than it is for you to delve into your pocket and put another $50 note in the machine. Just as casino chips were invented to de-personalize a player's cash, so credit on a card widens the gulf between playing just figures on a screen and parting with hard-earned cash.

While we're on the subject of Slots Club cards and loyalty cards, my advice is not to start playing any Slot machine without applying for one. Every time you play, even one credit, this is registered on the card and contributes to benefits for you. These may include cash-back, free meals, accommodation, invitations to casino functions and the like. And the key is: these benefits accrue to you while you are playing your usual game.

In terms of deciding what to offer you, the casinos do not look at how much you win or lose. Based on the percentage payout of any given machine, they know what to expect from you in the long run. By reading this book and applying its methods you will ensure that the casino makes a good deal less than it expects from you. But, that won't affect how much action you show the casino – and that is what the loyalty card monitors.

Imagine that you take $500 and decide to play Video Poker at a $1 machine. You will play five coins per play and you will win and lose – at a fairly even pace. You will probably play through your 100 spins in 30 minutes so, and after a couple of hours of play you will have shown the house $2,000 worth of action. At most casinos, that level of play will be sufficient to earn you a free meal. Play for several hours per day and you can see that soon the resort will be offering you free accommodation, a meal for you and your friends, or some other similarly valued bonuses. In the meantime, most casinos will be offering you free drinks, perhaps also free light meals. If you follow the correct strategies and enjoy all these perks – and walk away in profit – you'll be the one smiling and, just for a change, not the casino.

So, in short, make it your business to research the most comfortable, generous casinos which offer you the best conditions in which to play with the best perks to be accrued. However, never play at a higher stake just because you think it will lead to more benefits from your Slots Club or loyalty card. Unless you happen to strike lucky at just the right moment, this strategy will lead to fast losses and upset your carefully planned strategy.

If you have to wait to receive benefits, you don't have to play while you wait. Take a break, grab a drink, or just use the rest room. Then, collect your complimentary gift from the casino personnel.

Above all, pick those machines which offer the games with the best payouts for you, the player, because that is a decision which could cost you thousands, if not tens of thousands of dollars!

Coin Slots and Note Acceptors

Where cashless gaming is not in operation, the coin slots and note acceptors will be found on the front of the machine, usually to the right of the screen. Once you have fed in your coins or notes, the number of credits that you have available to play will appear, usually in the bottom right-hand corner of the screen. As you press the play buttons, you will see your credit total decline. When you win, you will see it rise, usually accompanied by some trilling electronic sounds or music.

Even using the most advanced technology, many note acceptors are temperamental. Be prepared to have brand new – or worn old – notes rejected time after time. Some note acceptors require that the note is placed in it a certain way; others are less discriminating. If the acceptor is awkward to use, either change machines, or summon casino personnel to help you.

Video Poker Areas

Video Poker machines tend to appear in groups, or banks or carousels, of machines in a casino. Usually they are grouped together in the same denomination of stake, and in groups of similar or identical game variations. If you cannot find the machine you are seeking, or a denomination that suits your pocket, ask a casino employee where your chosen machines are located.

Never play for a higher stake than you feel comfortable with, even if it means leaving the casino you are in and going elsewhere. Gambling beyond your means almost always results in ruin and, not insignificantly, will fill your session with anxiety and not pleasure.

Before playing, these are the key elements you should establish when you first look at machines:

The Game Offered

There are many different types of Video Poker, including Jacks or Better, Deuces Wild, Jokers Wild, Bonus Poker, Double Bonus Poker, Super Double Bonus Poker (and so on), Progressive Jackpots, Pick Five, 3-line, 5-line, 10-line, 25-line and 100-line Video Poker. We will look at a good selection of these in the forthcoming strategy section. Pick a machine which offers the game you would like to play, and for which you have an accurate strategy.

Increasingly, casinos are offering machines, such as "Game King", which gives multiple variations of Poker games (and sometimes other casino games too, such as Blackjack, Roulette, Keno and Craps). Not only can you select from up to 40 different games on some machines, but you also have complete freedom as to which denomination of stake you wish to play. These machines are set to become more and more popular, since they allow players the maximum choice of games, all within a single unit.

The Denomination of the Machine

This may be 25c, $1, $5, $10, $50 or $500, or variants according to the country in which you are playing. As you will see, the usual recommended action will be to play maximum coins, which on most machines means five. Therefore, a $1 machine represents a $5 wager per "spin", or play.

Your chosen stake must fit in with your planned bankroll for the session. It is advisable to have a minimum of 50 times your basic play stake to allow for short-term losing streaks. Therefore, to play a 25c machine, at $1.25 per play, you require a minimum bankroll of $62.50; for a $1 machine, at $5 per play, a minimum bankroll of $250; for a $5 machine, at $25 per play, a bankroll of at least $1,250.

Multi-line machines may show much lower stakes, such as 5c. However, if it is a 25-line machine, and you play five coins per line, this actually amounts to a stake of $6.25 per play! A 100-line machine would cost $25 per play, even though the denomination on the front of the machine says just 5c. So, be aware of the stake for each play.

The Payout Scale

This is absolutely vital since the deal of the cards is as random as a computer can make it. So, the way the manufacturer (or casino) can alter their percentage edge is by altering the payout.

For a basic Jacks or Better machine, the key payouts to look for are the Straight and Flush wins, and perhaps also for the jackpot, a Royal Flush. On other machines, for example, those which offer Progressive payouts, or bonuses for making Four-of-a-Kind or a Straight Flush, the payouts must be studied to ensure that you are getting a good game. What to look for will be discussed in a moment in our strategy briefings.

The payout schedule for Poker machines is absolutely vital if you are to beat the machines and make money. Poker machines in big gambling towns, such as Las Vegas, tend to be more generous than in individual shops or clubs, or in casinos where there is little choice for players to make. For example, in pubs and clubs in the United Kingdom, Poker machines frequently take between 8 per cent and a truly gob-smacking 27 per cent. To play these machines is to give up any hope of seeing your money again.

In small casinos, bars and independent shops in Las Vegas, on cruise-line casinos and river-boat gambling, the house edge might range between 4 and 13 per cent – still an absolutely unbeatable disadvantage in the medium or long term.

In casinos and resorts where the gambling public has a choice of machine and a choice of venue in which to play, the Poker machines are likely to be much more competitive. Some Vegas casinos have machines which, played properly, actually offer the player up to 2 per cent in their favour (although this is based on a big Progressive Jackpot, which is very unlikely to hit). Nonetheless, you are gambling within a couple of percent of an even-money game. This, together with benefits, free drinks, and the enjoyment derived from the game, seems like a pretty reasonable gambling deal.

Video Poker Machine Strategy

The strategy for best play on individual Poker machines can get quite complex. Since my aim is to give everyone who enters a casino a decent chance of success, each of the following strategy briefings is simplified to ensure that you will remember it and be able to apply it every time you play. Following these guidelines will significantly increase your chances of winning on Video Poker.

All successful strategies should acknowledge that your real goal is to hit a Royal Flush, since this pays by far the biggest prize. In some cases it will pay a truly enormous prize, based on a Progressive Jackpot which is linked between a bank of machines, throughout a casino or casino group, or even throughout a national casino network.

While the chances of hitting a Royal Flush, with the cards appearing in any order (there are some giant Progressives which require to hit the Royal Flush in a precise order of cards across the screen) being approximately 1/35,000, a regular player can expect to hit a Royal at some point. There are plenty of stories of players hitting two or even three Royal Flushes in one session although, as you can imagine, this is a rare occurrence.

A friend of mine in South Africa missed his first flight home when he hit a Royal Flush as he was about to leave the resort. A few hours later, preparing to depart for the last flight of the day, he hit another one on an even bigger machine and ended up staying an extra night when he realized he wouldn't make his later flight either!

You can abandon all standard – some might say, rational – plays in favour of trying to hit the Royal Flush, but a mildly ambitious strategy, backed up with good sense, ensures that your playing time is extended, and your chances of hitting the jackpot increased.

The good news is that there are just three golden rules which apply to all Video Poker machines. If you ignore these, you might as well just hand your money to the casino without wasting time.

1 Select Your Video Poker Machine Carefully

A few minutes taken to select your machine, or bank of machines, can make the difference between a profitable, enjoyable session and a losing, miserable one. In any case, becoming used to the casino atmosphere, finding out from regulars if there are any trends worth following, and generally assessing where you plan to gamble is a good idea.

As you will see, the payout schedule will guide you as to the house edge for any given machine. Check with the individual strategy notes to ensure that you are getting the best deal for your money.

If you are visiting Las Vegas, or another major casino resort, check online for recent reviews of Slot machines and payouts in one of many different free newsletters indicating the best casinos in which to play.

2 Play Maximum Coins

This is a general rule with very few exceptions. You will notice on the payout schedule that most machines pay the same award for each combination, simply multiplied by the number of coins played. Hence, on many machines Two Pair will pay:

with 1 credit played	2 coins
with 2 credits played	4 coins
with 3 credits played	6 coins
with 4 credits played	8 coins
with 5 credits played	10 coins

However, for the Royal Flush, the payout usually looks markedly different:

with 1 credit played	250 coins
with 2 credits played	500 coins
with 3 credits played	750 coins
with 4 credits played	1,000 coins
with 5 credits played	4,000 coins

The leap for the jackpot for five credits played provides a substantial advantage to the player. Playing five credits on this type of Jacks or Better machine, providing you follow the simple strategy, will pay close to 99.5 per cent back to the player. This makes it as good a game as any you will see in the casino, but one which, usually, will see your money last longer, while still giving you a chance of a substantial win (800 times your stake if you hit the Royal Flush).

3 Bankroll Management

It's dull, it's boring, it's spoiling your fun. Protecting your bankroll might not be exciting but if you want to be a winner it is essential. The casinos have spent decades working out the best way to protect their bankrolls, and if you want to beat them at their own game, so must you.

- Decide on the amount of bankroll for a session. Make it between 50 and 100 times the stake for each play you plan to make.
- Do not add to that bankroll under any circumstances. If you lose the session bankroll, take some time off, gather your thoughts, and consider going to play at a lower stake for your next session. Do not believe that your Video Poker machine is any more likely to pay simply because you have lost some money. There is no correlation whatsoever.
- If you find that you have made a 50 per cent profit on your session bankroll at any time, take out half this profit plus your original bankroll. If you do not touch this money now you will leave the session a winner. There is nothing more foolish than to make a profit

through sensible, skilful play, and then to lose it back to the casino through indiscipline.

- Play the remaining money (25 per cent of your original bankroll), and if you triple it then remove the original stake (25 per cent of your original session bankroll) and add it to your winnings. You have now made a 50 per cent profit on your session bankroll, and you still have 50 per cent of it to play with. Continue repeating this until you decide to bank your winnings and add them to your profits, or you lose the additional winnings and end your session.

To protect your bankroll, you must be prepared to close a session early. If you end one session early with a profit, it means you'll have more time for your next session, be it on Video Poker, another Slot machine, or at the tables. You can, of course, also spend that money on presents, a luxury meal, or some other way of remembering that you beat the casino at its own game.

How To Pick The Best Value Poker Machines

To begin, let's take a look at the most important pre-play decision you can make: which machine to play.

The industry standard Video Poker machine is Jacks or Better. This is a machine with no wild cards, which deals from a new virtual 52-card deck for every hand. A wild card is a card, often a joker, but sometimes a 2, which will substitute for any card required to make a winning hand. The Poker machine automatically uses it to produce the highest winning hand possible. Hence, if you are dealt king, king, joker, 5, 3, the joker substitutes for a king, and you will be paid for Three-of-a-Kind. The moment that there are wild cards, the odds of each particular hand vary massively and this will be reflected in the payouts for each combination. For "pure" Poker machines, there is a standard pay table which guides you as to how profitable each machine might be.

There are several varieties of the Jacks or Better machine and a relatively simple way to identify which one you should play. As discussed earlier, the key is the payout schedule. This is how it will appear on the vast majority of machines:

Jacks or Better (9/6)

Play/Coins	1	2	3	4	5
Royal Flush	250	500	750	1,000	4,000
Straight Flush	50	100	50	200	250
Four-of-a-Kind	25	50	75	100	125
Full House	9	18	27	36	45
Flush	6	12	18	24	30
Straight	4	8	12	16	20
Three-of-a-Kind	3	6	9	12	15
Two Pair	2	4	6	8	10
Jacks or Better	1	2	3	4	5

As you insert more coins, a vertical bar illuminates the column of the set of prizes you stand to win if you hit a winning hand. If you consistently play five coins per play, the far right column will remain illuminated. Notice that the jackpot for the Royal Flush is not sequential. When you play five coins, if you hit you will be paid 4,000 (not 1,250) coins. This is a substantial advantage to you, and the key reason why you should nearly always play maximum coins at Video Poker.

The key indicator as to whether you should play these machines, however, lies in the payouts for the Full House and the Flush. Often referred to as 9/6 machines, they offer a payout of nine coins for a Full House and six coins for a Flush. This is the industry standard, and it is usually the maximum payout you can hope to find for these combinations. With this 9/6 payout, and a fixed 4,000-coin jackpot for maximum coins played, these machines produce a house edge of only 0.5 per cent, providing you play the correct strategies. In other words, they offer a decent shot at taking the casino's money.

When you seek out Jacks or Better machines, make the payout schedule your first check. You may discover a less generous scale of prizes – what experts call the 8/5 payout, or Short Payback:

Jacks or Better (8/5)

Play/Coins	1	2	3	4	5
Royal Flush	250	500	750	1,000	4,000
Straight Flush	50	100	150	200	250
Four-of-a-Kind	25	50	75	100	125
Full House	8	16	24	32	40
Flush	5	10	15	20	25
Straight	4	8	12	16	20
Three-of-a-Kind	3	6	9	12	15
Two Pair	2	4	6	8	10
Jacks or Better	1	2	3	4	5

Notice that on this payout schedule the prizes for the Full House and the Flush have been reduced from nine and six coins respectively, to eight and five coins. This makes a substantial difference to your chances of emerging a winner from a session, increasing the house edge to 2.7 per cent. These machines are therefore a poorer prospect than most Tables Games, making them undesirable to play.

However, there are many forms of Video Poker machine offering an 8/5 payout that also offer a Progressive Jackpot. If the jackpot is higher, then the lower payouts for the Full House and the Flush are acceptable since, if you hit the jackpot, you will win even more money. Indeed, if the jackpot is high enough, the 8/5 payout schedule may still result in a machine that is offering an edge to the player! In a moment, we'll look at how high the jackpot needs to be to make these payout schedules worth your while playing.

Unless there are compensating payouts, such as increased prizes for Four-of-a-Kind, or a Progressive Jackpot, do not play the 8/5 machines Remember what the casinos do not want you to know: that you are very unlikely to hit a Royal Flush. So, increase your chances of winning at Video Poker by hunting down machines offering a 9/6 payout instead.

Jacks or Better (8/5 with Progressive Jackpot)

The key to deciding whether or not to invest your money in these machines will be the size of the Progressive Jackpot. You need to be savvy here, because most often the Progressive Jackpot is not shown as a number of coins, but as a cash total. It may be unique to a single machine, be linked across a bank of machines, or even throughout a casino or group of casinos.

This is what you should be looking for:

- A Progressive Jackpot usually starts at **5,250 coins**; at this level, the machine is taking 2.2 per cent from the player, and the machine is still not a good proposition. This is the level at which the Progressive Jackpot will be re-set following a Royal Flush being hit.
- When a Progressive Jackpot reaches **7,900 coins**, the machine is taking only 0.5 per cent from the player – the same as a standard 9/6 payout Jacks or Better machine, and it has now become playable.
- When a Progressive Jackpot reaches **8,700 coins**, the machine is taking no percentage from the player and you are playing an even-money game.
- When a Progressive Jackpot is **higher than 8,700 coins**, you are playing the machine with – in the long term – a positive expectation. You, the player, has the edge.

You may find it hard to seek out a Jacks or Better Progressive with a total higher than 8,000 coins, but they are around and they are worth finding. If you have a choice of casino, spend some time searching for the most profitable machines. Make the hunt for positive expectation machines part of your battle with the casinos for supremacy.

Please remember that, even if you find a really profitable-looking machine, you may not win. Unless you hit the Royal Flush, the 8/5 payout schedule is not generous. However, at least when you do hit the Royal, you will be paid handsomely and it will fund many more happy sessions, or some nice gifts for you or your loved ones.

These are the Progressive Jackpot totals you are seeking on a Jacks or Better machine with a standard 8/5 payout schedule:

25c machine:	7,900 coins	$ 1,975	0.5 per cent house edge
	8,700 coins	$ 2,175	No house edge
	8,800 coins+	$ 2,200+	Player edge upwards
$1 machine	7,900 coins	$ 7,900	0.5 per cent house edge
	8,700 coins	$ 8,700	No house edge
	8,800 coins+	$ 8,800+	Player edge upwards
$5 machine	7,900 coins	$ 39,500	0.5 per cent house edge
	8,700 coins	$ 43,500	No house edge
	8,800 coins+	$ 44,000+	Player edge upwards

As well as Progressive Jackpots, there are many other varieties of Jacks or Better machines, even without the addition of wild cards. The most popular of these variations do not feature Progressive Jackpots, but do offer big payouts for specific big hands, such as Four-of-a-Kind. Some offer the bonus for any quads hand; some offer different size bonuses depending upon which Four-of-a-Kind hand you hit.

These machines go by the name of Bonus Poker machines, and include: Double Bonus, Double Bonus Plus, Double Bonus, Super Double Bonus, Super Double Double Bonus and Bonus Poker Deluxe. Confused? I don't blame you. It benefits the manufacturers and casino operators to offer as many variations as possible and to change up the machines regularly. This ensures that players don't become bored by playing the same game forever (although players often become loyal to one type of machine, and game, over any others), and it ensures that learning the correct strategies for every new game is virtually impossible. More importantly, one machine may sound like another but offer a far poorer rate of return. Casinos love their punters to be uninformed and confused. Do not play if this is how you feel. Consult the information here and play only those machines that are recommended. We have picked only the best for you.

Of these varieties:

- Double Double Bonus offers only a 1 per cent edge to the house.
- Super Double Double Bonus offers only 0.7 per cent to the house.

However, as with the Progressive Jackpot machines, these low percentages to the house will only be realized if you both play the correct strategies and also hit one of the bigger bonus combinations. Otherwise, as you will see from the payout tables below, you will actually receive smaller payouts for the most common winning hands – the bigger payouts being reserved for the less likely, big winning hands.

Bonus Poker Deluxe Jacks or Better (8/5)

Credit/Coins	1	2	3	4	5
Royal Flush	250	500	750	1,000	4,000
Straight Flush	50	100	150	200	250
Four-of-a-Kind	80	160	240	320	400

	1	2	3	4	5
Full House	8	16	24	32	40
Flush	5	10	15	20	25
Straight	4	8	12	16	20
Three-of-a-Kind	3	6	9	12	15
Two Pair	1	2	3	4	5
Jacks or Better	1	2	3	4	5

Notice that the big bonus here is for any Four-of-a-Kind, paying 80 coins per credit bet (instead of the standard 25). This is offset by the lower 8/5 payout, and a reduction from two coins to one coin for Two Pair.

If you hit Four-of-a-Kind, this makes such a payout schedule attractive; if you don't, you will struggle with 8/5 payout and the money-back prize for Two Pair.

Double Bonus Jacks or Better (9/6)

Credit/Coins	1	2	3	4	5
Royal Flush	250	500	750	1,000	4,000
Straight Flush	50	100	150	200	250
Four Aces	160	320	480	640	800
Four 2s, 3s or 4s	80	160	240	320	400
Four 5s–Ks	50	100	150	200	250
Full House	9	18	27	36	45
Flush	6	12	18	24	30
Straight	4	8	12	16	20
Three-of-a-Kind	3	6	9	12	15
Two Pair	1	2	3	4	5
Jacks or Better	1	2	3	4	5

Notice that in this standard Double Bonus payout schedule, the payout for Two Pair has fallen from two coins down to only one coin. So, in order to make a profit from a play, you must hit Three-of-a-Kind or better. In return, the machine offers you at least double the prize for Four-of-a-Kind, rising to over six times the usual payout if you hit four aces. However, if you don't hit quads at any time, you will suffer from this lower payout.

Please note that some Double Bonus Jacks or Better machines make up for the lower Two Pair payout by increasing their payout for a Straight to five coins. This is worth looking for since Straights will occur regularly, whereas a Four-of-a-Kind of any sort is a rare occurrence.

There is one final Double Bonus payout schedule which you increasingly see offered, particularly in US casinos. It is a **10/7** based pay schedule, and it is very good for the player.

Double Bonus Jacks or Better (10/7)

Credit/Coins	1	2	3	4	5
Royal Flush	250	500	750	1,000	4,000
Straight Flush	50	100	150	200	**239**
Four Aces	160	320	480	640	800
Four 2s, 3s or 4s	80	160	240	320	400
Four 5s–Ks	50	100	150	200	250 **(239)**
Full House	**10**	20	30	40	50
Flush	**7**	14	21	28	35
Straight	**5**	10	15	20	25
Three-of-a-Kind	3	6	9	12	15
Two Pair	**1**	2	3	4	5
Jacks or Better	1	2	3	4	5

There are several elements to note here. Firstly, as before, Two Pair is relegated to a push, but a Straight pays five coins, a Flush, seven coins, and a Full House, ten coins. These are all excellent payouts. There is one anomaly, which is the payout for the Straight Flush with five coins paid at $5 per coin. Instead of 250, this pays only 239 coins. The reason for this concerns the American Tax system. All Slots wins of £1,200 or over must be reported to the Internal Revenue Service (IRS). At a $5 denomination, 239 coins equals $1,195, and therefore falls beneath this threshold. This payout is also sometimes for the Four 5s through Kings, for the same reason.

Played with correct strategy, these machines offer the player a real chance to beat the house, since the casino edge is only 0.21 per cent.

> As you can see from the payout schedules, all these machines demand that you play five coins in order to benefit from Royal Flush jackpots, both standard and Progressive. If playing five coins exceeds your session bankroll, seek a lower-stake machine.

Best Strategy for Jacks or Better Machines

If every Video Slots player followed a Basic Strategy when they played the machines, the casinos would make far less money. They might even tighten up the returns on Video Poker. But right now you have a chance to improve the odds against the house considerably if you follow these simple strategies for each of the main games.

If you are a high roller, playing at $5 machines or higher, you should take the time to learn the strategy and to research further for advanced "pro" strategies, which will enhance your edge even further.

Why doesn't everyone use these strategies? For exactly the same reason that players give casinos their money at Blackjack, Craps, Roulette and many other Table Games: they can't be bothered to do a little work to make themselves money. If players choose to ignore scientifically backed strategies, then they hardly deserve to win.

Once you have selected the machine which offers the best payout schedule for the game you want to play, you need to follow a simple strategy to give yourself the best opportunity to win. You can copy the charts in this book and take them with you. The casino will not mind – indeed some casino shops even sell strategy charts (at high prices) for players to buy.

The key to a successful strategy is that it is effective: that is it emphasizes your desire to hit the Royal Flush without making the game too much of a negative expectation, and that you can learn it and play it fluently quickly. The strategies presented in these sections fulfil all these needs.

Jacks or Better Basic Strategy

Play *every* hand following this order of priorities, HOLDING and DISCARDING cards. Check and play each hand from the top of the list downwards.

HOLD	Four of a Kind, Straight Flush, Royal Flush	HOLD ALL CAREFULLY*
HOLD	4 to a Royal Flush	DISCARD fifth card, even if it provides a paying combination

HOLD	Three-of-a-Kind, Straight, Flush, Full House	HOLD ALL CAREFULLY
HOLD	4 to a Straight Flush	DISCARD fifth card, even if it provides a paying combination
HOLD	Two Pair	
HOLD	Pair – Jacks or better	
HOLD	3 to a Royal Flush	
HOLD	4 to a Flush	
HOLD	Low Pair – tens or lower	
HOLD	4 to an open-ended Straight**	
HOLD	Two suited cards – Jacks or better	
HOLD	3 to a Straight Flush	
HOLD	Any two cards, Jack or higher	IF more than two cards Jack or higher, HOLD the two lowest cards***
HOLD	Suited J10, Q10, K10	
HOLD	One card, Jack or better	
HOLD	NOTHING	DISCARD ALL FIVE CARDS

*When you are dealt a big winning hand, it is easy to get over excited and fail to hold one card, or to press the hold button twice by mistake (this cancels the hold), and then to lose your big win. Although some machines automatically hold winning combinations, others do not, so you must be careful to hold the big win when it comes along. ** An open-ended Straight is one which can be completed by two cards. For example, if you have 7, 8, 9, 10, then if you hit either a 6 or a Jack you will make your Straight. In contrast, a "Gut-Shot" or "Belly-Buster" Straight is one where there is only one card you can hit to make your Straight. For example, if you have 5, 6, 8, 9, only a 7 will complete your Straight. *** This combines payout for pairing Jacks or higher, and maximizes Straight opportunities.

Deuces Wild – Full Pay Machines

These machines offer excellent value for the player, providing that they give a full pay schedule as detailed below. If you follow the strategy shown, a house edge does not exist! Instead, you, the player, hold a long-term edge over the machine of 0.7 per cent.

The industry-standard payout schedule should look like this:

Deuces Wild (Full Pay)

Credit/Coins	1	2	3	4	5
Royal Flush (natural)	250	500	750	1,000	4,000
Four Deuces	200	400	600	800	1,000
Royal Flush (wild card)	25	50	75	100	125
Five-of-a-Kind	15	30	45	60	75
Straight Flush	9	18	27	36	45
Four-of-a-Kind	5	10	15	20	25
Full House	3	6	9	12	15
Flush	2	4	6	8	10
Straight	2	4	6	8	10
Three-of-a-Kind	1	2	3	4	5

Notice that natural payouts (those not involving wild cards) pay by far the biggest prizes. The natural Royal Flush (not involving a wild 2) still pays 250 coins, and 4,000 for maximum credits played. Once again, this means that you must play the full five coins for each spin, so that you benefit from this massively increased jackpot. Four Deuces pays the second jackpot, but without a bonus pay for maximum coins.

Royal Flushes and Five-of-a-Kind, involving at least one wild card, pay relatively low prizes since you will see these hands reasonably frequently.

Usually rare hands such as Straight Flushes, Four-of-a-Kind and Full Houses become regular occurrences with the addition of four wild cards into the pack.

Deuces Wild with Progressive Jackpot

Deuces Wild can also be found with a Progressive Jackpot and, unless you catch the machine just after the Progressive has been reset (following a jackpot win), you will find these machines offer a great deal for the player. Usually, the machines are reset to the standard 4,000 coins after a jackpot and, at that point, the house holds an edge over the player of a little higher than 1 per cent.

As usual with Progressives, the key to deciding whether or not to invest your money in these machines will be the size of the Progressive Jackpot. Remember that the Progressive is nearly always displayed as a cash total and not as a coin value.

This is the payout schedule for a Full Pay machine with Progressive Jackpot:

Deuces Wild with Progressive Jackpot (Full Pay)

Credit/Coins	1	2	3	4	5
Royal Flush (natural)	250	500	750	1,000	Progressive
Four Deuces	200	400	600	800	1,000

Royal Flush (wild card)	25	50	75	100	125
Five-of-a-Kind	15	30	45	60	75
Straight Flush	9	18	27	36	45
Four-of-a-Kind	4	8	12	16	20
Full House	4	8	12	16	20
Flush	3	6	9	12	15
Straight	2	4	6	8	10
Three-of-a-Kind	1	2	3	4	5

Notice that although the payout for Four-of-a-Kind has fallen from five coins to four coins, the payouts for Full House and Flush have increased from three to four, and two to three coins, respectively.

A Progressive Jackpot usually starts at 4,000 coins. At this level, the machine is taking 1.1 per cent from the player, and the machine is only a reasonable proposition. This is the level at which the Progressive will be re-set following a Royal Flush being hit.

When a Progressive reaches 6,400 coins, the machine is taking no percentage from the player and you are playing an even-money game.

When a Progressive is higher than 6,500 coins, you are playing the machine with, in the long term, a positive expectation. You, the player, has the edge.

Remember that, even if you find a really profitable looking machine, you may not win. Unless you hit a natural Four Deuces or a natural Royal Flush, the payout schedule is not generous. You will, however, see a lot more premium hands than you would usually see playing Video Poker with no wild cards, or just one.

These are the Progressive totals you are seeking on a
Deuces Wild machine with a Full payout schedule:

25c machine	4,000 coins	$1,000	1.1 per cent house edge
	6,400 coins	$1,600	No house edge
	6,500 coins+	$1,625+	Player edge upwards
$1 machine	4,000 coins	$4,000	1.1 per cent house edge
	6,400 coins	$6,400	No house edge
	6,500 coins+	$6,500+	Player edge upwards
$5 machine	4,000 coins	$20,000	1.1 per cent house edge
	6,400 coins	$32,000	No house edge
	6,500 coins+	$32,500+	Player edge upwards

Deuces Wild Basic Strategy

Play every hand following this order of priorities,
HOLDING and DISCARDING cards. Check, and play
each hand from the top of the list downwards.

With four Deuces showing
HOLD   Four 2s (Deuces)   5th card irrelevant

With three Deuces showing
HOLD   Royal Flush with Deuces   HOLD ALL CAREFULLY

HOLD   Three Deuces   DISCARD 4th and
                                      5th cards

With two Deuces showing
HOLD   Any pair with your two
        Deuces (Four-of-a-Kind)

HOLD   Two cards for Royal Flush, plus your two Deuces

HOLD   Two consecutive suited cards, plus your two Deuces –
        for Straight Flush

HOLD   Two Deuces   DISCARD 3rd, 4th and
                                            5th cards

With one Deuce showing

HOLD   Trips, plus your Deuce   DISCARD 5th card

HOLD   Three Royal Flush cards,
        plus your Deuce   DISCARD 5th card

HOLD   Made Full House

HOLD   Three consecutive suited cards,
        plus your two Deuces – for
        Straight Flush

HOLD   Any Pair plus your Deuce, made
        Straight, or made Flush

HOLD   Two Royal Flush cards,
        plus your Deuce   DISCARD 4th and
                                            5th cards

HOLD   Deuce only

With no Deuces showing

HOLD   Four cards to a Royal Flush

HOLD   Made Straight Flush; made Three-of-a-Kind

HOLD   Four cards to Straight Flush

HOLD   Three cards to a Royal Flush

HOLD   Any Pair

HOLD   Four cards to a Flush/
        four cards to a Straight/three
        cards to a Straight Flush   DISCARD ALL CARDS

Joker Wild (Full Pay)

There are many variations of Joker Wild. The game is dealt from a single pack of 52 cards, plus the addition of a 53rd – a joker. This card is wild, linking up with other cards to form the best possible hand.

Some machines start paying on pairs of kings or aces, and move upwards. These machines – if you can still find them – offer the player a tiny long-term edge (about 0.5 per cent), but only if Four-of-a-Kind is paying 20 coins. If you find these machines, check that the payouts offer this, then go ahead and enjoy. These are excellent machines for the player.

More commonly, however, Two Pair is the starting point for payoffs in the payout schedule. These machines, if accompanied by a Full Pay schedule and played sensibly, offer the player a game where the house edge is a little over 1.2 per cent.

The Full Pay schedule should look like this:

Joker Wild (Full Pay)

Credit/Coins	1	2	3	4	5
Royal Flush (natural)	250	500	750	1,000	4,000
Five-of-a-Kind	100	200	300	400	500
Royal Flush (with joker)	50	100	150	200	250
Straight Flush	50	100	150	200	250
Four-of-a-Kind	20	40	60	80	100
Full House	8	16	24	32	40
Flush	7	14	21	28	35
Straight	5	10	15	20	25
Three-of-a-Kind	2	4	6	8	10
Two Pair	1	2	3	4	5

Notice that the payouts for Full House and Flush are eight
and seven coins respectively and these, together with the
wild joker card, make these machines likely to prolong your
playing pleasure. You will hit the mid-range hands quite
often and these pay well. Once again, the massive bonus for
playing five coins is achieved when you hit the Royal Flush
(without the joker). The Royal with the joker and Straight
Flush (with or without the joker) both pay a healthy 50
coins, and Five-of-a-Kind pays 100 coins.

Joker Wild Basic Strategy

Play *every* hand following this order of priorities,
HOLDING and DISCARDING cards. Check and play
each hand from the top of the list downwards.

With Joker Showing

HOLD   Five-of-a-Kind/Royal Flush/Straight
        Flush/Full House/Flush

HOLD   Three-of-a-Kind, plus joker   DISCARD 5th card

HOLD   Three cards to Royal Flush,
        plus joker   DISCARD 5th card

HOLD   Three cards to Straight Flush, plus joker

HOLD   Made Straight

HOLD   Pair, plus joker

HOLD   Two suited high cards, plus joker (for Royal Flush)

HOLD   Two suited cards, plus joker (for Straight Flush)

HOLD   Three suited cards, plus joker (for Flush)

HOLD   Four consecutive unsuited cards, including
        joker (for Straight)

HOLD   Joker only   DISCARD
                                            remaining cards

With No Joker

HOLD   Four cards to a Royal Flush

HOLD   Made Four-of-a-Kind/Full House/Flush/
        Straight/Three-of-a-Kind

HOLD   Four cards to a Straight Flush

HOLD   Two Pairs

HOLD   Three cards to a Royal Flush

HOLD   Four cards to a Flush/Four cards to a Straight

HOLD   Three cards to a Straight Flush

HOLD   One Pair

HOLD   Three cards to a Flush/two cards
        to a Royal Flush/three cards
        to a Straight Flush/   DISCARD ALL
        two cards to a Straight Flush   FIVE CARDS

There are a vast number of variations now available, based on the original-style Poker machine. These include Deuces and Joker Wild, Full House Bonus Poker, Five Aces Poker, Sevens and Joker Wild, Sequential Royal Bonus Poker...The list is almost inexhaustible.

If one of these myriad variations is your favourite game, research the best strategies online or purchase computer strategies from leading gaming bookshops. Study of these will inevitably lead you to lose less and, if your choice of machine is one with an edge available to the player, make much bigger profits over time.

Multi-Line Machines

With the advent of advanced touch-screen technology and the desire to keep players in front of the machines for even longer, gaming manufacturers and casinos alike wanted to invent machines to tempt players to make far bigger bets than they might have planned. They achieved this by creating multi-line machines, where players have the option to bet, not just on a single line of Poker action, but on three, five, ten, 25, even 100 lines of action simultaneously.

The attraction of these games is that the base stake seems quite modest and, once you work out how the game works, the chance to win seems big. The reality is that you might as well be playing 100 Poker machines simultaneously when you play one 100-line Poker machine, because your chances of winning or losing are exactly the same.

Multi-line Poker machines come in many variations, from standard Jacks or Better to many of the complex variations now on offer for single-line machines. The difference is that you can opt to play multiple lines based on your original hold/draw decision. Let's see how a multi-line Poker machine works, starting with a 3-line Poker machine – Jacks or Better.

As usual, you select to play one to five coins (and, as usual, you should nearly always play maximum coins to take advantage of the big Royal Flush bonus for five coins). However, on this machine, you will have to play three times five coins – namely, 15 coins – to cover all three lines at five coins each.

Having done so, the machine deals five cards into the bottom hand. From this hand, you choose which cards to hold or discard, and this choice is replicated in the other two hands above.

You now draw cards from separate decks (minus the cards you have discarded) to each of the three lines in play. All wins are paid off, the prize being indicated on the screen next to each hand before credits are added to your total.

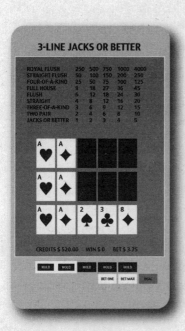

The excitement of a multi-line machine is that if you have a winning combination – say, a Pair of aces – when you hold this pair it is also added to the two other lines, so you are guaranteed a win on every line, plus three chances to make Three-of-a-Kind, Full House, or Four-of-a-Kind. If you can hold four cards to a Straight Flush or a Royal Flush, you have three chances to hit your card for a really big payout.

However, if you cannot hold a winning combination, then you may suffer a multiple line loss. So, the simple result is that you win more quickly, and you lose more quickly. That, generally, is a bad idea in a casino.

If you choose to play multi-line machines, check carefully the payout schedule for the game you plan to play, and reject the machine if it does not match up to the payout schedules shown earlier in this chapter. You will find that most multi-line machines do not offer the best payouts – the casinos are hoping that, amid the excitement, you do not notice this. Also, check the denominations very carefully. If you play a 10-line Poker machine, you are committing yourself (if you are giving yourself the best chance) to playing five coins on ten lines – making each bet 50 coins!

If you choose to play a seemingly low-rolling denomination of, say, 25c, this still equates to $12.50 per play. That's a high roller's stake.

At a $5 machine, you are talking $250 per play! That is a massive stake and, although you could be lucky and double or triple your money on the very first play, you could also loose all, or nearly all, of it if your original line contains nothing much worth holding.

The big trick in all of this, from the point of view of the casinos, is that these multi-line machines usually offer a payout schedule that is worse than optimum for the player. They justify this by claiming that the stake is so low (maybe 5c) that the payouts must be reduced to increase the house edge. Of course, if you are playing ten lines at five coins per line, that "tiny stake" is actually $2.50 per play – a perfectly decent stake per spin for the casino.

There are also instances of multi-line machines featuring a maximum total payout per play, meaning that, if you were lucky enough to get dealt a Royal Flush on your original line and you held it over to all the other lines, you wouldn't even get paid the full amount. This is tantamount to thievery.

So, in short, I do not recommend multi-line Poker machines. You would do better to play slightly higher stake single-line machines and hunt down the best payout schedules and the highest Progressives available. In Las Vegas, you will soon be able to track down online references and newsletters which tell you at which casinos the best machines are located, where the Progressive Jackpots are highest, and which casinos offer the most rewarding Slot Clubs and loyalty schemes. Success on Video Poker machines must be worked at, but it can be achieved.

New Variations

As a general rule, new variations of Poker machine, at least in the last 20 years, have not offered the player a better chance of success than the original-style Jacks or Better machines and the innovation of one or more wild cards added to the deck.

Machines which offer you multiple chances to place ever-more obscure bets are there simply to tempt the player into making greater numbers of wagers with the odds more heavily stacked against them. A good analogy can be found on the Blackjack tables: this game played sensibly can be made almost an even-money proposition, and with a little skill even a positive expectation game for the player, and so the casinos have introduced side bets, which usually grab for the casino a massive house edge. So it is for Poker machines.

Stick to the original games and follow the guidelines here, and you will truly enjoy your Video Poker play.

Double or Nothing Feature

From quite early on in the evolution of the Poker machine, many varieties have offered an extra gambling opportunity when you make a winning hand: a simple double or nothing option. If you opt to take this chance, the screen clears and five new cards are dealt. The card to the left is face up; the remaining four cards are face down. You can choose any one of the four hidden cards and, if the card is higher than the one showing, you double your money; if it is lower than the one shown, you lose your prize.

On almost every machine, aces are played as high; 2s are low. Therefore, if the card showing is a 2, you cannot lose; if the card showing is an ace, you cannot win. If the card showing and the card you select are the same value, it is a push, and you are invited to gamble again, or collect the original prize.

Most machines offer you the chance to continue gambling, doubling your money, right up to the point that, if you won, you would exceed the machine's natural jackpot.

Some machines only offer you the chance to double three times, or five times, or to a pre-set limit. This limitation seems to appear more in online than in land-based casinos.

Some players love this feature and claim that it is the way to beat the machine; others never use it and believe that it has nothing whatsoever to do with the game and may even affect the machine and the likely outcomes in the future.

According to the machine manufacturers, this gamble is a genuine even-money proposition, based on a random visible card and randomly dealt hidden cards. It is also completely separate from the standard Poker game, which is dealt from a different virtual pack.

Personally, I have experienced much success using this double or nothing feature on many Video Poker machines, and I like it. My impression is that it is not random and that if you gamble and lose repeatedly, at some point you become more likely to win than previously. Since I have played (in statistical sample terms) only very few hands, this is not suggested as fact, merely as an observation. The effect I have observed could also be replicated in the comparatively short-term by a totally random allocation of cards. Nonetheless, the double or nothing feature can add excitement to a game where, generally, the prizes are very small in relation to the stake placed.

20
Hybrid Games

EVEN TODAY, when I speak to lady gamblers, they tell me that they feel intimidated by Table Games. They are afraid of making a mistake and having it pointed out publicly; they are apprehensive of being at a table full of men – sometimes quite drunk men – and above all, they come to a casino to escape the worries of everyday life and just to enjoy some solitude, or the occasional interaction with other women.

It has taken casinos ages to work out that plenty of women would gamble at Table Games if they felt more secure. To this end, Slot machine versions of virtually every Table Game have become available in the big casinos, allowing gamblers to play Blackjack and Roulette, to name but two, in privacy and without needing to interact with a judging audience.

However, casino research found that many women are suspicious of computer gaming in casinos (although plenty play online) so the casinos came up with a near-perfect solution: hybrid games. Bets are placed electronically, using touch screens, retaining a gambler's privacy, but the game itself is played live. Hence, for Roulette the usual layout is to have a ring, or horseshoe-shaped arrangement of betting machines, surrounding a real Roulette table. Every 90 seconds, the live dealer spins the real ball in the real wheel and the result is obtained in the usual way. Big screens display the wheel in motion so that everyone can see the action. The result is then fed into the computer and all the winning bets on your touch-screen are paid out, either in coins or credits.

Naturally, the casinos love these hybrid games. Instead of eight or ten players at one table, you can have 20 or 30 betting consoles where people can play. Instead of a supervisor and at least one dealer, if not two, a single member of staff can handle the entire operation. Better still, the consoles can cope both with small bettors and the occasional high roller. This means that the hybrid games are a perfect way for people to learn the games at low stakes (I've seen 25c Roulette bets available), become used to the action, and then, if they choose, graduate to the full, live Table Game.

Many casinos in the United Kingdom now offer a hybrid Punto Bunco (Baccarat) game, with rows of betting desks, so that 30 or 40 players can bet on each coup. The hands are dealt from a standard eight-deck shoe, monitored by cameras. The players watch the hands forming on the screens in front of them and join in on the excitement of trying to break a good opponent's hand, or hit just the right card to make their chosen hand the winner.

For me, one of the pleasures of gambling is the social interaction and the chance to meet people whom one might not usually get the chance to find out about. The shared experience of being at a Blackjack table, or playing dice – when the going starts off bad, but slowly the players turn it around and then hit a hot streak – is unbeatable and it is part of the huge excitement of winning. So, despite the fact that Slots and electronic consoles offer the casinos 24-hour non-stop gambling, with no risk of fraud, no chance of dealer-player collusion, low wages and maintenance costs, it still lacks something key.

There is also the matter of addiction, which is a very real problem, and which affects a far higher percentage of gamblers than casinos, or governments, like to make out. There is not only compulsive gambling – a truly horrendous affliction which can destroy lives – but there is also excessive gambling, where players just about live within their means but spend every spare penny (and every penny that is not spare) on gambling, and forgo all of life's other pleasures. At least having dealers and supervisors, friends and fellow gamblers around you, gives you the chance to talk about these problems and receive advice and an opportunity to control such urges. The faceless machines just take and take and take, and no one looks out for you.

However, assuming that you are a determined, but recreational, gambler, these hybrid games do provide an excellent opportunity to practise casino games, for low stakes, and without too much supervision. Naturally, I hope that before you try any of these games you study this section of the book so that you not only know the best strategies, but also feel confident enough to play in any casino in the world. And, don't forget, if you want to practise these games for free, there are a multitude of online gaming sites where you can play in practise mode without risking a penny.

Playing and Betting Strategies for Hybrid Games

All these games follow exactly the same rules as for the standard Table Game. In the case of Roulette, you should check if the wheel being used boasts two zeros (in which case, do not play it), or only a single zero.

A word of warning, particularly with Roulette: one of the best features for the casino about touch-screens is the ease with which you can place bets (just by a fingertip). For this reason, casinos have found that the average number of different bets placed is higher on a touch-screen than at the table. So, resist placing extra bets on the touch-screen. Keep your main bets for the High/Low, Odd/Even, Red/Black bets, where the odds are least against you, and place bets on numbers only for small amounts.

Similarly, at Baccarat do not be tempted to stick a couple of dollars on the terrible Tie (or Égalité) Bet, just because it is so easy to do so. Stick to betting on Bank or Player, and you will stand the best chance of walking away from the betting console with more money than you arrived with.

With both these games, if you are winning you can increase your bets moderately to try to hit a hot streak and carry on increasing your bets while it lasts. However, once you lose a bet, return to your base stake and begin again. This will lessen your chances of being wiped out if the casino hits the hot streak and not you.

Bankroll

Use the hybrid games as a chance to practise playing while keeping your bankroll small. As usual, a minimum of 20 times your base bet is the minimum bankroll to ensure that you withstand a poor run of luck before, hopefully, recovering your position, and possibly building on it.

21
Multi-Game Video Slots

I N THE GAMING industry, the greatest revolution is the massive increase in the popularity of video gambling. Instead of having to provide tables, manned by at least two members of staff, over three 8-hour shifts, scrutinizing every transaction by camera to control fraud, the casino installs an almost maintenance-free Slot machine, and it sits there enticing gamblers to sample its charms 24 hours a day, without complaint, every single day of the year. And players seem to love them.

What started off simply as Video Poker, has now blossomed into Video Blackjack, Video Keno, Video Roulette, Video just-about-everything. I love Slots and Video Poker but, for me, the other games are Table Games and should be played in the company of fellow gamblers. So, personally, I'm not keen on these video games. Apart from anything else, you could play the same games, often for better odds, at an online casino in the comfort of your own home. However, as we will discuss shortly, online gaming cannot always be guaranteed to be honest, whereas you would have to be exceptionally unlucky to come across a dishonest video machine in a casino. Particularly in Nevada, the state in which Las Vegas sits, the Gaming Commission takes its responsibilities very seriously and goes the extra mile to ensure that the gaming is fair in its casinos. Machine software is regularly tested and verified and any casino found to be defrauding their customers (you might argue that they all do, one way or another) by displaying odds which are incorrect, face massive fines or even closure. That extra assurance of security and honesty is often reason enough for players to visit the casinos rather than to play at home.

As with all casino gambling, you should join the Slots Club, the loyalty card scheme, so that every bet you make registers on the systems and accrues benefits for you. It is as close to free money as you will ever find, because if you were going to gamble anyway the casino will now reward you automatically. And, somehow, if you lose $100, but you are offered a free lunch, the pain of losing doesn't seem so great. The better the casino, the more carefully they will look after you, however modest your gambling budget. Whereas in the past, Slots players were considered unimportant, nowadays these same players are looked upon as the mainstays of the casino, and generally you will find that you are offered plenty of benefits, and incentives to play.

How the Games Work

Most Table Game Video Slots look exactly like Video Poker machines, but advertise themselves as Video Blackjack, Video Keno, Video Baccarat, etc. You insert your coins, tokens, notes or Player's Account card, plus your Slots Club card. However, before you begin to play you will be offered a number of different options and you must choose carefully to ensure that you get the game you were looking for.

Multi-Game Machines

Many manufacturers now provide casinos with machines that will play a range of different games on the same console. Players touch the on-screen button for "Main Menu" and are then offered a choice of games. On a typical multi-game machine, you might be offered six different Blackjack games, another six Keno games, a couple of Roulette games, and up to 20 different Video Poker games.

At first sight this may seem daunting, but just think carefully about the game you want to play. If it is Video Poker, check the pay tables for each game and ensure that they match up to the recommended variations in the Video Poker chapter in this book.

For Blackjack games, check the options available. A little later, I'll show you exactly what to look out for to get the best game and provide the highest chances of success.

I don't recommend playing Keno at any time, but at least the video version is usually less horrendously mean than the live game.

Multi-Denominational Options

Many Table Game Video Slots and Video Poker machines offer the player a choice of denominations within the same machine. You might choose to play a Video Poker game at 25c per credit, or one where each credit is worth $5 or $25 or even $100. You are in control, and you can select the bet size and the overall denomination that you want for any game you choose. Just be careful you don't hit the button without studying the stakes, as you may run through your $100 bankroll in two spins and not the 200 for which you had planned.

Despite the fact that you are within a maze of Slot machines, there will still be casino staff around to help you. If you can't work out how to operate a particular feature of a machine, instead of wasting your money experimenting ask for guidance from a staff member. The casino staff will be happy to help you, and they can also be asked to attract a cocktail waitress, arrange a Slots Club card for you, and guide you to the cashier for change, or to cash in your winnings.

Cashless Gaming

Increasingly, casinos worldwide are reducing staff and increasing security and efficiency by introducing cashless payouts and cashless wagering.

In some casinos, instead of paying out cash, Slot and Video Poker machines are printing out special paper tokens with the amount of your winnings. These tokens can then be exchanged for cash at the cashier's desk, or in some cases re-inserted into another machine to provide new credit. Each token is printed by the machine and will contain a barcode and unique combinations to avoid fraud.

When the machine you are playing provides this option, your winnings on any bet will not be paid out immediately in the form of coins, but will be added to your total bankroll in terms of credits available to play. When you are ready to finish your session, you press the "Cash Out" button and then the machine will print out your token and you will be ready to change this token into cash, or move on to a different machine.

Where cashless gaming is in operation – in South Africa for example – players have their loyalty cards charged up with a bankroll at the cashier's desk before play. You present your card (temporary cards are available for occasional visitors) at the desk, hand over cash or a credit card, and your card is then charged up with whatever amount you choose. At no time will you need to insert cash into the machines or use it at the tables (although many casinos do allow you to buy chips with cash and buy credits on Slot machines with cash if you wish to top up your card). All winnings are paid by using the "Cash Out" button on the machines, directly onto your card. This allows you to move easily on to the next game without the bother of buckets of filthy coins, or the need to stand in line for ages while over-worked cashiers count up thousands of low denomination coins.

Most casinos will allow you multiple cards so that, if you must, you can gamble on two machines simultaneously, or play Blackjack while your credits disappear on a nearby Slot machine.

In terms of efficiency and security, cashless gaming is a beneficial innovation. However, the casinos know full well that it is much easier for you to slip a card into a machine and play the remaining money on it than to have to visit an ATM for more cash, or unpeel more greenbacks from the wedge in your back pocket. For this reason alone, more and more casinos are introducing, in effect, debit-card gambling.

Video Keno

In short, don't play it. It will almost always offer the worst odds of any machine in the entire casino. If you must play, stick to small denomination bets and play slowly. One of the features of Video Keno is how much faster it is than the real game, and it is simply because the casino knows you can place so many more bets per hour that they offer you marginally better odds on these games.

Video Roulette

Only play if a single-zero wheel is offered and then only place small bets, preferably on the Red/Black, Odd/Even and High/Low options. This reduces the casino's edge to a minimum. If you must bet on numbers, try to bet on a few numbers only and do not become carried away by the touch-screen and find yourself placing far more bets, for more money, than you would normally do.

Research has shown that touch-screens do indeed increase the number of betting actions made by most players, and this is why casinos love them. The more action they get from you on their high-earning games, the more money they make.

Video Poker

As discussed in the earlier chapter on Video Poker, you need to know the game you want to play, what payouts you are seeking and at what denomination you wish to play. Do not start to play until you have located a favourable game. This may involve looking through the Main Menus of many different machines and then checking pay tables, but it's a small price to pay to offer yourself the best chance of winning. Is five minutes worth it when it could gain you hundreds, thousands or even hundreds of thousands of dollars? I always think so.

There are many multi-game Video Poker machines out there now. These machines offer not only Video Poker, but many variations of the game, from the standard Jacks or Better, right up to Multi-Line Bonus Poker. I've seen a 99-line multi-line game just recently (not recommended), as well as some newfangled variations. As a rule (though it is not set in stone), the more lines on offer, the more variations provided for the player, the poorer the overall odds will be. Stick to the games recommended in the Video Poker chapter and you will do pretty well.

Video Blackjack

These machines, whether stand-alone Video Blackjack machines, or multi-game machines, have become increasingly popular of late. For many gamblers, the deciding factor is the speed at which you can play Blackjack against a machine as opposed to against a dealer, perhaps with a full table of other players. The danger of this, of course, is that bankrolls fluctuate far more quickly and, if you are having a bad run (and they certainly can occur at Blackjack), you will lose all your money almost before you've got into the game. So, be aware of the high-speed nature of Video Blackjack.

Many Video Blackjack machines offer you extra gambling opportunities in the form of a High/Low Bets to double the winnings from any hand. My advice is to reject these extra opportunities and to stick to the classic game, played as well as you possibly can.

Next, you should consider the safety of gambling at Video Blackjack. If the machine contains a verified computer chip – and all casino machines should have exactly this – then the cards will appear as close to a random selection as it is possible for a computer to produce. As we will discuss in the main Slots chapter, it is almost impossible for a casino to "fiddle" with the computer chip, and there is no dial which alters the odds for the player and the casino. In other words, the game you play on Video Blackjack is as fair as the games that are dealt out of shoes and dealing machines.

Most Video Blackjack machines use a system where each new hand is dealt from a "newly shuffled deck of cards". That is to say that each hand is entirely unrelated to the proceeding one or the one which follows. This renders counting and card-tracking utterly useless and it is another reason that the casinos love the video versions of the classic Table Games.

On the other hand, no one will object if you sit at your Video Blackjack machine with this book open at the Basic Strategy section for Blackjack, or if you have a chart, or other aide-memoiré, sitting in your lap to guide you to the correct plays.

What will be important, however, is that you select the correct game from the choices available via the Main Menu. If you come across an older-style machine where only a single game of Blackjack is offered, just check that the game offers you rules that are favourable to you, the player. Rules for the game will either be printed on the machine itself or, if it is a multi-game machine, be available by pressing the "Help" button, or the "Game Rules" button, on the touch-screen.

Favourable Rules for the Player

Here is the checklist of features that you should look out for. By the way, you'll see that the percentage advantage to the player for each of these factors seems very small – just fractions of 1 per cent. However, trust me, these tiny edges soon add up. Just remember the hundreds of billions of dollars made by the gaming industry each year is on the back of games which shouldn't be offering the house more than about a 3 per cent edge. Anything that you can do, at any time, to reduce that edge, will benefit you for certain in the long run, and usually in the short-term too.

The Essential Rules

- **Blackjack pays 3–2.** This is the way it has always been. On principle, never play Blackjack if the casino, or Video Blackjack machine, is not offering these odds when you make Blackjack. A Blackjack game which is offering you only 6–5, for example, is adding over 0.5 per cent to the house edge.
- **Dealer stands on all 17s.** If the dealer on your machine hits Soft 17, this is a disadvantage to you, since the dealer may improve his hand and beat you (he may also bust, but he is more likely to improve his hand). If the dealer does stand on all 17s, this is worth 0.2 per cent to you, and is a very desirable feature.
- **Dealer takes hole card.** Another vital element; if the dealer has a Blackjack, you won't lose your split or double-down bets because the dealer will expose his Blackjack before you need to play out your hands. If the dealer does not take a hole card, but waits until you have played out your hand(s) first, he can still make Blackjack

and you can lose all your bets. The dealer taking a hole card – as in all American casinos – is worth approximately 0.2 per cent to you.

- **Double after split.** This is pretty much essential, since you are splitting against the dealer's weak cards, such as 4, 5 and 6, primarily to get as much money on the table as possible in a favourable situation. To succeed in a session of Blackjack you need to come across some favourable opportunites, exploit them by doubling down or splitting pairs, then doubling on at least one of the hands, and going on to win the hand. If you lose the double downs and both split hands, then you are on your way to a losing session. So, if your Video Blackjack machine does not allow you to get plenty of money down in the good situations, then walk away. The option to double down after splitting is worth approximately 0.12 per cent.

- **Surrender.** This is the offer to forfeit half your stake in return for giving up against the dealer's powerful card, such as 9 or 10, when you hold 15 or 16. This can save you money and is worth about 0.1 per cent to you.

Other Rules

These rules are good if you can find them:

- **Early surrender.** This rule is increasingly difficult to find in casinos now. It allows you to surrender your hand for the loss of half your stake, even if the dealer is showing an ace, before he checks to see whether or not he holds a Blackjack. This provides an excellent player advantage of approximately 0.7 per cent. If you find this rule in operation, it is a big advantage to you, but check that there are no negative rules to compensate for it.

- **Doubling on three cards or more.** A double-down rule which permits you to double down at any time against the dealer gives an advantage to the player of approximately 0.25 per cent.
- **Drawing more than one card to split aces.** The vast majority of Blackjack games only permit players to take one card on each hand when they have split two aces. If you can find one which allows you to continue to take cards – and therefore probably improve your hand – this is a considerable advantage. There is nothing more frustrating than splitting aces against the dealer's 8 and finding that you have been dealt A2 and A4, the dealer turns over a ten, and you have just lost both hands. This advantageous rule, when you can find it, adds about 0.15 per cent to your edge.

Side Bets

The following statement, although a generalization, I have found to be true in my experience: all side games offered to players at the Blackjack table – whether it is live, on Video Blackjack, or online – offer significantly poorer odds than the main game and should be avoided. Not only will these side bets eat up your bankroll almost without you noticing, but they also distract you from the main business in hand, which is to play perfect Basic Strategy at all times.

Shop Around for the Best Deal

If you are unhappy with the rules offered by a particular machine, then search for a different one. As we will discuss shortly, one of the casinos' main weapons with Slots is to provide some loose (generous) Slot machines next to some tight (mean) Slot machines. If you can pick the loose ones, you are winning the battle already. Unlike standard Slot machines where, usually, it is impossible to tell which is tight and which is loose, the pay tables on Video Poker machines immediately show you the game you are getting. Similarly, with Video Blackjack some machines will have unfavourable rules and should be avoided; others will have more generous rules and can be played for a decent game.

If you are unhappy with all the machines in the casino, change casino. Make finding the best games for you part of the fun of gambling. When you beat the casino as a result, the feeling will be even more sweet.

Picking a Machine

Other than the differences in rules between games offered and machines generally, there will be no advantage to picking one machine over any other: they will all offer you the same odds of winning or losing. It makes no difference if a previous player has been winning or losing: the same odds will be available to you.

Playing Strategy

Use Basic Strategy at all times. To play any other way is to hand the casino your money. Of course, on any given sequence of hands you might guess what to do yourself, without using the correct strategy but, in the long run (and that is quite quickly at Blackjack), you will start to lose far more money than you need to.

Take this book with you to the casino and follow the strategy as set out on pages 77–78.Take along a chart or an aide-memoire.Almost all casinos permit this at Video Blackjack machines, and many allow it at live tables too, but check with a supervisor before you do it.

Any departure from Basic Strategy will, in the long run, cost you money. There is no debate about this. It is cold, hard scientific fact.

Betting Strategy

No betting strategy will improve your odds of winning. Even played with perfect Basic Strategy, the game will still hold a 1–1.5 per cent edge against the player (more if the rules are unfavourable). Nevertheless, the best way to benefit from a hot streak, if you are lucky enough to hit one, is to increase your bet size modestly after each winning bet. Return to your base stake whenever you lose, and start again.

Note that in the long term you are just as likely to lose or win as much if you are betting one chip per hand, every hand, forever.

Bankroll

For a proper session, take 40 times your base stake. If you lose this, walk away and wait before you start to play again. Generally,Video Blackjack offers games at lower stakes than at the tables. There are often $1 machines in casinos. However, higher-stake machines are being introduced to cater for the medium-rollers who prefer to play their favourite games on machines.

If you manage to double your initial bankroll, reserve half the profit, together with your initial bankroll, and do not touch it. If you wish, continue to play with the remaining 50 per cent of your profit, and keep putting half aside every time you double it. Ensure that, having made a profit, you leave the machine with a profit. That is how you beat the casino.

22
Slots

SLOT MACHINES began life as one-armed bandits, entertaining the wives and girlfriends of the so-called serious male gamblers. The stakes were small, the prizes modest (at one time, due to State legislation, the prizes consisted of nothing more than bubblegum). The various fruity flavours of the gum were incorporated into symbols on the reels, hence the name "Fruit Machine". Nowadays, some Slot machines still feature fruit, but many do not. As symbols, Sevens have stayed popular (supposedly the perfect number) and Bars – single, double and triple varieties. Slots have been transformed from three-reel mechanical devices to multi-reel, multi-line, video-screen, electronic, computer-controlled machines, with bonuses and features, Progressive Jackpots and payouts which can benefit an entire line of Slots players.

The demographic of the Slots player has changed too and, although the ladies still dominate, there are more and more men taking Slots-filled vacations. Twenty years back, most Slots players would have been, let's say, of a "certain age". These days, many more are younger and more affluent.

Personally, I have very mixed emotions towards Slot machines. I have mentioned some of these thoughts earlier, but I'm going to spend just a moment talking about them here because, if you play the Slots regularly, I think they are worth thinking about.

The Slots in a casino are, without doubt, among the worst bets in the casino. Although the individual stakes can be low, the speed of play possible on modern Slots is very fast, so you can find yourself losing a sizeable bankroll very quickly. Add to this the modern multi-line Slot machines and, while you may be playing a 25c machine, if you play all nine lines at ten coins you will be betting $22.50 per spin – and that is serious high-roller stakes.

One of my major problems with Slots is that they are so addictive. There are more gambling problems surrounding Slot machines than any other form of gambling – and it is going to get worse. Unsupervised, individuals can lose everything on the Slot machines. This is not simply a socio-economic problem as it affects wealthy, educated people just as often as poorer, financially desperate people. The lack of human interaction means that there is rarely someone to say: "Enough... take a break; can you afford this...?" and so on. One of the hazards (and joys) of playing Slots is that it can be a very solitary experience: a battle between man (or woman) and machine. However, that isolation can lead to mental problems and certainly to bankroll difficulties.

Having said all this, and being a man who gambles only small stakes at any game where I do not perceive a possible advantage, I totally appreciate the lure of the Slots. Certainly, there have been times when I have played Slots for hours on end, very happily, except when I checked my bank balance. On one occasion years ago, a big jackpot win in Las Vegas was massively exciting and paid for many luxuries around my house. But, am I ahead playing Slots? Not even close. I'm a very occasional, modest bettor, who has been lucky, and I am still way down on the Slots. Hopefully, that tells you something.

So, is there a magic way to win on Slots? No. If anybody ever tells you that they have a system – they don't. If anybody ever tries to sell you tips, don't buy them. Every day, online, I am offered a foolproof way to win at Slots; free systems, pamphlets of systems costing $49.95, DVDs of Slots systems for $299 – everything. And every single one of them is complete rubbish. There is no magic system to beat Slots – and if there was, do you think anyone would be foolish enough to share that advice, so that the casinos themselves could see? Here's a tip: if you ever find a way to beat the Slots (legally), don't tell anyone. Just travel the world in luxury, topping up your bank account with jackpots as you go. But sadly, it's a halcyon dream. There is a reason why the casino business is so successful – awe-inspiringly, gob-smackingly successful – and, these days, that reason is almost entirely the Slots.

There is a very tiny and select group of Slots players who, because they hit it really big, have beaten the Slots, and the casinos, and can live the dreams of the mega-jackpot winner. For the rest of us, there are ways to understand the games you play, pick machines and strategies carefully, manage your bankroll effectively and lose far less money, while still holding onto the chance of winning a big jackpot, or a life-changing Progressive.

In this chapter, I want to explain to you how Slot machines really work, what the odds are, and how to get the best for your money. I want to explode some misleading myths, and allow you to enjoy your gaming unencumbered by foolish misunderstandings and false logic.

In researching this chapter, I have reviewed books and online sites from Slot machine manufacturers, software researchers and testers, gaming regulators and independent authors. If there is one thing about writing this book that has shocked me more than any other, it is the unbelievable rubbish that is published on Slots. In half a dozen books dedicated to Slots, I have found lies, misleading system suggestions, illogical advice, and, in many cases, advice that will cost you, the player, even more money. It came to the stage where I was so astounded by what I was reading, I had to research whether these books were being backed by some unscrupulous casino chain or Slots manufacturer.

To make clear my own situation, I have no connection to any casino at the time of writing (although I have been consulted by a couple of online casinos and been involved in associated projects with casinos in London and Monte Carlo).

As you will see, I will suggest that you bet less and more prudently so you may enjoy your Slots play even more.

Hard Slots Facts

First I will show you how a Slot machine works and try to dismiss the superstitious and silly ideas held by some people. There is so much gossip and folklore surrounding Slots that a few good solid facts are needed to help you.

What You Are Seeing Has Already Happened

Unless you are playing a classic Slot machine, from the early 1970s or before, Slots machines are not mechanical. Whether it is a classic-style machine with reels that spin, or a Video Slot with the appearance of spinning reels on a screen, what you are seeing happening has nothing whatsoever to do with the prize you are about to win (or not win).

All modern Slot machines select what will appear on the reels, or on the video screen, the millisecond you touch the start button (or pull the handle). The moment that happens, the computer takes a random number for each reel (or video "reel"), which is assigned to a particular "stop", and it then displays this in the glass, or on the video screen, in front of you – as a particular symbol or blank.

A Video Slot machine is no more artificial than one with reels. Those reels are merely displaying what, in a Video Slot machine, the computer has selected, and their spinning has no more significance than decoration.

Every second the Slot machine is switched on, the Random Number Generator (RNG) inside the machine generates thousands of random numbers. At the precise moment that you hit the start button or pull the handle, one number is selected for each reel and this is what eventually appears on the screen in front of you. Long before you can see any given combination, the computer has determined whether or not you have won a prize. So, what you are seeing happening in front of you is merely a record of what has already happened. There is no point shouting at the last reel to put in the symbol you want because, not only can it not hear you, but it already "knows" what symbol it will put in even before the symbol on the first reel appeared.

The appearance of each number is as close to completely random as it is possible to be but, crucially, this does not mean that every symbol on the reel is as likely to appear as any other. Why this is, I'll explain in a moment.

Superstition Must Play No Part in Your Slots Decisions

You cannot predict what a Slot machine will do, other than that, in the long run, it will make the casino the percentage it is supposed to make. In the short term, you may lose for 25 spins in a row, or win a jackpot on consecutive spins. The former is far more likely than the latter (but I have seen the jackpot being won twice in a row in a casino!). There is no way you can predict a hot run, or a cold run. You can only assign these terms after you have played the spins. You could lose consistently for ten hours on a Slot machine and then win consistently for half an hour and end up making a profit. More or less anything is possible. However, these cold, hard facts mean that superstition must be abandoned. You will find that, free of it, you are actually much happier – and I recommend such a state of mental clarity to you wholeheartedly.

Here are some facts to help dispel the myths:

What a Slot machine has done on the previous spin, spins or multitude of spins, has absolutely no bearing on what will happen next.

A Slot machine is not more likely to pay out if it hasn't paid for hours or days or even weeks, than if it has been paying well all that time. What it does in this short period of time is completely insignificant in the long term. And a short period of time may mean years.

A Slot machine might as well be played just after it has paid the jackpot as at any other time.

It doesn't remember that it has paid a jackpot; it doesn't even know what a jackpot is! You are just as likely to win immediately after a jackpot as when there hasn't been one for months. Surely, you may say, when a jackpot is won, the machine goes tight to recompense itself for the jackpot and try to return to the advertised percentage payoff? Well, the answer is no. The machine just carries on producing random numbers; the stops on each reel and the payouts awarded for certain combinations ensure that, in long run, the machine will come very close to the expected percentage payout.

Many players believe that Slot machines work on pre-determined sequences, albeit very long ones. This is not true.

Every single spin is completely unpredictable and random, and has no relation whatsoever to the previous or subsequent spins. Indeed, the machine doesn't even know what a previous or subsequent spin is!

There is no point asking casino personnel which machines are "hot" and which are not, because the information they give you (even if it is accurate) is irrelevant to you.

All it tells you is what they have been doing in the past and that in no way influences what they might do when you play them now. Incidentally, in a High-Roller Slots section of a major Strip casino, I saw a guy win $250,000 on a $100 machine one day and the next day heard a Slots host telling another high roller to play the same machine because it had paid nothing for weeks! Maybe it was an honest mistake, or perhaps the Slots host thought he could get this punter to re-fill the machine. Either way, the information was bad, but it didn't really matter; the gambler was no less likely to win as a result of it.

It is commonly believed that if you leave a machine and someone comes up to it, plays it once and wins the jackpot, you have been incredibly unlucky; it was your jackpot. This is complete nonsense.

Unless you had pressed the start button at the precise millisecond that the next person did, you would *not* have won the jackpot. It is not in the least bit unlucky for you, but it is incredibly lucky for the next person. They happened to play a machine and hit the button at the right millisecond to get the three (or more) random numbers which equated to the jackpot. However, that outcome had, and has, nothing to do with you. So, you can sleep easy. You would not have won it had you carried on playing it yourself.

Also completely wrong is the belief that the longer you play your machine, the more likely you are to win.

The longer you play any Slot machine, the more likely you are to win a prize, because, by the law of averages, the more you play the more random numbers are converted into outcomes and the more likely it is that one of those outcomes will be a nice big win. However, the longer you play, the more likely you are to lose overall, because the house, in effect, takes a percentage of every bet you place. It makes no difference whatsoever which machine you are playing.

By the way, there may be a difference in the financial result if you stay on the same machine and it has a

Progressive Jackpot, or a banking style bonus, but your chances of winning one of these are no greater on one machine than on another.

Here's another myth to dispel: when you get a jackpot symbol on the first reel and a jackpot symbol on the second reel and then a blank on the third reel (with the jackpot symbol just above the pay-line), you were very close to winning the jackpot. No, sorry, you weren't.

You were lucky to get two jackpot symbols, but on the final reel the random number assigned was not the jackpot, but a blank. A jackpot symbol showing just above or below the line in no way suggests that you were close, or closer to, winning the jackpot than if it was nowhere to be seen. This is an illusion based on thinking that the machine is mechanical and the reel could have stopped one "stop" later. The machine is not mechanical, and it will never stop on the jackpot symbol unless that was the symbol selected by the random number. These "near misses" provide maximum adrenalin boosts for the player, and if you think you are close to the jackpot it is understandable that you want to keep playing. The Slots manufacturers know this and they design their machines accordingly.

In the old days, Slot machines only displayed the symbol actually on the pay-line. Why do you think they show you the symbols above and below the pay-line? To tease you, that's why (and of course there are machines with more than one pay-line). Just remember, you were not close.

The casino cannot alter the payouts.

This fact is very important to understand. Many people wonder whether the casinos have "twiddled a dial" in the back and made the machine tighter on weekends and public holidays, so that they can make more money when the casinos are busy. It's a lovely idea, and it often feels that way. However, the way that Slot machines are manufactured means that to alter the payout percentages the casino would have to replace the computer chip in the motherboard with a completely new chip. While this is not impossible to do, it is not a quick alteration and, if the supervising body found out that casinos did this, they would be in big trouble, facing massive fines, possible closure and certainly jail terms for anyone involved. So, you can be 99.9999 per cent certain no has "twiddled" with the dial.

The way you push the button, or pull the handle, affects the outcome.

Yes, this is kind of true. The millisecond at which you push the button or pull the handle is vital, because that is the moment when the random numbers are decided. Can you know when this moment is? No. Could you work it out? No. Can you practise at home, pushing buttons? Sure, but I can suggest better things to do with your time.

All these facts apply to all Slot machines, online and in live casinos, video screen or classic-style reels.

How the Random Numbers Select the Symbols

This is technical stuff, but the better your understanding of everything in a casino, the more you will be able to control your emotions and make sensible decisions.

Every Slot machine works the same way but, for this example, let us imagine a three-reel Slot machine with standard symbols: blanks, cherries, single bar, double bars, triple bars, Sevens and double jackpots.

The number of "stops" on any given reel will vary, but 40 stops are about average. If the result depended upon every symbol, and blank, having the same chance of appearing, then the machine would pay out way too much money (I know that is a lovely thought, isn't it?). To prevent this from happening, the reels are "weighted". That is to say, while each "stop" looks the same, some stops have far more random numbers applied to them than others. So, for example, the stop which features:

- double jackpot
- **blank**
- single bar

may appear whenever one of dozens of random numbers is selected. Only the middle symbol hits the payline, and this reel is showing a blank, but the players can see the jackpot symbol just above the payline, which excites them, provoking misguided thoughts of a near miss.

Whereas, the stop featuring:

- blank
- **double jackpot**
- blank

with the double jackpot on the payline, may have only a single random number applied to it, making its appearance most unlikely. In simple terms, the less valuable the "stop", including a blank, the more frequently it will appear, since it has the most random numbers applied to it; the more valuable the "stop" the less likely it is to appear since there will be very few (or only one) random numbers applied to it.

This is all worked out by the Slots manufacturers so that they can provide the casinos with machines which are programmed to produce the required payback percentage in the long term.

As long as the near-miss effect is created through a random selection of numbers, it is not considered a fix and gaming commissions permit it. But, as you now know, it is done deliberately to tempt and tease you, the player.

The Laws of Attraction

One of the great excitements of Slot machines is that fraction of a second that it takes your brain to register what the eye sees. The creation of a string of matching symbols is, psychologically, very compelling. This is why seeing three matching symbols often produces a greater feeling of euphoria than mixed symbols which still pay a big prize. It is for this reason that many Slot machines feature symbols of the same colour, and symbols which, at first sight, look quite similar: to reproduce that feeling of excitement in the player, even though the combination showing is not a winning one.

For example, most Slot machines feature red cherries, which are exactly the same tone of red as the jackpot symbol of a red Seven. This is done so that as the reel is spinning (or appears to spin) the player can see the red colour and imagine that it is going to stop on the reel. If the red does stop on the reel, it is far more often a red cherry than a jackpot red Seven.

One psychologist-author has also suggested that the use of bright, often primary, colours is particularly attractive to people who want to regress to a simpler life – to childhood, if you like. The spinning reels, with their tantalizing glimpses of colour, stimulate memories of kaleidoscopes, turning mobiles and cartoon characters. In turn, a bank of Slot machines waiting to be played, flashing carefully calculated combinations of colour, suggests festive lighting, fairground rides, Christmas trees and celebratory occasions. You think this sounds a little far fetched? The author worked for a Slots design team!

Tips: Bad and Good

Another author, whose biography on the back of his expensive book claims that he is a mathematician, makes a series of misleading suggestions to players. This one is a classic misconception and to see it repeated yet again in black and white is truly depressing (especially if you've paid good money for this nonsense):

"Whenever a Progressive Jackpot is close to the base amount, it means there was a recent win and the next win is not likely to occur for some time."

The first part of this sentence is correct: if you see a Progressive Jackpot close to its reset level (assuming, of course, that you know the reset level), then it has indeed paid the Progressive Jackpot recently. However, this in no way affects the probability of the jackpot being won again, on the next spin, or in three years' time. A mathematician should know this.

No wonder there are so many disappointed Slots players out there. Not only are Slots among the worst bets in the casino, but the Slots players are lulled into thinking that after a jackpot there won't be another one or, after a long period without a win, it is more likely that there will be one. This is simply not true.

Here are a couple more misleading statements from books by other "experts" on probability, expectation and Slots:

"Play each machine for six spins; if you don't win, the machine is 'cold' and you should leave it."

I mean, how silly is that? Why six spins? And, after six spins, how do you know that it's cold? You can have no idea what the machine will do on the next spin, so trying to assess the state of a machine by playing six spins is ludicrous. Yet this book sells many copies.

"Increase the number of credits you play because the longer you are not winning, the more likely it is that you will win now, and you want to win big."

This is also rubbish. As we have discussed, and logically proven, it makes no difference to you, or the machine, what happened on the last spin, or the last ten, one hundred or one million spins. It is just about what happens now. It cannot be right to increase your stake because you lost in the past.

Incidentally, this wrong advice is really the opposite of sensible play because it will increase the chances of you being wiped out. If you must suddenly increase the size of your stake (say on a multi-line, multi-coin machine), the least damaging time to do it would be after winning some money. Taking a big gamble, you could decide to risk the profit you have just made on getting another win at a much higher stake. If you then failed to do this, you should return to the base stake once again.

Personally, if I win on a Slot machine, I am delighted with whatever I get. Since you can never know when it is right to raise or lower your stake, the easiest thing to do is not to change it.

A popular tip shown on websites is that you should not insert your Player's (loyalty) Card in a Slot machine, because it makes it less likely that you will win.

This seems silly even before you look at the facts. If I was a casino owner, I would want my regular loyal players to win more, not less, than anyone else. Then they would play more, encourage more people to the casino and make me richer. As it is, it makes no difference at all whether you use a Player's Card – other than the fact that if you do not, you are throwing away a chance to pick up a few benefits. The Random Number Generator is not affected by whether a Player's Card is inserted or not. It doesn't "know" about Player's Cards, it doesn't "think" about it. It just sits there, spewing out random numbers.

Finally, here are some sound tips for when things aren't going so well:

After a long, losing session, do not go to the cashier's desk, or the ATM, and change some more money.

Never change more money thinking that, because you have lost for so long, the machine is bound to pay out now; that it would be a terrible mistake to leave the machine; that it is more likely to pay out now and how awful it would be if someone else won your money. It's not "your" money, and someone else will have to be lucky to win anything out of the same Slot machine. If they do, it doesn't mean that you would have won had you carried on playing.

It makes no difference to your chances of winning whether you continue on this machine today or another machine tomorrow, or next week, or next year.

Your chances of winning are exactly the same. So, tell yourself that it's not been your lucky day, and go and do something else. Relax and enjoy the facilities of the hotel or resort, go out for a meal, go home and relax. It's been a bad day, and there's no need to play any more today.

Types of Machine

Having looked at many of the negative factors surrounding Slots, it's time to turn our attention to the more positive ones and look at some tips which could save your bankroll and increase your chances of winning.

It makes no difference whether the machine you choose to play is a classic-style spinning reels machine, or a Video screen Slot machine. The percentage paybacks will likely be very similar. However, there are some differences in the symbols they carry and the style of the machine, and it is worth looking at these.

Special Symbols

Most machines carry special symbols linking them to the theme on which they are based. For example, the popular "Cleopatra" Slot and its impersonators nearly all use pyramids. Many big casinos ask the manufacturers to add a house symbol, often for the jackpot, to personalize the machines. Ultimately, it makes no difference what the symbols are since they are merely representations of the random numbers produced by the Random Number Generator within the computerized centre of the machines.

Wild symbols: any symbol described as "wild" is one that substitutes for any other symbol to create a winning combination for you. Be aware that some machines specify that their wild symbol does not replace cherries, or jackpot symbols, or feature-launching symbols. You just have to read the small print to avoid being disappointed.

Multiplier symbols: these have become increasingly popular on modern Slots, particularly those using classic spinning reel-style displays. Since there is a limit to how much excitement these simple-style Slots can produce, having a symbol – usually the jackpot symbol – which is wild and multiplies any completed winning combination certainly has the potential to create some nail-biting outcomes.

"Double Jackpot", "Double Win", "Double Trouble", "Double Diamond" are all machines which, as you might have guessed, have double symbols. The appearence of two double symbols multiplies the corresponding win by four, and three of these symbols will be the jackpot.

"Triple Jackpot", "Triple Gold", "Triple Diamond" and "Lucky Trebles" all offer three times payouts for winning combinations that include one symbol, and nine times the advertised payout if you have two of these symbols on the payline.

"Five Times Pay" multiplies wins by five, and with two symbols showing, by 25.

"Ten Times Pay" multiplies wins by ten, and by 100 times, when two of these symbols complete the paying combination.

The higher the multiplier symbol, the less likely it is that you will see it, and the meaner the majority of the payouts will be. Playing a double or triple multiplier is the highest recommended multiplier that you should play.

Styles of Machine

Here are some of the different styles of machine you may encounter.

Classic 3-Reel with Fixed Jackpot

Usually geared for you to play one, two or three coins per spin, all wins increase proportionately to the number of coins played. The jackpot, however, may increase disproportionately for the third coin played.

There are also machines which allow between one and nine coins to be played. Again, all wins increase proportionately, except for the jackpot, which is usually increased markedly by the playing of maximum coins.

However, this is not a good reason to play maximum coins. Many guides advise you always to play maximum coins to ensure you get the maximum jackpot, but the chances of the jackpot are very small, and the increase for maximum coins may be very modest. Playing maximum coins might shave 0.2 per cent off the house edge. But, if you lose three, or nine, times as many coins, is that worth it? Probably not.

Classic 3-Reel with Bonus Awards for Maximum Coins

These machines, now already dating, offer a set of payouts for one coin or two coins, but extra possible winning combinations for playing the maximum of three coins. In effect, you buy the chance for extra prizes. On these machines, it is advisable always to play maximum coins or you risk missing out on the extra, usually biggest, payouts. If you cannot afford three coins, try playing another style of machine.

Classic 3-Reel with Progressive Jackpot

Progressive Jackpots are very popular with players because the sight of the jackpot total increasing all the time is an exciting concept. In this section, we will deal only with machines that either carry independent Progressive Jackpots – usually displayed on an LED screen at the top of the machine – and Progressives which are linked across a bank, or carousel, of machines, with the Progressive total indicated, again on a big LED sign, but this time usually above the entire bank of machines.

On these machines, the Progressive Jackpot is only paid when maximum coins are inserted. To make the machines worthwhile, only play them with the maximum coins, unless the Progressive Jackpot has just been won and the advantage of winning it is not much greater than a win playing with one or two coins.

Machines which carry extra large jackpots are generally much meaner with smaller wins (which tend to tide over players and keep them playing for longer). Slots with Progressives tend to be meaner with their small wins because, for each dollar staked, a proportion goes into the Progressive total. Hence, more from each wager needs to be taken, and you win less on smaller bets. The bigger the Progressive Jackpot, the fewer other prizes you are likely to win, which tends to encourage a strategy of all-or-nothing. Either you will lose everything more quickly than usual, or you will hit the jackpot and leave the casino a rich man (or woman).

WAPS (usually 4–Reel Classic Slots)

Back in the mid-1980s, machine manufacturer IGT invented the first of a breed of Slot machine that would come to be called WAPS machines. WAPS stands for Wide Area Progressive Slots, a term which indicates that the Progressive Jackpot is not accumulated from merely one machine, or one bank of machines; indeed, not even from one casino. The Progressive in this case is formed from carousels of Slots from casinos throughout a State, or even the entire country. There are WAPS in operation in the USA, UK, South Africa and Australia. The chance of hitting the Progressive Jackpot is truly tiny – even less likely than winning a National Lottery – but at $3 a play, as many of them are, a chance to win 4, 8 or 12 million rand, Australian/US dollars or pounds seems a pretty exciting prospect.

The big problem with WAPS is that for every dollar you insert in the machine, a proportion of that goes into the jackpot. Because most ▇▇▇▇ are not managed by the casinos themselves, but by the Slots manufacturer or distributing company, there are higher overheads in maintaining the system, ensuring its security, and paying out big winners. All this means that, even more than on stand-alone or linked Progressives, a sizable proportion of every spin made must be reserved for the Progressive, the operators and the casino profits. So, apart from the jackpot itself, the general payout on these machines is considerably poorer than on other machines with lower jackpots. Therefore, if you play machines like this you are playing for the tiny, tiny chance of winning the big one, and (assuming you don't win big) you are likely to lose your bankroll pretty quickly.

On "Megabucks", the first of the truly massive ▇▇▇▇ jackpots (the jackpot is reset to $10,000,000 after it has been won, and it grows from there), the expected payback, not including the jackpot, is 84–5 per cent. This makes it one of the worst bets in the entire casino, unless you become the one in ten million players who hits the big one.

Also, since the Progressive is the only real reason to play these greedy machines (they are often four-reel monsters) you have to play maximum coins, which may be three, four, or even five coins, to be able to collect your winnings should you hit the miracle random numbers. For this reason, I recommend a short session to see if your luck is really in, and then retreat to the less stingy, more modest machines elsewhere in the casino.

By the way, if you do hit the jackpot on some ▬▬▬▬ machines, you won't necessarily get all your money straight away. Firstly, there will be a lengthy delay while your win is verified and the machine is checked for tampering. Then, the body who controls the ▬▬▬, will usually pay you part of the jackpot (sometimes 20 per cent; sometimes $1,000,000) and then the rest will be paid to you in installments over a period of years. On some of the smaller ▬▬▬, you may get the whole jackpot in one go, which certainly benefits you. If you do have to wait, I doubt you'll be too worried about this if it happens to you, but I thought I'd tell you, all the same.

Does the size of the Progressive Jackpot make it any more likely that it might be won? Whether you are talking about a single machine with a Progressive, a linked carousel of machines or ▬▬▬▬ the size of the accumulated jackpot makes no difference whatsoever to the likelihood of winning the big prize. Just because it hasn't been won for months, or even years, does not mean that it is anymore likely to win now. All it does is make the big prize bigger if you do manage to hit the magic combination.

Classic Slots and Video Slots, with Accumulator Bonuses

These machines are sometimes described as "Variable State Slots" because, depending on the moment you choose to play such a machine, it may be more or less favourable to you.

The principle behind these machines is that the bonus is paid to the player only when he has accumulated a number of symbols or combinations in a "bank" to trigger the bonus. The idea, from the casino's point of view, is that this will tempt you to remain playing the machine for longer than you might have done, because you won't want to relinquish a machine with part of the bonus bank filled. Instead, you will want to continue playing until the bonus is released.

Many guidebooks and system sellers trumpet the idea of these machines as representing a major chance for "skilful" players and an important breakthrough in Slots tactics. Search the casino, they tell you, looking for machines where the bonus banks are half filled, or three-quarters filled. This is equivalent to saying: "If you see a $1 note on the sidewalk, pick it up." The advice is so obvious it is almost an insult. Anyone who has the remotest interest in Slots could work this out for themselves. In every casino I have been in, I have seen Slots players searching the machines for those which offer some of the bonus bank filled. By all means, do this yourself, but the chances of finding such a machine is pretty small. And, if you do, don't get into fights with another player which such situations have sometimes caused!

Furthermore, I cannot recommend these bonus bank machines, featuring accumulator bonuses, because of what they represent: you shouldn't be tempted to stay on a machine once you have exhausted your planned bankroll. This style of machine is geared to making you change more money, to over-spend your budget, and to take more from you for the casino. On the other hand, as with most bonus machines, if you don't hit the bonus, you are playing a machine with a poorer than average return, so it is in your interest to go for the bonus payout. This is a blackmail style of Slot because, unlike any other kind of Slot machine, the more you play an individual machine, the more likely it is that you will win the accumulator bank. However, be wary. The manufacturers have worked this out too and, just because an accumulator bank appears half full, it does not mean that you are half way to winning the bonus. I have seen players part with five times the amount of money the bonus will pay, just to grab it for themselves. The designers have spotted another way to exploit the Slots players. No one, they think to themselves, will want to leave a machine when they believe they have just set it up for the next player; they will never leave that machine until the bonus is won. And, that indeed, does seem to be the effect.

For this reason, I recommend that you do not play Slots with accumulator banks – they almost inevitably tempt you to play for too long.

3- and 4-Reel Classic Slots, with Bonus Games

These machines are becoming the mainstay of many casinos' Slots stables. They offer a fairly classic Slot machine of three or four reels, with the addition of a bonus game if you hit a certain combination or a particular symbol on one of the reels (often the fourth reel). The key to these games is that unless you hit the bonuses quite regularly, you are likely to find yourself losing pretty quickly, because a good number of the worthwhile payouts occur during the bonus games.

Many of these Slot machines are based on famous American television shows and films. Knowledge of the shows is not a pre-requisite for playing the machine, because the vast majority of Slots require absolutely no skill or knowledge whatsoever. As a general rule, the bigger the advertising on the machine for a particular bonus, the worse the general payout will be, excluding the bonus rounds. Since the bonus could appear repeatedly, or not at all, it is impossible to know when to play the machine.

On one classic machine, there is a "wheel of fortune" feature above the main machine, which comes into operation if you hit a particular symbol. As with the effect of spinning reels, the illusion that the light is illuminating prizes in sequence, or an arrow is moving around the face, is nothing more than a special effect. The ▬▬▬▬ has selected a number the moment you hit the button, and it is that number which the light will eventually illuminate. As before, each "stop" on the wheel is not equally likely to occur, since the lower payouts will have many more random numbers assigned to them than the high payouts. This is why, when you look at the bonus prizes paid out on these machines, you can usually see that most of them are for the smaller prizes. As with the main machine, what you are seeing is merely a bit a fluff covering up the result which was determined the moment you hit the start, or stop, button.

Video Slots, with Multi-Line and Multi-Coin Functions

These games are exceedingly popular because (as everyone loves to win) manufacturers have invented a machine that pays a lot of the time. Sadly, your winnings are usually less than the amount you put in, but at least the lights are flashing, the buzzers sounding and the credits whizzing up and down.

There are some variations between machines, but this description covers most of the machines you are likely to find.

Each machine is for one denomination, which may be 1c, 5c, 10c, 25c, $1, $5, or even higher. Be aware that these machines use many credits per spin, so even a 25c machine may end up being very expensive for you.

Play one to ten coins per spin. Some use touch-screen buttons but, currently, most have buttons on the console for you to increase or decrease the number of credits you are prepared to stake on each game.

Play one to twenty paylines (including the centre line, the top and bottom lines, diagonal lines, zig-zag lines, lines with a drop in the middle, lines with drops at the end and at the beginning). Some use touch-screen controls, but most still have buttons on the console beneath the screen for you to adjust incrementally how many lines you wish to select. If you want to see which lines are available, there will either be a diagram on one side of the console showing you the shape and position of each line which can be played, or there will be an actual, or touch-screen, button to push, marked "Help" or "Lines Available".

The effect of these options means that you can play between one coin and 200 coins. The casinos, many of the guidebooks, and most of the so-called Slots experts will all persuade you to play maximum coins. If you don't, they will preach that you will be missing the chance to win on the lines you didn't play, or you will only win X1 with one coin, but X10 with ten coins. This is nonsense. It is like saying: you had better play every single Slot machine in the entire casino because if you don't you might miss some wins. Clearly, this is ridiculous.

Look at the payout structure. Does it reward you for playing ten coins rather than just one? Almost always the answer is no. Therefore, there can be no logical, strategic reason to play more than one coin. Play more if you want to, if you can afford to, but don't feel that you have to. You don't.

Will playing all 20 lines make it more likely that you will win compared to just playing one line? Yes, far more likely. But it will also cost you 20 times the stake to play those extra lines.

However, since you have chosen these machines for their action, it seems sensible to play at least ten lines, probably at one coin per line. If your bankroll allows, play all 20 lines, but for one coin only. There is no advantage to playing more coins other than to increase your exposure and your possible (but unlikely) gain.

Most of these multi-line, multi-coin Video Slots carry a bonus game. This is usually activated when three or more symbols are scattered across the win lines. Some machines offer you a choice of "boxes" with hidden amounts behind them; you just touch the screen to reveal the amounts. Some offer a chance to try to gain free spins by selecting hidden awards on the touch-screen. Many offer free random spins, during which the payout is doubled, tripled or multiplied by up to ten times the usual amount.

Once again, it is these bonus games which offer the player the best chance of winning, and without them you will be struggling. Where there are bonuses which involve free games paying out multiples of the usual prizes, the average payout outside these bonuses may be very low – and your money may disappear very quickly. However, hit a big bonus, or get a repeat bonus within the bonus spins, and this is the one time when you can win big.

Incidentally, I have played one version of this machine and have suffered five occasions when the bonus spins paid absolutely nothing – and nothing tripled is still nothing – and enjoyed one occasion when I won the second jackpot within the bonus spin and got it tripled.

Note that at Blackjack – a Table Game holding perhaps only 1 per cent over the player (played properly) – you can have long stretches of terrible luck, where it seems as if the deck must be stacked against you. Imagine for how long a terrible run might last at a game where the house edge is more like 10–14 per cent against you, as in some of the Video Slots machines? It could be a very, very long time indeed. So, be prepared for bad streaks and hope to hit the bonus rounds hard when they do finally arrive.

> **Whenever the emphasis is placed on the bonus rounds, machines tend to be pretty mean and can cost you a lot of money.**

House Edges and Machines to Play

The house edge is usually expressed in terms of percentage payback a machine will make. In Las Vegas, these paybacks tend to vary between 83 per cent and 93 per cent across the board, meaning a house edge of between 7 and 17 per cent. Even at the bottom end of the scale, these are big figures and insurmountable over even the medium term for most gamblers.

However, there are casinos on the Las Vegas Strip which claim to have Slots offering 99 per cent returns. Be wary. This may apply only to one machine in a bank of machines, or to just a few machines scattered throughout the casino. If they advertise a particular payback, they are required to indicate to which machines this applies, so ask a Slots manager to show you.

Online, and on the streets in Vegas, there are newsletters indicating in which casinos the best Slot machines are located. You can subscribe to some up-market newsletters. Assuming that they know the paybacks for these machines (which is not always clear), the information may be outdated very quickly, as casinos regularly change their layouts of machines and the machines themselves. If reports are going simply on who has won what recently, this information is completely useless to you. Just because machines have been paying out well in the past is no guide to their future performance. However, there are respected sources which provide good information, if you hunt it out, which can be worth a lot of money to you.

As a general rule, the tightest Slots in Las Vegas casinos are in the big, luxury Strip resorts, where many guests stay without ever leaving the property. Generally, the casinos downtown – on and around Freemont Street – are looser. Better still are the casinos which cater for the locals and know that they have to provide more action if they are to keep their customers. Take a 10–15 minute cab ride out to some of the smaller casinos around the Strip and enjoy some personal attention and more home-style welcome. When the Slots are looser, you'll enjoy your gambling more.

Wherever you go to play Slots, ask the Slots manager what the paybacks are. He may not want to tell you, but he, or his boss, will know, and you can always see if he is willing to share that information.

Choose Denomination Sensibly

The most important piece of information concerns denominations. As a general rule, the higher the stake, the higher the percentage payback. So, using US Slots as a guide:

If the average payback from 25c machines is, say, 87 per cent, then:

- from $1 machines, it may be 92 per cent
- from $2 machines, it may be 93 per cent
- from $5 machines, it may be 94 per cent
- from $10 machines, 95 per cent
- from $25 and $50 machines, 96 per cent

and so on.

After all, as a casino owner, which would you rather have: 13 per cent of 75c per maximum spin (about 10c), or 4 per cent of $75 per maximum spin (about $3)? You get the general idea.

So, assuming that you are playing machines without a Progressive Jackpot, it is usually better for you to play one coin on a higher-denomination machine than three coins on a lower-denomination machine. Find out whether you need to play maximum coins for extra payouts and bonuses, and stick to simple machines, without too many bells and whistles, so that you know you are giving yourself the best chance of success.

> It's much better to play one coin on a $5 machine than three coins on a $2 machine.

Do not use this information to increase your bankroll. If anything, you should reduce your exposure on the Slots and try Blackjack, Craps or Baccarat.

Slots Temptations

In the old days (and sometimes still today), casinos would pump oxygen into the casino to keep everyone awake and gambling. Pheromones attractive to humans were tried in one casino's air-conditioning system. Slots were placed strategically: between the buffet and the elevators, blocking the exits, next to the queue to check in. Slots were everywhere to tempt you.

These days the machines themselves, plus the Player's Card benefits and the free drinks, all make for a pleasant experience when playing Slots. The Slots manufacturers still use simple, but persuasive techniques to keep you coming back to their machines. Slots which are not being played are set to produce a tantalizing lightshow, the ▬▬▬ selected for their attraction and sense of optimism.

Sound is widely used these days, especially on the new-fangled multi-line Video Slots. Enticing sounds echo through the casino air, luring players in who are attracted by a sound they associate with a big win, or a small win, or a bonus win. Gamblers begin to crave the sound of the machines.

I spoke to one lady in South Africa who plays the multi-line Slots at least three times a week at her local casino. She told me that she goes to sleep at night dreaming that she can hear the bells that sound when she hits three pyramids which trigger the bonus round of free spins tripled. There is nothing that she does recreationally, she said, that gives her as much pleasure as that sound. That's no coincidence; people have devised this effect for good reason.

Many casinos have some monster Slot machines on display. These novelty machines are nearly always tighter than the normal machine and are merely there to get people in from the street and playing. Some casinos offer free spins to win a big prize. The prize is a universe away, but the casino has succeeded in getting you inside and probably primed to play some more Slots while you are there.

Warning: Slot machines are mean anyway, but Slot machines outside the casino environment are extra mean. Don't play them!

It is tough enough to win on the Slots without handicapping yourself from the outset. Slot machines in bars, shops, convenience stores, at airports, garages – anywhere out of a casino – will be tighter than usual, often very tight. This is simply because you are a captive market and you have no choice of where you want to gamble. You are often stuck there for a while, with nothing to do. As always with a monopoly, they try to exploit you.

In the United Kingdom, there is a long history of fruit machines in fairgrounds, sports clubs, pubs and bowling alleys. In the past they used to be called ▆▆▆▆ – Amusements with Prizes – a dirty little name for some dirty little machines. Their average payback was an amazingly awful 72 per cent (meaning a 28 per cent edge to the house) and they were the simplest way to lose your money quickly and without debate. Many establishments even said that if the machine malfunctioned while paying out, then too bad – you lost your money anyway. Wow! But, that was all we had, and I well remember losing my pocket money for weeks on end on two machines strategically placed next to the cafe at the sports club.

Pubs and bowling alleys still have these terrible machines and, although on many of them the payback has increased to a percentage somewhere in the low 80s, they are still terrible machines. *Never play them.*

In casinos in the United Kingdom, the Las-Vegas style machines are moving in. We don't have Progressives yet, but they are on the way. There are, however, machines offering thousands of pounds in jackpots, with house edges ranging from nearly 20 per cent down to a more reasonable 7 per cent. They are still a really bad bet and are not recommended.

Likewise, never play Slot machines on cruise ships. Although it is very difficult to get accurate figures from the companies operating casinos on cruise ships, all the evidence points to Slots on board being the meanest machines around. If you look at the rules for Blackjack, Roulette and other games, you will find that they are strongly casino-weighted and not player orientated. The cruise ship is the classic monopoly–captive audience situation. They don't have to compete with anyone.

Incidentally, this applies to cross channel ferries, just as much as to hyper-luxurious mega-cruise ships. Their Slots are tight and they offer a really lousy gamble for your money.

Slot Positioning

Many myths surround how Slot machines are positioned and, unless you are the Slots manager of any given casino, you will not be certain of which machine offers the best prospects. Slots located on the ends of rows used to be thought to be the looser Slots in a particular column of machines, but then there is good reason to place a noisy paying Slot in the centre of an area so as to attract players into that particular corridor of machines.

Slots managers usually mix up a variety of Slots: those with a more generous pay table, and those which are tighter. The problem for Slots hunters is that it is almost impossible to discern which machines are loose and which are not. Take a classic, very popular machine such as (gaming company) ███'s "Red, White and Blue" – a classic-style spinning reels machine. This machine comes in a variety of denominations, including a multi-denominational variation, and the payback varies between 85 and 97 per cent. The latter is clearly a pretty good gamble for a Slots player; the lower figure a disastrously bad one. How can you tell which payout structure might be in operation?

The only way to have any idea is through the denomination of the machine – the higher the denomination per credit, the higher the return will be to you.

If the casino in which you are playing is reliably reported as offering generally looser Slot returns, then you can assume that one of their machines might pay back 1–5 per cent more than the same machine, at the same denomination, in another casino. For example, an off-Strip casino in Las Vegas might offer the same machine but with a higher payoff schedule. Clearly, those casinos keener to drum up business, especially loyal business, will offer better payouts.

Slots Tournaments

One of the most surreal sights to greet gamblers in a big casino is to stumble upon a Slots Tournament. Properly organized, it will be noisy, colourful and packed with action.

You may be able to enter a Slots Tournament when you arrive at the casino, but regular Slots Club members will usually receive advance notice of such events, together with free entry, or cut-price accommodation, or casino tokens.

A casino will usually rope off a section of the main casino floor and set it up with banks of special Slots for the event. You can often hear the action from all over the casino floor. A typical event, if well run, will feature cries of "jackpot!" every few minutes, and general excitement, punctuated by screams of delight and sighs of disappointment.

A Slots Tournament can run over one session, or over several sessions during the day and evening, and in some cases over several days. There is no skill involved in these events whatsoever, unless you consider pressing a start button as quickly as possible skilful, or sitting on a stool. Instead, this is a chance to enjoy a lot of Slot action for a fixed entry fee. On top of that, the Slots used for these events are quite different from usual Slots. Firstly, they take no money and, secondly, they pay far more freely and generously than the real money Slots. (There are Slots events when you do gamble with your own money on standard Slots, but these are relatively rare and tend to attract only higher rollers.)

You can see the psychological advantage in this system for the casinos. You play loose, generous Slots and win lots of credits for an hour of Slots Tournament and then, while you are waiting for the result, or for the next round, you go off to play the real Slots – quickly, enthusiastically, and probably for higher stakes than you might usually.

The leading players (those who have won the most credits) at the end of each qualifying session often move forward to the main final (or sometimes semi-final stages) and play all over again, bashing the start buttons frantically, entertained by a loud chatterbox on the public announcement system. Good hosts, or commentators, will whip up the action into a frenzy, jog around the room with their microphones, chatting to players and encouraging them to play even faster and with even more gusto. You can also expect to see the appearance of party hats, streamers, blowers, balloons and the like.

Now, if this appeals, the best advice is to look for events which offer all the entry fees back in prize money, retaining none for the casino — so called, 100 per cent equity events. Also, check whether the entry fee includes beverages and perhaps a buffet for all the players. You can usually expect prizes for the top 10 per cent of the field, as well as spot prizes and sometimes even a booby prize. Free gifts, generally of a very modest value, usually abound and the whole event is very sociable, save for the time you are actually playing when you can retreat to your own world and watch the reels line up far more than is normally the case.

Personally, Slots Tournaments do not do it for me, but I do know a very high-powered UK lawyer who makes a point of visiting casinos which have them on, proving that really there's no accounting for tastes. If the idea of a Slots tournament appeals to you, your best bet is to join your local casino's Slots Club, or, ahead of a Vegas visit, to research online, or call up, various casinos and see which are offering an event around the time you plan to travel. On rare occasions, you may be able to walk into an event and sign on at the time, but usually the events are full up well in advance.

23
Table Games
Tournaments

WHILE SLOTS TOURNAMENTS have been around for some time, many casinos are now branching out and offering their regular players opportunities to enter competitions for Table Games. These events vary from those which are great fun and offer good value for money to players, to those which are nothing more than an attempt by the casinos to lure you through their doors and keep you there for as long as possible.

The most popular varieties are Blackjack and Roulette. In South Africa, the leading casino operator, Sun International, offers one million rand (about $100,000) as first prize for its nationwide events and, as a result, attracts good-sized fields, offering qualifiers as well as direct entry.

As with Slots Tournaments, there is an entry fee and then no further financial outlay. Players compete during time-limited sessions and those with the most chips, either at the Blackjack tables or the Roulette wheels, move forward to the semi-finals and finals. These later stages take place at residential casinos, where accommodation is paid for, but you are stranded there for some time, ensuring that you gamble on their premises.

As with Slots events, you should seek out those competitions which offer 100 per cent of the entry fees back to the players in prizes and perks. Beware especially of one-day events where the prize money seems to come up way short of the total of entry fees – there are plenty of smaller casinos quite happy to use these events as money-making exercises, rather than as promotional tools.

For both Roulette and Blackjack events, following the strategies outlined in this book will certainly give you the best chance of success. However, over short periods of time, anything can happen, and you can play perfect Basic Strategy and hit a terrible run of cards. Worse still, you can watch someone with no idea of the correct plays rake in the chips. Nonetheless, in the long run, those who play best will rise to the top, and if you enter a few of these events you will discover that, far more often than not, the skilful players are generally those who reach the finals.

Here are some tips if you enter one of these events:

- For Blackjack Tournaments, bet bravely, since others will be betting for large stakes too, but follow Basic Strategy for play decisions. Take every correct opportunity to double down since, to qualify for the finals, you will need to amass a large stack of chips.

- For Roulette Tournaments, try to focus on the even-money bets, such as Red/Black, Odd/Even and High/Low, since these bets offer you the best odds. Be prepared to bet maximums because if you can win just a few of these big bets you will then be in a strong position to build your chip stack. Just hanging on to a few chips will certainly result in your elimination. You should be focused only on one thing – qualifying for the final and heading for the big prize money.

- For all tournaments, some research and smart questioning will benefit you and increase your chances of success:

  - Be completely clear as to how many of the competitors qualify from each heat, or what proportion of competitors qualify. These events are all about comparing results between competitors, and not the usual player vs casino battles.

  - Ask tournament officials for winning totals in previous years, so that you can set yourself a target.

  - If playing in qualifying heats, try to discover the chip totals of those who have already played or, at the very least, the number of entrants, so that you can assess what would be the average chip count, and therefore what you would need in excess of this average amount.

  - Stay alert to those around you. If you discover that everyone else is losing their chips quickly, be prepared to play conservatively to protect your stack. If, on the other hand, other players are making a lot of chips, you cannot afford to guard your stack. You must gamble to ensure that you amass sufficient chips to qualify. Remember that, in theory, every competitor could lose his or her chips, while possibly a tiny minority do really well. Your concern is only to achieve what is required to get you to progress through the events to where the cash prizes are awarded.

Finally, remember that the casinos offer these events to persuade you onto their premises to gamble. Be careful when you swap from playing with "play money" back to your own hard-earned cash, and do not become impulsive or over-aggressive when you return to the real Roulette and Blackjack tables. This is what the casinos are hoping for: that you will finish your tournament, and then move to the cash games with the same over-aggressive, money-no-object attitude and try to win a huge prize – and probably lose your entire bankroll in trying – as opposed to gambling sensibly and building your profits slowly.

24
Online Gambling

THIS SECTION WILL show you the best opportunities for gambling online and taking the maximum benefits. Online strategies will also be revealed. However, I must begin with some important background information. Although it is neither ▬▬ nor glamorous, I urge you to read this part and, if any of it affects you in any way, to take note and act upon it.

For me, Las Vegas is the ultimate gambling city. I approve of it, not only because it does what it does brilliantly, but also because gamblers must make a conscious effort to go there. Gambling is restricted to those over 21 and, as adults, we must take responsibility for our actions. Gamblers must fly in or drive for five hours across the desert. They must book motel or hotel rooms and take days off work to do it. In other words, anyone going to Las Vegas should be prepared for the constant battle with the casinos and they should know what to expect. Gamblers should take only their prepared-for bankroll and no other credit cards or access to borrowed money. Take some precautions, know what you are doing, and Vegas is fun and exciting and an amazing holiday (see chapter 29 for more information on visiting the city).

Online gambling is accessible 24 hours a day. It requires no preparation, no organization. It is there all the time and it is markedly more addictive and destructive than gambling in land-based casinos. Personally, I believe that this is a huge step in the wrong direction.

It says much for the world that the two most popular uses for the Internet are ~~pornography~~ and gambling. However, whatever your views of both these pastimes, it is clear that there is a demand for them, and that people find that accessing them through the Internet is the most convenient method they know.

Nonetheless, online gaming has at least three serious inherent flaws. I urge you strongly to consider these before you play and, if you are already a regular player, to re-assess your view in the light of these key points. I love gambling, and I believe that the vast majority of people can enjoy it modestly. However, I am also aware that gambling addiction is affecting far more people than casino operators and governments would care to admit. It is a problem that must be faced by everyone who gambles and, I believe, we also have a duty of care to our friends and acquaintances with whom we gamble.

Gambling online is the ultimate solitary gambling experience. There is usually no one around to warn you that you are wasting too much time and losing far too much money. Online casinos must, under the conditions of almost all their licensing authorities, provide backup for those gamblers who are playing too long, offer deposit limits, and self-barring options for those who believe that they may have a problem. But, I can tell you right now, most online casinos pay only lip service to these requirements and couldn't care less if you lose everything, including the roof over your head, providing that you lose your money to them.

Secondly – and directly connected to the above – online casinos operate almost entirely using credit cards. Most of these casinos offer you the chance to wire money to them, use debit cards and bank transfers, as well as to ultilize online payment systems. However, research shows that the vast majority of online gamblers use only credit cards. This means that they are borrowing money to fund their gaming habits and there is no way to know whether these players have the capital to re-pay these debts or whether they are bankrupting themselves with their habit. Remember that interest rates on credit cards are among the highest anywhere on offer. In fact, there are drug-riddled loan sharks who offer better deals than these companies! So, while you certainly should never borrow money to gamble, if you absolutely must, then never use credit cards, because almost all of them offer you the worst deal going.

Finally, online gambling operates at a pace of which land-based casinos can only dream. Every game can be played at break-neck speed, so that, even if you are betting small amounts, the sheer volume of bets placed will ensure that the casino gets its predicted percentage edge against you, and more. Since, if you bet $100 in $1 or $2 amounts, you will soon be betting this money over and over again, on average losing 2–3 per cent every time. This is why casinos hope to hold 20–30 per cent on average against you, every time you play their games.

Unless you have an edge over the house, which online is not possible, then, quite simply, the more often that you gamble, and the more bets that you place, the more certain you can be that you will lose your entire bankroll.

Blackjack hands can be played four times, six times, even eight times faster than in real life. Usually, you are the only player at a table, the "dealer" deals his cards much faster, you make quicker decisions, and the payouts are made much more rapidly than in a real casino situation. At Roulette in a land-based casino, the croupier will wait for everyone to place their bets, spin the wheel and take time to pay out winning wagers. Online, usually you are the only player at the table, the spin is quick, the payouts instantaneous. And off you go again. This increased volume means that online casinos make more money per hour, based on the volume of small bets, than the land-based casinos operating the same games at the same, or higher, stakes.

So, before playing another hand of Blackjack, or spinning another reel of Slots online, please think carefully about the financial impact of your actions.

As you will see later in this section, there are now hybrid games: online games which are being played live. These have the dual advantages of greater integrity and slower game pace. Both of these factors can increase your enjoyment of the session.

How Safe and Secure is My Money Online?

This is one of the most asked questions by online gamblers and it is not a straightforward question to answer. However, since you may be risking quite substantial sums, it is vital to know whether you are taking extra inherent risks when you make a transfer from a bank account or credit card, or even online payment method, to the online casino you have chosen.

Before I answer this, let's just reflect on one fact. I have spoken with computer experts (of all kinds) and they all tell me the same thing. Any home computer, like just about any company or governmental computer, can be hacked. There is, at the time of writing at least, no cast-iron guarantee that your information online is safe.

However, these same people have also explained that, for most serious online criminals, home computers, and the information contained on them, are not of any interest. High quality computer and Internet protection will keep out most amateur crooks and these systems should be checked regularly to ensure they are updated and are functioning properly.

So, everything on your computer is under constant threat but, decent Internet protection should safeguard you against most attacks, save the most determined professional criminals. It doesn't sound very comforting to me, but I guess we all take calculated risks every day of our lives and this is just another which, taking everything into account, we are prepared to shoulder.

This assumed, our next concern must be the legality and reliability of the online gaming sites themselves. Will they steal your money? Will they pay out your winnings?

Once again, there are elements of risk. However, if you stick to the big, well-established, mainstream companies, your money is probably as safe in their hands as it is with any other vendor. The good news is that in the last few years several websites have sprung up which review online casinos, follow up complaints from customers who feel that they have been, in some way, cheated, and chase down missing payments. Any decent search engine online should offer you a choice. Be aware that, unless they can prove otherwise, there may be a conflict of interest in these sites, since they may be sponsored by other sites. However, by and large they make sensible recommendations which, when double- and triple-checked, appear to be correct.

Since online gambling took off, there have been scores of smaller online casino businesses that have gone bust, some taking their customers' money with them. Some major players in the past have also gone down and refused to pay out players' winnings, and there have been online gambling sites which have been hacked into, exploited by employees and programmers, and defrauded by their very own customer service personnel. However, as so often in business, the tougher economic climate has weeded out many of the weaker operations and left a large handful – closer, in fact, to an armful – of major players in the marketplace. Stick to these big names and you should encounter no problems with security, payment of winnings, and being offered decent complimentary perks.

At the time of writing, there are bills before legislators to legalize US citizens' gaming online, with a particular emphasis on playing online Poker. Other countries which ban gambling online are beginning to realize that they may as well attempt to regulate it and enjoy some tax benefits from it, rather than driving it underground through prohibition.

Having researched hundreds of sites, and played on quite a few, my only complaint about some of them is that they take too long to make their payments. Most, however, are efficient and prompt and helpful – just as they should be.

Are the Online Gambling Games Honest?

In theory, yes. There is really no need for online casinos to cheat their customers using fraudulent software. With the volume of business – and the way so many gamblers bet poorly – they are making so much profit that they are rolling in it. If any claim of dishonest software could be proven, it would shut a site down within a few days and seriously damage the reputation of online gaming for years. It is a risk, which, to me at least, makes no sense.

Like the Slot machines in casinos, all the online gambling games are controlled by a █████ (Random Number Generator), which, although not 100 per cent random, is certainly random enough to ensure fair play for all games. Whether you play Blackjack, Roulette or Slots – or any other game – they are all operated using the █████.

Furthermore, when you question online casino personnel about their software, as I have done, you discover that almost no one knows anything about it, other than to quote a pre-arranged company answer. The fact is that almost everyone who works for online gaming companies knows relatively little about the software, how it works, or even how the games work.

This seems odd, I know, but go back to the example of land-based casino personnel, the people who deal and supervise the games all their working lives. Have they picked up the key knowledge and observed the winning ways? Do they understand the odds of the game, the bets good and bad? Usually they do not. Will casino staff give you good advice? I'm certain that many mean to, but in reality almost no one gives accurate answers to the important gambling questions. So, do not expect customer helplines or even senior management to know what is happening "behind the scenes" of their websites. They are there to lure more people in and keep the profits rising and rising.

In the past, reported both in the national press and online, there have been instances of employees breaking into the software to divert funds. There have been cases of expert hackers discovering the "seeding code" to the logarithms used in the RNG and therefore being able to predict future outcomes. There have certainly been cases of player collusion on online Poker sites. However, without almost any exceptions, no one has proved, or got close to proving, that a site's software was inherently biased (other than to the extent all gambling games are inherently biased against the player – their house edge).

I have received many emails in the last few years from online Poker players and casino gamblers about what they perceive to be cheating by the casinos. Let's take a couple of them, since they well reflect impressions that many players get when they play online:

"I played Blackjack online and lost 14 hands in a row. I then reduced my stake and started to win... I increased my stake, but then I lost my entire bankroll."

This is a classic enquiry from correspondents. I know how they feel and I sympathize. Blackjack (and any seemingly 50–50 game) can be brutal at times. My personal record was 17 hands in a row lost in a live game of Blackjack, and 23 in a row without winning a hand (I had two or three stand-offs against the dealer). This can happen and is completely within the laws of probability. It is very unlucky to happen to you straight away, but it can be expected if you play Blackjack a lot.

Let's just talk a moment longer about this correspondent's comments. He lost 14 hands in a row, and then reduced his stake! I hope that as a reader of this book you would be on a minimum stake to start with and would not increase the stake until you started winning. This would save you quite a bit of money during a bad streak. Then he reduced his stake and won – that is frustrating. Then, he increased it again and lost all his money. To what did he increase it? And why was it not reduced again when he started losing? I suspect that the correspondent was frustrated to have been unlucky, but compounded it by playing unwisely. Finally, of course, I don't know whether this player knew Basic Strategy or was a complete Blackjack maniac.

In short, be prepared for both long losing periods, long-ish winning periods, and a lot of choppy waters in between you and a profit.

"I played dice on [name of site] and every time I loaded up the table with bets, the dice rolled 7. It is obviously fixed. What do I do about it?"

Have you felt like this when you have played online? Most gamblers certainly have when they play live. This is what happens. You seem to be going along nicely, you win a bit, you press your bets and get into a really good-looking position, and then it all goes wrong. That is a big part of gambling. It is why it is so exciting and so frustrating. However, the house has the edge, so it's not surprising that it wins more often than we do.

I replied to this correspondent asking for how long he had played and what bets he was placing, but he didn't respond. I suspect that this was one short session and, if so, this is what happens regularly to everyone. It is completely within expectation for the dice to seven-out on a regular basis (very roughly, once every six throws). Maybe he made many really poor bets, instead of playing the best strategy; maybe he pressed the size of his stake too hard. At the end of the day, at Craps, one in every six rolls will be the dreaded 7.

From the contents of this letter, there was no one single thread of suggestion, let alone proof, that the site was in any way dishonest.

Be prepared to face seemingly unlikely outcomes all the time, because within the normal variance there are both long periods of relative calm and long periods of wild fluctuation. In the short term, whatever the odds, anything can happen – and it usually does.

Licensing Authorities

Every online gaming site must be registered by a national gaming authority. Many online casinos, including the big ones, use small offshore authorities, not only for tax purposes, but also for regulatory ones: islands off the British coast, in the Caribbean, off North America, Malta, Israel. All can be used as the base for a casino's online licence. In return for the pretty small annual and monthly fees, these authorities promise the consumer that they will supervise the operation and ensure fair gaming.

Do I believe them? Absolutely not. I have dealt at length with two national licensing authorities and have found them to be unhelpful, totally uncooperative, ignorant of their responsibilities and, in my opinion, negligent of their duties. However, this does not mean that the casinos are cheating their customers. I suspect it just means that these jurisdictions have put in some pretty incompetent people to run what must be a cash cow for their economies.

Can an ▮▮▮ be cracked? A major Australian company which supervises and tests ▮▮▮▮ for big companies worldwide certainly thinks so and uses the fact to promote their work in testing and reporting all aspects of the ▮▮▮▮ in use.

Random Number Generators for casino sites should be tested for compliance, licensed and then regularly checked. The company in Australia which undertakes this work tells me they suspect that many smaller online casinos have no licence for their ▮▮▮▮, nor any desire to have one checked and tested at a cost to them if they did have one. What then are the licensing authorities of the various jurisdictions doing? Seemingly, very little. Certainly, not carrying out their self-professed duty of care to the clients of these online casinos.

However, this same company reported that the major players seem to comply voluntarily with such requirements and that their software is well tested and periodically checked.

The bottom line is that the vast majority of major online casino sites operate well tested and maintained software offering you, the player, a fair game.

Are the Odds at an Online Casino Worse Than in a Real Casino?

No, usually quite the opposite. Online casinos should pass on more of their profits to players because, unlike a land-based casino, they have no huge real estate or staffing costs. They are not offering you free drinks, meals and accommodation. Even the carpets and chandeliers don't need cleaning or replacing.

Most online casinos offer a wide variety of options for all games, from Blackjack through to Slots. As a consumer, your job is to find the best bargains out there and to make the most of them. Below, I'll show you what to look for and how to benefit from the offers available to you. Because there are so many online casinos – even among the reliable, big players in the market – there is a good deal of jockeying for position, trying to attract your money. You must take advantage of that to give yourself the best chance of winning.

What Should You Look For as a Sign-Up Bonus?

The one time the casino appears to give you free money is when you sign up and join a new site. This sign-up bonus will vary between $10 and a 100 per cent match of your first deposit. Indeed, just recently, I have seen sites offering you 150 per cent, 200 per cent and even 300 per cent bonuses on your initial deposit. You would think that this would mean that if you joined the site and deposited $500, they would give you another $750, $1,000 or $1,500 to play with. But, it usually doesn't mean that at all.

Sign-Up Bonus Scams

These sign-up bonuses are as fickle as any promotional advertising and the people behind it are hoping that you won't bother to read the small print. Buried somewhere in the terms and conditions you will discover that in order to "earn" this bonus (and there we were thinking it was a gift) you will have to play tens, if not hundreds, of thousands of dollars' worth of chips to qualify for slow, incremental releases of your bonus. And, you will have to do it within a specific timeframe – often one month… Oh, and certain games you play will not count towards the release of your bonus: games like Blackjack, Craps and Baccarat – in other words, all the good games. These bonuses are simply not worth having in the first place. They encourage you to gamble too much in too short a space of time and to play the games which offer the biggest edge for the casino instead of the best chance for you. In other words, they get you to do everything exactly opposite to my advice in this book. Strikes you as suspicious? It should do.

Then, there is the immediate bonus offered by many sites, including one UK Bookmaker's online site. You get £25 released over a very short period of time. I read the terms and conditions, I thought carefully, and decided to take advantage of this offer. I played Blackjack on this site and doubled my £200 to £400 in a short time. I decided to withdraw my profit, leaving my original £200 in my account. But, when I tried to do this I was told that I couldn't withdraw any money until I had played sufficient credits to release my £25 bonus. I told them they could cancel my bonus, I'd just take my money, and they referred me to a section of the small print that was even smaller than the usual small print. And there it told me that I couldn't do that. So, not only was my bonus not mine until I'd played a lot on their site, but my own money wasn't mine until I did this. I played some more Blackjack, very luckily won another £400, fulfilling my bonus qualification play, and cashed out my money. I won't ever play there again.

Watch out too for the apparently very special offer of a free $500, or $700, or $1,000 to play any games you like for the first hour, and you can keep the profits. This sounds like a great idea because you could place a couple of $250 bets at Blackjack and then, if you won even one of them, you could cash out $500. But you can't do this, of course. Firstly, you have to play lots of different games, and you have to play a lot of each of them. Often you have to play your money at least 100 times through the casino to qualify for anything. Then, some games are excluded from this offer, like Blackjack, Craps and Baccarat – them again – leaving just the very poor odds games left. Oh, and finally, hidden away in what are often pages and pages of terms and conditions, it says: you can only cash out a maximum of $50!

Picking the Best Sites and the Best Bonus

When you first approach online gaming sites, check the terms of any offer very carefully and do not be swayed to play at one site rather another just because of a sign-up bonus. It is much better to play a site that a friend has recommended to you (they may get a bonus for the referral too).

- Check whether the bonus is paid as a lump sum, or incrementally depending upon how much you play,
- Check how many times you must play through any bonus funds before withdrawing your money. If it is more than 50 times, that requires too much play to make it worthwhile.
- Check that you can withdraw your money, and any profit made, at any time (probably giving up your bonus entitlement). If they lock your money in until you have qualified for your bonus, this is a very bad feature and you should reject the site.

It can be beneficial to shop around, depositing small amounts in different casinos in order to benefit from as many offers as possible. By doing this, you will be able to judge the true terms of the bonus offer, check how easy it is to make deposits and withdrawals and, once you are on their list as a playing, paying customer, they will send you emails with special offers, like free gaming chips and bonuses paid into your account.

One site which I played for a while, losing only a little, sent me an email after I had not played their site for some time, saying that to welcome me back to them they had deposited a free gift in my account. I expected $10, so was very surprised to find $200 in my account – about the amount I had lost to them overall. The play-through conditions were generous: I had to play the money through ten times to be able cash out. This I did, with a small profit. I'm waiting hopefully for my next free gift from this site.

If you want to approach online gambling professionally – and since you are risking your own money I would recommend this – it is also a good idea to email the customer service department of any site you plan to use to test their responses. If they are quick and efficient, that is a good sign. If they take four days to reply and then don't answer your question, don't play on their site. What is more, you can use your email to them to ask for any special promotions and offers they might like to make to you. You will be surprised how often, if you ask, some far better bonus is offered to you.

- Email the customer service department, asking them to explain simply the terms of their bonus offer. If they reply quickly, and the terms are acceptable, you have the first indication that the site is well run and properly managed. If not, walk away from this site and find another one.

While you wait for the reply, use the casino's "play money" to try out their software. Some sites have beautiful software which is a pleasure to use and adds to the excitement of the game; others have lousy designs, and annoyingly fiddly interfaces which become unpleasant to use very quickly. Don't commit yourself to a site until you've tested that it suits you.

- Use play money to try out the software and check that you like it. If you are new to trying to gamble sensibly and win, you have the chance to practise the correct strategies from this book and see the positive effect they have.

Incidentally, it is against the regulations for an online casino to make its "play money" games looser, or more generous, than the real money games. Some sites have been caught out doing this, as an obvious way to attract players to wager real money, and this is one of the elements the licensing authorities should be paying close attention to. Are they? Not the ones I have dealt with. Most of the people I have spoken to don't even understand the difference between play money and real money wagering. It is as if they have never seen an online casino site!

- If you are a Slots player, ask customer services to tell you the relative percentage payback and whether it makes any difference at what stake you play. I have found that many sites are prepared to give this information out to players and it can help you decide on which site to play.

By the way, I am amazed how many people tell me that they have played a particular Slot machine on a particular site and they are doing very badly and they want to change sites, but they are worried that they might miss the jackpot on their machine. The machine doesn't know how long they've played or what they have lost. The machine doesn't know who they are. It is just as likely to pay out now as it is to pay out in 100 years' time. If you aren't happy with a site, leave it, join a new one and find a Slot you enjoy playing. That should be why you are gambling: for pleasure. If it provides no pleasure, please stop – right now.

Loyalty Bonuses

My advice is to play only a little when you gamble online. Remember, the more you gamble at games where the house holds an edge against you, the more certain they are to win, and you are to lose. However, even if you plan to gamble only a relatively small amount of money over what you hope will be a decent period of time, be aware that all good online casinos should pay you a loyalty bonus, reflecting your level of play. If you are playing Blackjack for $1 per hand, you will have to play a fair amount before you see much by way of bonus points. But, if you are betting $20 on each spin of the Roulette wheel, then your points will add up quite quickly.

These points will appear in a bonus points account, and they are usually paid to a player as a percentage of expected revenue for the casino. Depending upon how much you bet and at which online casino you play, you can expect between 1 and 10 per cent of the expected casino win to be paid back to you in bonus points. This is not a dissimilar scale to that used by Vegas casinos to calculate complimentary benefits to players.

These points can then be converted into cash (real cash that you could choose to withdraw immediately), used to buy gifts from the casino shop (some have them now) or to enter Poker tournaments and other special events, or to buy tickets into a prize draw. One site even offers to convert points to their partner airline's frequent flyer club at quite a preferential rate.

Note, however, that different sites award points of different value, which produce completely different redemption totals. For example, one site might give you 10 bonus points, which could be converted into $10. Another might give you 5,000 bonus points, which was only worth $5.

- If you plan to play seriously on any one site, check how many points you are awarded for your action (an efficient customer service advisor should be able to tell you) and how many points are required for each dollar, pound or euro.

Currency

Many sites now offer gambling in multiple currencies. To avoid charges from some credit card companies or banks, and to escape from the vageries of the currency fluctuations, stick with your local currency at all times.

Online Strategy

One of the biggest advantages of playing online is that you can take your time, study the best rules and strategies, and consult notes you have taken directly from this book. No one else will hurry you (some sites do operate a time limit for bets and decisions – steer clear of these sites if you want to play at your best). As a result, you can play perfect Basic Strategy at Blackjack, and all the Blackjack variations on offer. For any Table Game in a casino, you will find an online casino which offers the same game. Use the winning strategies from this book at all times to ensure that you offer the casino the smallest house edge possible. At no time do you have any excuse to place a bad bet, or make the statistically incorrect decision. For each of the games described in the following pages, we'll look at the rules and payouts you should seek, and the strategy you should employ.

My advice is do not play any game online until you have tested at least four sites (by using play money and contacting

Customer Services – do not deposit any money yet!) to find the best rules for whichever game(s) you enjoy playing. If you are expecting to lose, or playing to lose, then you might as well not bother. But if you are playing to win, you want to win as much as possible. The difference in odds and payouts can be enormous and finding out the best rules is essential.

Blackjack

This is an excellent game to play online, since you will be able to find the most favourable rules. However, unless a site tells you otherwise, all hands will be dealt from a new "deck" of 52 cards, so there is no opportunity to count cards or to track shuffles. Good Basic Strategy will keep the house edge hovering around 1 per cent, and that gives you a decent shot at beating the casino out of quite a lot of money.

Check the rules of the game; there are many variations. These are the most significant:

1 Does the house pay 3–2 for Blackjack? If not, do not play this game.
2 Does the casino take a hole card? If so, this is good. If it waits until you have played your hand(s) before taking a second card, this is poor.
3 Does the dealer stand on soft 17? If not, this is disadvantage – you will need good compensating factors to make this game worthwhile playing.
4 Are you permitted to double down after splitting? If not, this is a poor game.
5 Can you split aces more than once? If not, this is a poor rule for you.

6 Does the game offer a surrender facility? If so, this is a benefit.

Most online casinos display all their house rules as signs at each table, usually beneath the table minimums and maximums. If you cannot see these rules, check with customer services before you play the game. The difference between a favourable game and an unfavourable one could be worth hundreds or thousands of dollars to you.

Remember:

- **Follow the Basic Strategy advice and charts in the Blackjack section of this book.** Do not depart from this strategy. Even though it will not work perfectly all the time, in the long run it is scientifically proven to be the best way to play every hand.

- **Never increase your bet size unless you are winning.** Statisically, you could bet the same amount every hand and it would amount to the same potential win or loss as increasing and decreasing your bet. This is because the outcome of every hand is random. However, by increasing your bet when you are winning, when you hit a hot streak (which is what all gamblers really want to see), you will be rewarded with bigger profits than flat betting. My suggestion is that if you start with a base bet of, say, $10, and you win this bet, then increase your bet to $15, then to $20, and so on. Always return to your base bet if you lose.

  Incidentally, many online casinos will allow you to play $1, and then increase your bet to $1.50, so you do not need to risk huge sums to enjoy playing Blackjack. Take pride from making a $20 profit and locking it away. Any profit is a victory over the casino. Enjoy that moment, whatever your stakes.

- **If you make a 50 per cent profit, lock away your original stake, plus half your profit.** If you wish, continue playing with the remaining half of your profit, until you double it again. Then, lock away another 50 per cent of your profit, and so on.

- **If you lose the remaining profit, do not dip back into the profit you have set aside.** There can be no advantage whatsoever in continuing to play at this moment. Since each deal is completely random, you can play another time. However, if you get into the habit of locking away profits and ceasing play afterwards, you will become one of a very rare, but achievable, breed – a winner.

Craps

Played correctly, following the strategies outlined earlier in this book in the main section on dice, you can play this game offering the house only a small edge. Depart from the correct bets, however, and suddenly you are playing a game heavily weighted in the casino's favour.

Check that the game is well displayed. Some online casinos have really rotten graphics for Craps, while others show three-dimensional dice spinning and rolling and the game looks, and feels, very realistic. Next, as always in any casino, check for some crucial rules:

1   How much can you place behind your original Pass
    Line wager in Odds? If the casino allows you only Single
    Odds (the same bet in Odds as you placed on the Line)
    reject this casino and play Craps elsewhere. You want at
    least Three Times Odds, and ideally the Vegas Strip
    Standard: X3 on numbers 4 and 10, X4 on numbers 5
    and 9, and X5 on numbers 6 and 8. Many online casinos
    offer these odds, and these are the sites you seek out.

2   Check that these Odds are also available for Come
    Bets, since these are part of your best strategy.

3   Although the Field Bet is not the best bet on the layout,
    many players like it. If you must make bets on the Field,
    check that your site offers a 2–1 payout on 2 or 12, plus
    a 3–1 payout on the other number. This reduces the
    house edge on this bet to 2.7 per cent, which is
    acceptable. If you can find a site offering 3–1 on both 2
    and 12, this reduces the house edge still further. In the
    past, I have found online casinos offering this bet.

4   For other bets (which you should generally avoid),
    make sure you pay close attention to the style in which
    the payouts are displayed. Remember that "10 for 1"
    means that for one chip, if you win you receive ten
    chips. Whereas, "10–1" means that for one chip you
    receive ten chips, plus the one you wagered. That is a
    10 per cent difference and vitally important to note.

Baccarat

Baccarat, or Punto Bunco, is a low-edge game which requires
no skill or understanding on the part of the player. If you tire
of your usual game and want to try something different, this

is a good game to play. If you are a regular Slots player, I advise that you put some of your bankroll aside to play a game like Baccarat as, with its favourable odds, you will preserve your bankroll and may even be able to top it up substantially.

Check that the game is well displayed and that you understand the basic principles (there are no advanced procedures for this game). There is a tiny advantage in consistently betting on the Bank rather than on the Player, but both wagers offer among the best bets in the casino.

In terms of rules, there is only one which you should seek out: can you find a casino where the house takes less than 5 per cent commission on winning Bank bets? If you can, this is excellent and you should happily play there; if you cannot find less than 5 per cent, do not worry, since this is the industry standard. You are still playing a game with an edge to the house of only a fraction over 1 per cent.

Incidentally, the casino may not clearly display the 5 per cent commission on winning Bank bets. If in doubt, email, or initiate a live text chat, with a member of the customer support staff and find out the house commission.

Never bet on a Tie (or Égalité) since this is the worst bet on the table by far, offering the house an in-built edge in excess of 14 per cent!

Roulette

Roulette is, to me, one of the less successful games to play online. Nothing quite replaces the beauty of the traditional wheel spinning and the excitement of watching the ball drop into one of your chosen numbers. You will need to select a site carefully if you wish to play Roulette online, since many of them offer very poor graphical representations of the wheel. This, I am certain, will improve rapidly in the coming years, as computer graphics and processing power advance beyond recognition.

Remember that Roulette holds a substantial advantage over the player, amounting to a minimum of 2.7 per cent on bets placed directly on the numbers layout. Therefore, play for small stakes, and be prepared to leave quickly if you are lucky enough to make a profit.

In terms of House Rules, there are a few factors worth researching before you play. Remember that you can discover the answers to these vital questions, either by practising the game using "play money", or by consulting customer services for your site. If they do not answer promptly and courteously, then the site may well not be worth playing.

1   Most online casinos offer Roulette on a standard American-style wheel, and also on a European-style wheel. Only play Roulette on tables which offer a wheel with a single zero. These tables are usually described as European Roulette. Never play Roulette with two zeros on the wheel, since the house edge is so great that you will almost always lose your entire bankroll.

2   Does the house offer 50 per cent of your stake returned on High/Low, Odd/Even and Red/Black bets, if the ball lands in zero? If not, all bets, including the even-money ones, carry a house advantage of 2.7 per cent. This makes it an expensive game, and you should try to seek out a casino which does refund half your bets in these even-money situations.

3   Check that you understand how to remove chips from the layout as well as to place them. This is because,

when placing chips on a Roulette layout using a mouse, it is quite easy to place a chip in a different position from the one you wanted. If you do not know how to move a chip, or take it off the layout, you will end up placing more bets than you planned to make. Most online casinos use a right-click of the mouse to remove chips, but check how to do it on your site.

Keep your bets small and try not to press too hard if you hit a big win. Instead, lock away the profit, and leave the table when you lose any extra profit with which you have been playing. If you do not leave the table with a profit, you can never win.

Three-Card Poker

This attractive and simple game is not the best for the player but can, when you hit a hot streak, win you quite substantial sums. If you are lucky enough to win several hands in a row, lock away profits to ensure that you leave the table with money.

The big danger of this game played online is that you are nearly always playing a single hand on your own. This means that the action can move very quickly and the number of hands played per hour is many times more than in a casino. In a land-based casino situation, there are likely to be several players at the table. The dealer has to wait for the dealing machine to produce hands and he takes his time making the correct payments to each player.

If you are going to play Three-Card Poker online, it is vital to your chances of success that you seek out the best pay schedule for both the bets available: the Ante/Raise Bets and the Pair Plus Bets.

1 The Ante bonuses payable for premium hands on the standard Ante/Raise Bet should be:

Straight	even money, 1–1
Three-of-a-Kind	4–1
Straight Flush	5–1

If the online casino at which you play offers less than these payouts, they are being greedy and increasing their edge on a game which already favours them handsomely. Find another site which offers the industry standard payouts.

2 The bonuses payable for premium hands on the Pair Plus Bet, should be:

Pair	even money, 1–1
Flush	4–1
Straight	6–1
Three-of-a-Kind	30–1
Straight Flush	40–1

If the casino is offering less than these payouts, again, it is being unduly mean and you should play elsewhere.

You may find the Three-of-a-Kind and Straight Flush payouts altered to, say, 33–1 and 35–1. This is acceptable, because these payouts rarely occur and will not affect the house edge too greatly. The payouts on which to focus are those for the Flush and Straight. These are the hands that you will see regularly and for which you must be paid properly if you are to have any chance of ending up a winner. If these payouts are reduced to, say, 3–1 and 5–1 respectively, this increases the house edge substantially, and you must not play Three-Card Poker at online casinos offering these payouts.

Because the game operates at a fairly large edge over the player, keep your bets small and increase them only modestly if you find that you are being lucky. Return to the base stake immediately if you lose. Any profit is an achievement at this game, so lock it away and do not play it back.

Avoid all side bets offered, since these represent even poorer value for money than the main game.

Caribbean Stud Poker

This isn't a great game for the player and it becomes a little bit worse online where, once again, the speed of action means that you will be spending more per hour than you would do in a land-based casino. The casino owners love this, which is why online gaming is so profitable, but it is a matter of concern for players.

Your prime areas of research should concern the payout schedule for made hands when the house qualifies, and also the size of the Progressive Jackpot and payout structure of the side bets.

1 The industry standard payout schedule is:

Royal Flush	100–1
Straight Flush	50–1

Four-of-a-Kind	20–1
Full House	8–1
▬▬▬.	6–1
Straight	4–1
Three-of-a-Kind	3–1
Two Pair	2–1
One Pair	1–1
Ace-King High	1–1.

Pay particular attention to the payouts for the Flush and Full House, since these are often reduced in order for the casino to increase its edge over you. If, for example, the payouts for these wins are 5–1 and 7–1 respectively, you are being diddled – and you should reject this game on that site.

2   If you plan to place a bet – usually $1 – on the Progressive Jackpot, ensure that you are aware of the payout schedule and, since you are playing for a miracle result, ensure that you will be well rewarded if those beautiful cards all line up in your hand perfectly for you. The standard payout schedule for the Progressive is as follows:

▬▬▬▬	Progressive Jackpot
▬▬▬ ▬▬▬	10 per cent of Progressive Jackpot
Four-of-a-Kind	$500
Full House	$150
▬▬▬	$50

If the Full House and Four-of-a-Kind payouts are markedly less than this, you are missing out on two of the better elements of this particular bet. In terms of the overall Progressive total, you would like to see something in excess of $100,000 to make the bet even close to worthwhile.

As mentioned earlier, I have a soft spot for this otherwise pretty poor wager, since online I hit a Straight Flush. I did this when the Progressive total was very high and hence won a substantial prize. Hitting the hand was pure luck, but ensuring that I would be paid well if it happened was down to research and site selection. Failure to research sites for your favourite game can cost you thousands, even tens of thousands, of dollars. Make site research part of the fun of taking on the casinos.

Let It Ride

Not a great game to play, but one that continues to be popular online. Again, the speed of play increases your overall exposure and makes it more likely that the casino will triumph. If you do want to play, there are payouts you should seek out.

Check the payout schedule for made hands is similar to the following:

~~Royal Flush~~	1,000–1
~~Straight Flush~~	200 –1
Four-of-a-Kind	50–1
Full House	11–1

	8–1
Straight	5–1
Three-of-a-Kind	3–1
Two Pair	2–1
One Pair (10s or higher)	1–1

Once again, it is the mid-range payouts, for Straights, Flushes and Full Houses, that are most significant, since these are the big wins you have some chance of hitting. If the payouts are less than those indicated here, then the odds against the player at this game become prohibitive, and I strongly recommend that you do not play Let It Ride in those circumstances.

Do not play side bets at this game, since they are almost all very poor games taking far too high a percentage for the casinos.

Spanish 21, or Casino Pontoon

This is one of the best games for the player with house edges well under 1 per cent if the player adopts the correct strategies. Since it is a complex game to assess at the table, and the strategies are quite tough to remember (they can easily become confused with standard Blackjack Basic Strategy), this makes Spanish 21 an ideal game to play online.

Not all online casinos offer this game, partly because relatively few gamblers know how it works, and partly because it is too good a game for the player, but there are plenty which do, and they are worth seeking out.

1 Check payouts and rule variations at the table. These are emblazoned on the baize in a semi-circle near the dealer. If you see "Dealer Stands on All 17s", this gives the player a further 0.4 per cent advantage over tables where "Dealer Hits Soft 17s and Stands on Hard 17". It is very good for the player, but may be hard to find online.

2 The following are the standard payouts for hands, even after a split (but not when doubles have been used):

- Blackjack pays even money (some sites offer 3–2 payouts on Blackjacks made after splitting – this is a very favourable rule to the player indeed).
- Five-card 21 pays 3–2. This is for a five-card trick totalling 21.
- Six-card 21 pays 2–1.
- Seven-card 21 pays 3–1.
- 21 composed of mixed suits 7, 7, 7 or 8, 7, 6 pays 3–2.
- 21 composed of same suit 7, 7, 7 or 8, 7, 6 pays 2–1.
- 21 composed of 7, 7, 7 or 8, 7, 6 pays 3–1.
- Check for a Super-Bonus payout. Most casinos should offer this, although only a few provide the so-called "envy-bonus" to all other players competing. A Super Bonus is paid if you make a same-suit 7, 7, 7 and the dealer's up card is also a 7, of any suit. This is not paid when hands have been split or doubled. Bettors staking below $25 are usually paid $1,000. Bettors staking $25 or above are usually paid $5,000.

Other side bets are, as usual, best avoided.

Blackjack Switch

Since the secret of keeping the house edge to a minimum is to know the correct time to switch, and when to keep your two original hands, this game lends itself perfectly to online play since, through the Internet, you can access a Blackjack Switch calculator which shows you when it is right or wrong to switch. The calculator can be downloaded in a couple of seconds from several different sites and is free to use. Using this additional piece of software reduces the house edge to a very playable 2 per cent.

1   Use a Blackjack Switch calculator to ensure that you make the correct decision at all times.
2   Be fully aware of all the differences between this game and other Blackjack variations by reading the description and strategy decisions in the chapter on Blackjack Switch (page 196).
3   Pay careful attention to the House Rules as these will affect your overall chances of winning quite considerably. Some online casinos offer Early Surrender, which includes surrender against the dealer's ace (providing he does not hold Blackjack). This rule reduces the house edge still further. An online site offering this may be the perfect place to play Blackjack Switch.
4   Of all the side bets available, the Super-Match Side Bet on this game is a decent bet, providing that the pay schedule is generous. The industry standard payouts are the minimum you should accept if you plan to make this bet (see top of next page). Any less, and the house edge rises too high to make the bet worthwhile.

Any Pair	even money, 1–1
Three-of-a-Kind	5–1
Two Pair	8–1
Four-of-a-Kind	40–1

Sic Bo

Sic Bo is not a good game for the player, offering the house too big an edge to give you even a medium-term chance of making money. The best bet available (High or Low) takes 2.8 per cent; then there are other bets on offer, ranging from the bad to the truly awful, which take 18 per cent or more!

If you want to play for small stakes for a short while, there are some factors which you should look out for to ensure the best possible playing conditions:

1   **Proposition Bets on precise numbers.** Beneath the Totals Bets is a row of 15 Proposition Bets, where you can predict which numbers might show on two out of the three dice. Every combination possible is represented, without the doubles (which can be covered at the top of the layout). All these bets pay the same: 6–1 if you bet on the correct outcome. These are some of the best bets on the layout, as the house edge is a meagre 2.78 per cent, but check the payout carefully online – many online casinos pay 5–1, making it a terrible bet (16.67 per cent house edge). Even worse is that some casinos, which display all their payouts in standard odds (5–1),

change the display for this set of bet, offering 6 for 1, which is only 5–1 in normal odds.

2   **Number Appearances.** If you place a bet here you are backing the appearance of a number on one of the three dice. This is usually a bad bet (7.9 per cent edge), but if the online casino offers a bonus for that number appearing on all three dice, this reduces the house edge somewhat. Look for payouts of 6–1 or better if your number shows on all three dice. Otherwise, stay clear of this bet.

Sic Bo is a game of sucker bets, but unlike Craps there are no really good ones to even it out. It's a different type of game, offering its own thrills and a unique display. Although it warrants some action using play money, I would not risk very much real money on a game with such a negative expectation for the player.

Pai Gow Poker

Pai Gow Poker is a fun game, involving plenty of player decisions and a high percentage (40 per cent) of stand-offs between casino and player. This means that your bankroll will last longer. If you hit a run of good cards, you can also build up a good head of steam and take the house for a fair amount of money. The key to the game is how to place your cards correctly between the high hand (five-card hand) and the low hand (two-card hand). Since the exact science of this is very complicated, you can download from the Internet a Pai Gow Hand Setting tool, which shows you the statistically correct method of placing your cards. Using this ensures that you are giving the house as tough a game as possible and keeping the house edge to a minimum.

1   Fully acquaint yourself with the rules of the game and basic strategies by reading the chapter on Pai Gow Poker (page 211).

2   Use a Hand Setting tool to ensure statistically perfect play.

3   Avoid side bets, which are always poor odds.

Beware playing Pai Gow Poker for low stakes online, since if you bet less than $5 per hand, when you win the casino will usually take a minimum of 25c in commission even if you are only betting $1. In this instance you would be paying a 25 per cent commission and it would ruin you.

Keno

I cannot recommend playing Keno at any time. It is simply one of the poorest bets you can find. If you want to play a similar game, try one of the many Bingo sites which offer a multitude of different games, many for modest stakes.

Casino War, Red Dog

Both these games will bore you very quickly played online and neither offer a good gamble for your money. They should be avoided.

Online Slots

Generally, online casinos offer among the best Video Poker and Slots that you can find anywhere. It is up to you to try to ascertain the Slots payouts and to discover which are the loosest and tightest games – this may vary from online casino to casino, even if the machines seem identical. Try speaking to the Slots Manager of an online site (or the customer service advisor) and ask which machines pay what percentage. Some sites will tell you; others claim total ignorance as to which Slots pay what. Someone knows the answer, but they may not work with customer services.

My research has found that most online casinos are reporting paybacks of between 92 and 96 per cent for their Slots, which is better than most land-based casino Slots, particularly low-stake ones, but not as good as some. With the amounts of money passing through the online casinos' hands, these percentages will still yield them considerable profits.

Online casinos tend not to decrease their edge as the stake increases, although this is not universal, so playing low stake Slots is usually the best idea. Online Slots play even more quickly than casino Slots, so a lot of money can pass through them very quickly.

As with casino Slots, the higher the jackpot – including Progressives – the meaner the general payout structure of the Slot will be.

If you want a good game, where you receive plenty of small prizes, pick a Slot with a modest jackpot. Machines carrying jackpots (for one coin) of between 600 and 1,000 coins are best for this. The moment you play a Slot which offers more than 1,000 coins as a jackpot, you will find that the chances of winning – unless you hit the big one – become markedly less.

With multi-line Slots, unless you hit the bonus feature, the general payback will be meaner than on a standard Slot machine. Play a modest number of coins only, since these monsters can take up to 90 coins per spin, putting them into seriously high-roller mode.

Above all, remember that it makes no difference how long you play a particular Slot, or if you return to the same Slot another day. It isn't really a Slot machine (and nor are the ones you find in the casino). It is just a random number lottery, with a display that looks like a Slot machine.

- If you have lost consistently on a Slot machine, you are no more likely to win on the next spin than if you had been winning consistently. Do not increase your stake, or download more money, chasing your losses. You have just as much chance of winning another day.
- If you choose to play a Progressive Slot machine (with generally a meaner payout for smaller wins), pick one with a big Progressive total. Then, if you do happen to hit the jackpot, you will be paid off handsomely. A Progressive Jackpot is just as likely to hit straight after paying someone else as it is if it hasn't paid out for months, or even years. The difference is, the old jackpot will be big and the young jackpot relatively small – this affects your overall odds of playing that particular Slot.
- *Do not become over-excited by very large Progressive Jackpots.* The reason for the enormous total is because no one has hit the winning combination for months or years on end. That serves only to illustrate just how unlikely it is that you will hit it yourself.
- If Slots games are for you, look online for sites which recommend where to find the big Progressive Jackpots. Although many of these sites are closely

linked to online casinos, they can provide up-to-date information that is helpful for players.

- Check that your chosen online casino is rewarding you with worthwhile loyalty points and special offers, including free casino credits. If not, call customer services and ask for a bonus; if necessary, threaten (politely) to play elsewhere. You'll be surprised how often they will give a bonus if you ask for one.

Video Poker

Video Poker online is almost identical to a Video Poker machine in a casino. The program which controls the game will be the same, and the display on your screen will also be very similar (if anything, it will be higher quality since most casino Video games still use old-fashioned cathode-ray tube displays).

Although you can use this book and its strategy advice in the casino, or even purchase strategy cards and use those, many Video Poker players feel embarrassed to do this. The player on the next machine to me recently asked me the correct plays to make on his machine (we were playing reasonably high stake denominations). When I suggested that he used a strategy card, he said it would "spoil the glamour" for him. He told me that he had lost a lot of money playing Video Poker this year. From his play, I could see that he was making poor decisions, but he obviously preferred it that way than being seen with a crib sheet.

Online, it is easy to make every decision perfectly. This allows you to play a casino game with a small house edge and still give yourself the chance to win a big prize if you hit the Royal Flush, or one of the bonus big prizes on some machines.

As with Slots, a Video Poker game with a big Progressive Jackpot may compensate for this by making the smaller prizes worth less. This is why, as well as knowing the correct plays, the most important preparation when planning to play Video Poker online is game selection. Investigate different sites and the games they have on offer and check the pay tables to ensure that you are getting the best possible value for money and the best chance of winning from the casino.

There are many varieties of Video Poker games available. The following payout schedules are what to look out for in the standard, most popular games found in online casinos:

Jacks or Better

Play/Coins	1	2	3	4	5
	250	500	750	1,000	4,000
	50	100	150	200	250
Four-of-a-Kind	25	50	75	100	125
Full House	9	18	27	36	45
	6	12	18	24	30
Straight	4	8	12	16	20
Three-of-a-Kind	3	6	9	12	15
Two Pair	2	4	6	8	10
Jacks or Better	1	2	3	4	5

On this classic Poker machine, the key payouts to check are the Flush and Full House. If these payouts are 8 and 5 respectively, then this is a short-pay schedule (i.e. a meaner schedule of pay-offs than the industry standard) and should not be played; if they are 9 and 6, this is usually considered the full-pay schedule and the one to play.

Note that the only advantage to playing five coins, as opposed to any other amount, is if you hit the Royal Flush. If you have only a small bankroll you may find it more fun to play one coin and make your money last longer.

Jacks or Better Progressive

Play/Coins	1	2	3	4	5
~~████████~~	250	500	750	1,000	Progressive $6,867
~~████████~~	50	100	150	200	250
Four-of-a-Kind	25	50	75	100	125
Full House	9	18	27	36	45
Flush	6	12	18	24	30
Straight	4	8	12	16	20
Three-of-a-Kind	3	6	9	12	15
Two Pair	2	4	6	8	10
Jacks or Better	1	2	3	4	5

This payout schedule is ideal. It is a full-pay schedule with a Progressive Jackpot. Many Progressive Jackpot Jacks or Better machines offer the short-pay schedule and therefore return less to the player (unless you hit the Royal).

Assuming that this is a $1 Video Poker game, the jackpot shown here is sufficiently high to warrant playing 5 coins – 6,867 coins, opposed to the standard payout of 4,000.

If you find a payout schedule showing 8 and 5 for the Full House and Flush respectively, ensure that you play it only if the Progressive is significantly higher than the base setting of 4,000 coins.

Bonus Poker Deluxe Jacks Or Better (8/5)

Credit/Coins	1	2	3	4	5
~~Royal Flush~~	250	500	750	1,000	4,000
~~Straight Flush~~	50	100	150	200	250
Four-of-a-Kind	80	160	240	320	400
Full House	8	16	24	32	40
Flush	5	10	15	20	25
Straight	4	8	12	16	20
Three-of-a-Kind	3	6	9	12	15
Two Pair	1	2	3	4	5
Jacks or Better	1	2	3	4	5

This schedule pays only 8 and 5 for the Full House and Flush respectively, and, significantly, only one coin (your money back) for Two Pair. To offset these deductions, Four-of-a-Kind has been promoted into a significant win, greater even than a Straight Flush.

Once again, here you are playing maximum coins only for the Royal Flush jackpot and you may feel that playing one coin is quite sufficient.

Double Bonus Jacks Or Better (9/6)

Credit/Coins	1	2	3	4	5
Royal Flush	250	500	750	1,000	4,000
Straight Flush	50	100	150	200	250
Four Aces	160	320	480	640	800
Four 2s, 3s or 4s	80	160	240	320	400
Four 5s–Ks	50	100	150	200	250
Full House	9	18	27	36	45
Flush	6	12	18	24	30
Straight	4	8	12	16	20
Three-of-a-Kind	3	6	9	12	15
Two Pair	1	2	3	4	5
Jacks or Better	1	2	3	4	5

This schedule pays the full 9 and 6 for Full House and Flush respectively, but reduces Two Pair to a money-back win. In return for this, there are three stages of Four-of-a-Kind bonus wins: Four Aces (160 coins), Four 2s, 3s, or 4s (80 coins), and Four 5s–Kings (50 coins).

Watch out for online casinos which offer you this Video Poker, but with the Full House and Flush payoffs reduced to 8 and 5, making this style of machine a poor proposition.

The Video Poker payoff schedule to find, though, is the one below. I have seen it in casinos and on one online site. It may be tough to find but if found it is well worth playing, offering you a game where the house has less than a quarter of 1 per cent edge over you. This provides a real chance to beat the house out of quite a lot of money.

Double Bonus Jacks Or Better (10/7)

Credit/Coins	1	2	3	4	5
	250	500	750	1,000	4,000
	50	100	150	200	**239**
Four Aces	160	320	480	640	800
Four 2s, 3s or 4s	80	160	240	320	400
Four 5s–Ks	50	100	150	200	**239**
Full House	**10**	20	30	40	50
Flush	**7**	14	21	28	35
Straight	**5**	10	15	20	25
Three-of-a-Kind	3	6	9	12	15
Two Pair	**1**	2	3	4	5
Jacks or Better	1	2	3	4	5

Notice that, despite the poor element of receiving only one coin (money back) for Two Pair, the payout for a Straight is raised to

5 coins, and the Full House and ▆▆▆▆ payouts are scaled at 10 and 7 coins respectively. This is excellent for the player.

In land-based casinos in the US, you may well see that the 5-coin payouts for a Straight ▆▆▆▆ and the basic Four-of-a-Kind win are reduced from 250 coins to 239 coins. This is so that US taxpayers playing this machine at a $5 denomination do not pay tax on such wins. Online, you may find that these payouts are at their correct levels, namely 250 coins for a win when 5 coins are played.

This is another Video Poker game which will play just fine at one coin per play, allowing you to preserve your bankroll. Since the site on which I found this schedule offered $1 per coin as the minimum bet (a medium-roller stake), playing one coin seems even more attractive.

Doubling Feature

This feature is favoured by some Video Poker players. When selected after a win it displays one card and you must pick from one of four cards to find a higher card. If you succeed in finding a higher card, you double your prize; if you do not, you lose your prize; if the card value matches the exposed card, the bet is a stand-off or tie.

I have been unable to confirm to my satisfaction that the doubling feature available online is the same random feature offered by the casino-based Video Poker machines. All the indications are that it is and, personally, I have done very well online using this feature.

Many online Video Poker machines offer only a limited number of doubling opportunities, while others permit doubling until your reach the jackpot total, or when a double of your current total would take you beyond the jackpot total. At this point, the machine makes you take the prize.

Summary

Payout schedule selection and correct strategy will ensure that playing Video Poker is one of the very best bets online. If you can find a Video Poker machine with a sizeable Progressive Jackpot, backed up by a reasonable general payoff schedule, you could well be gambling with a statistical advantage – which is certainly very rare, especially online.

Do not feel committed to playing maximum coins, unless the Progressive Jackpot warrants this play.

Be wary of the multi-line Video Poker which, in effect, results in you playing several machines simultaneously. If you win, you may win more, but if you are losing, you will certainly lose more.

Ensure that you play the correct statistical strategy for whichever machine you are playing, otherwise you are offering the casino an extra edge, which they don't need! If you cannot find the strategy in this book, research online or purchase a strategy card from a good gambling website. To play incorrect strategy on these machines, when the correct one should be available to you, is just plain stupid.

General Online Gambling Policy

Because of the speed of action online, and the ease with which you can dip into your account money, or download more money to your account via a credit card or other payment method, you must be disciplined when you gamble online.

Use Well-Known and Recommended Sites

Once you start to gamble online, you will be bombarded with junk email telling you about a myriad of casinos and their special offers to you.

Firstly, have a secondary free email address for online casinos. This way, you will not have your main account taken up with junk. Secondly, check all boxes which request no publicity material to be sent to you. However, do glance at emails from your own chosen casino, since they may include good offers, payment and deposit confirmations, and even free money.

Ignore other casinos and their offers. Stick to a well-known online casino, or a casino which has been tested and recommended by friends. Above all, you want good customer service and as much reassurance as possible that the casino operates legally and reliably. Never be swayed to play at a casino because of special offers. In the long run, they are nearly always not worth it.

Deposit Limits

I strongly recommend using the Deposit Limit option which all good online sites offer. Within your account options, you should be able to set a limit for the amount of money you can deposit to the site in any given day, week or month. My advice is to strictly limit yourself. Most sites permit you to change these limits provided that you give one week's notice. This is a minimum precaution you should take.

Self-Barring

Use the self-barring mechanism to prevent you from returning to the site for the next week, month, or indefinitely if you lose too much money online.

If you have run up too much debt on your credit card, call the company and explain that you want them to bar any online activity on your part. Many major credit card companies will agree to do this.

Bankroll

Because online casinos usually allow you to play their games for quite modest stakes, ensure that you have sufficient money in your bankroll to allow for a minimum of 20 bets at your base stake; ideally, cater for 40 bets at your base stake. This will allow you to weather a poor run of form, and still emerge on the other side with money to build back up again.

Don't play Blackjack for $10 a hand if you only have $50 to play with. While you could win, because you only have five bets to play with you could easily be wiped out and have no money left. Far better to bet $1 to begin with and then increase your bet by a dollar every time you win a hand, returning to the base $1 if you lose. This, at least, rewards you when you hit a hot run of cards, which is what all of us want to do.

Never increase your bet when you are losing – this is essential. So many players try to get even by increasing their stake and end up losing four times, eight times, twenty times what they lost originally. It is one of the biggest money management mistakes you can make, and it nearly always ends in tears.

If you have lost money, never tell yourself that you are trying to get even. Just because you have lost previously, it is no more likely that you will win now. Accept that you have had a bad day and take a break.

Enjoy Your Profits

Because of the speed of action online, if you win, you may be tempted to race to another game and start playing that at a frantic pace too. If you win, allow yourself time to revel in the feeling and enjoy the power it gives you. Lock away some of the profit (or, ideally, withdraw it from your online account). Then, play some other games for lower stakes and see whether you can build up further profits. If you do, the feeling of satisfaction will be enormous; if you don't, you will only have lost a tiny fraction of your profit, and you won't feel bad about it.

The wrong thing to do is to use profits to increase your stakes well beyond your usual ones in an attempt to get rich quick. This may work, but for the vast majority of the time you will lose all your profits and more — and you will feel terrible. I've done it, virtually every gambler I know has done it,

Remember these two vital gambling truisms:

1 The greater the size of win you aim for, the more likely you are to lose.

2 If you set yourself modest targets for profit, you are much more likely to achieve them.

Betting Strategy

The best betting strategy is to play every game for a modest stake and retain the size of your bet whether you are winning or losing. Sadly, this is also a very boring way to bet and, when you hit a hot run, you will feel that you have not exploited it for maximum profit.

The simplest and safest way to play more aggressively and try to build profit is to use a gentle system of bet parlays to increase your stake when you are winning. When you lose, return to your modest base stake and start again.

For example, if you are betting $10 at Blackjack and you win, you increase your bet to $15; if that wins, increase to $20. If you win five hands in a row, you now increase your stake by $10, so you increase a winning bet at $30 to $40, and so on.

Now, if you hit a hot streak, you will cash in on it successfully. If you lose, return immediately to your original $10 wagers and stick to them until you start to win. This way, you are always betting the minimum while you are on a losing streak. This saving of money is often as important as the winning of money because, if you have saved, then that money is profit when you do win and not merely an attempt to get even.

The downside to this is when the session is very choppy: you win a hand, you lose a hand, you win a hand, you lose a hand. You may lose more than you would have done if you had stuck to a static betting amount.

Equally, you can find yourself up at $60 on a hand, and you are dealt 11 versus the dealer's 5 – one of the best positions in which to be, and you should definitely double down. Now, however, all the winning action from the previous number of hands is bet on this one hand. If you win, as you may well do, then you have a tremendous result (from a $10 wager to $120 on the board at the best moment); if you lose, all your hard work is undone. However, at least you have your maximum bet in play at the very best moment, statistically, for you to win. And this is what all successful gamblers achieve.

Remember that when you increase your stake, you increase your overall exposure, since you may have to make further bets to maintain your position:

- at Blackjack: double downs and splits.
- at Craps: Odds and Come Bets.
- at Three-Card Poker: Raise Bets for the same amount as your Ante Bet.
- at Caribbean Stud Poker: Raise Bets for exactly double the ~~Ante~~ Bet.

So, be aware of how much you are actually committing when you increase your base bet.

Profit-Taking

This is a simple statement, but its implications seem to elude many gamblers:

If you want to make money, you must leave the casino when you are in profit.

The plain fact is that you have to decide whether you want to win, or merely that you want to play. If it is the latter, none of this matters – play your games however you want; lose your money and don't complain.

But, if you want to win, when you are ahead, you must stop and walk away from the table, or from the casino altogether. If you keep gambling until you lose, you will lose regularly and consistently.

As a basic rule, this will assist you hugely: when you have 50 per cent profit on your game bankroll (regardless of what has happened at other games at other times), take away your original stake, plus half of the profit. This ensures a 25 per cent profit, which is a good goal to aim for on any given session.

Leave with the other 25 per cent profit too if you like, but if you want to keep playing limit yourself strictly to playing only what you have left. Lose that, and you must leave. But you leave in profit and it will feel good.

If you manage to double your remaining money, be disciplined and strong enough to take out half of that profit once more, and add it to the money you have already set aside. Continue playing only with the remaining money. This way you will guarantee yourself a 50 per cent profit on your original bankroll – and that is a tremendous result!

Follow this basic rule (or your own, carefully thought out one) or face constant losses. To succeed requires self-control, and the ability to fight the urge to have more fun when you are doing quite well.

Many gambling books advise you never to leave "while you are winning". I don't subscribe to this idea at all. If you are playing a negative expectation game – which includes, basically, every online game – you might win more if you keep playing, but the odds suggest that you won't, that you are more likely to start losing. You can't predict a winning streak, you can only look back on one. So, if you have made a profit, or got your money back after a long losing session, stop immediately. You have done really well and there is no need to press your luck.

It's Supposed to be Fun

This is crucial. Gambling is a pastime intended to be stimulating, exciting and, on occasion, rewarding. If at any time you find yourself stressed, unhappy or desperate when you are gambling, I urge you to stop. ~~and assess your position~~, and assess your position. If you think you might need some help and support, then I guarantee you that you do. Please take that action: it can be as simple as talking to a trusted friend and getting some good, objective advice. Non-gamblers do not understand the excitement and pleasure and, also, disappointment and frustration gambling can bring. Confide in someone who understands these emotions and, if you don't have friends like that, call a helpline. All land-based casinos, as well as online casinos, should offer the relevant contact numbers for gambling support.

25
Live Television and Online Hybrid Gaming

A T THE BEGINNING of the twenty-first century, the United Kingdom moved from a country with a conservative attitude towards gambling to one governed by politicians determined to milk the gambling industry – and the ever-increasing numbers of the general public who frequent it – for every last penny.

Online gaming sites are welcomed in the UK; land-based casinos can open far more easily; membership and registration requirements have all but disappeared. In the centre of London you can simply stroll into casinos without any ID and gamble for thousands of pounds.

Licences for mobile telephone gambling sites have been established, and television channels dedicated to encouraging people to gamble now thrive. Is this a good thing? Personally, I think it is a terrible idea. Gambling usually has its worst effect on those from poor socio-economic backgrounds; to encourage it is highly irresponsible. Have casinos, by all means, but regulate them well, ensure fair gaming, and make it a conscious decision for people to gamble, so that it is not too easy for them. I am a libertarian, but I do believe that some things should be made harder to do than others.

However, the fact remains that we now have casino channels broadcasting, all day and all night, mainly Roulette games, but also Blackjack variations, and Bingo-style games. More and more people are playing along online with these games and the average bet is increasing as people become familiar with this method of gambling.

Live Television Hybrid Gambling

This form of gambling combines the live broadcast, on a cable and satellite channel, of a simulated Roulette wheel. The actual result is defined by a Random Number Generator (████), with a jolly presenter announcing when the table is open for bets, when the betting must end, and naming the big winners. The end of the betting period is marked, not by the statement "No more bets", but, rather weirdly, by the phrase "Table closed". If I saw a "table closed" sign, I think I'd walk on to another one, but this is the terminology they use.

Each spin takes place at 90-second intervals. While bets are being placed, the presenter will run through how to sign up with the associated website, how to place the bets, and what the payoffs for each bet will be. There is also plenty of time to spread a bit of misinformation, such as noting which numbers are "hot" and which are not; persuading punters to bet on black when there have been a lot of red numbers recently, because "the law of averages says it's even more likely to come up black now", and so on.

Bets are placed via the website and the screen name you choose will appear onscreen with your bets and winnings. Occasionally, the presenter will mention you by name; the overall idea being that you should feel like part of a happy "gambling community". However, as with all online gaming, this activity is a solitary one, without the human back-up of a real community of friends, and the fail-safe advice that can sometimes stop you from losing far too much.

On the website for each of these channels is a fully-fledged online casino persuading players to try other games, and not just those that are combined with the television broadcasts.

The "wheels" are, at least, single-zero models and there is no reason to believe that this style of gambling is any more likely to be dishonest than any other online operator. If anything, the fact that the games are broadcast should ensure that the ████ is licensed and up to date, and that the game is free from interference. Since a minimum of 2.7 per cent is being taken by the house for every £1 bet made, the channel is probably doing very well.

Because the game played is nearly always Roulette, and this is a poor game for the player, I cannot recommend this form of gambling any more or less strongly than standard online Roulette games. Frankly, they are best avoided.

Interactive Bingo

Bingo and lotteries are the United Kingdom's national gambling pastimes, so Bingo channels were not an unexpected development. Currently, these are hi-tech affairs playing a Bingo-style game with several presenters and high-tech graphics.

You sign up online, download your money and start to play. There are a limited number of games available, with varying-sized jackpots. The numbers "drawn" appear on a giant screen in the studio (again using an ▓▓▓▓), and the twist is that when players get close to winning the action moves to another presenter in front of a map of the UK, who shows us where all those players, just waiting for one number, are located. This is quite fun (it also shows that the vast majority of players are located in the, generally, poorer North of England).

The stakes and the prizes are pretty moderate, and the presentation is such that it makes for amusing, if undemanding, entertainment – a modest gamble with plenty of razzamatazz.

Standard online Bingo sites, which also offer other games, often encourage online conversations and sometimes show video clips and even live feeds. Just keep your bets small, and these can be an enjoyable diversion.

Live Dealer and Wheel Online Gambling

Online casino operators vary from the opportunists who set up a site, promote it successfully and then let off-the-shelf software run the whole operation, and those who genuinely attempt to innovate. At the time of writing, the latest innovation addresses the concerns of honesty and reliability of the in-built RNG, by replacing it with a live dealer. In the case of Roulette, bets are placed as usual online, by placing chips via your mouse on the Roulette layout. However, instead of you then pressing an on-screen "Spin" button, when the betting has taken place the live dealer (appearing via webcam on your screen) announces that the betting is complete, and the spin will be made. The camera focuses on the live wheel, the ball is spun and everyone waits for the outcome. The result is fed into the computer, the program pays you off correctly, and betting for the next spin begins again.

There is no RNG involved; players can see all the action of a Roulette game played out in front of them while having confidence that the result is truly random and not at the mercy of some secretive computer. Already, this idea is proving popular and successful. The downside is that the online casino operators have to pay staff to run the tables instead of benefiting from negligible staffing overheads. However, the position is clear: the gambling public trust a real, live human being far more than a hidden RNG.

Game designers are already working on other human/online interactive games. It seems that the rise of computer gambling will be tempered by the need to see human beings in charge of the sensitive stuff.

Mobile Telephone Gambling

If online gambling in your own home on your PC or Apple presents a threat of ever-present temptation, then the almost inevitable "progress" to mobile gambling takes this a stage further. The casino owners would ideally like everyone gambling for every minute of the day and night. However, one of the ways that players give themselves a chance to win (or at least moderate their losses) is by understanding that they do not have to place another bet – they can just walk away. And they can then stay away for days, weeks, or even months. The advent of the facility to gamble wherever you are really cannot be a good thing. Even with improving graphics and expanding screen size, the whole experience will surely be a disappointing one, especially when you remember that all traditional online gaming is controlled by a RNG and is therefore little more than repeated games of Keno or a lottery, with flashy pictures appearing on screen to veil the reality.

This said, there is no reason to suspect that online gaming on your mobile telephone will be any more or less trustworthy than ordinary online gaming; it just isn't likely to be very desirable.

Television should, fundamentally, be a relaxing experience. I doubt that the increased stress levels of gambling "on TV" will be very beneficial. Similarly, if passengers on the bus and train are gambling as they travel to and from work, not only will they lose their salaries, but it won't be much fun sitting next to them. Sadly, making money from gambling is just too easy for the operators. As consumers we must try to ensure that only the best customer service and the most generous games are supported by our hard-earned money. Otherwise, who knows where it will end?

26
Online Poker

POKER ONLINE is a very different experience from a live game, especially if you are used to playing friendly Poker with your friends, regular group, or at a casual club.

This section is not for complete beginners. It assumes that you have watched plenty of Poker on television, or that you already play with a basic knowledge of terms and Poker ideas. The glossary on page 500 includes an explanation of basic Poker terms. Beginners should consult *The Mammoth Book of Poker* for a solid introduction and grounding in the basic skills.

As with gambling in general, you must decide early on whether you are playing for fun or for profit. Nearly everyone thinks that they are playing for profit when, in fact, nothing could be further from the truth. Playing Poker for profit, especially online, requires massive commitment, patience and self-control. Played in this way, it can be an easy way to make money – perhaps not as much money as you would like, but regular, reliable monthly profits. However, well over 90 per cent of online Poker players lose money – month in, month out. Many of these people truly believe that they are skilful, winning players, just going through a bad streak, or being very unlucky.

Unlike casino games, you are not playing against the house, with an in-built edge against you. Instead, you are, in effect, paying the casino, or online Poker site, a commission (on your winning pots, or as entrance fees to tournaments) to play against other gamblers. To succeed, not only must you win more than you lose, but you must also earn enough to pay the rakes – the small percentage the casino extracts from most pots as a fee for hosting the Poker game.

Many Poker players will claim that their game is not gambling. I disagree with this opinion strongly. Playing Poker is definitely gambling. However, unlike the vast majority of typical casino games, this is a gamble where your input can determine – in the long run – whether you end up in profit, or lose money regularly. For most amateur Poker games I estimate that there is a skill element of about 3 per cent and a luck element of about 97 per cent. When I first suggested these figures, many people told me that the skill figure was far too low. However, I believe that this figure is correct: apart from anything else, a 3 per cent edge at any game where the turnover of money is very high provides a very substantial edge indeed. If you could sustain a 3 per cent edge against your Poker opponents, you would be very wealthy, very quickly.

Online Poker

At the highest end of Poker skill, the skill edge against less skilled players will be far greater, and the luck element reduced. Against their peer group, expert Poker players use many additional factors to make decisions of which amateur players have no real concept.

In *The Mammoth Book of Poker*, I explain in detail the skill sets required for success at all forms of the game, from beginner to successful intermediate player. In this section, I want to explain how to join an online Poker club, or casino, and the best methods to ensure that you prepare yourself to play and win online. This advice is for players beginning Poker or who have played a fair amount but who are still losing. I suspect that there will be many readers who fall into the second category. Self-knowledge – and the acceptance that you might not be quite as good as you thought you were – is crucial to financial success at Poker, especially in the online environment. Be prepared to make the effort to learn the game properly, and you can succeed. Be arrogant, or in self-denial, and you may never become a winning player however long you try.

Joining an Online Poker Room

Pick a well-known Poker Room, where the software is trusted, the customer support is strong and the company behind it reliable and well funded.

There are many examples of lesser, start-up Poker sites failing to test their Random Number Generator (RNG) systems correctly, providing poor support, refusing to pay out winners, and ignoring suspicious activity. Even some mid-size online card rooms have been rocked by scandal:

interference and theft from employees, collusion among players, and companies declaring insolvency, refusing to pay back customers' money and then re-opening elsewhere.

The established Poker sites are, on the other hand, as reliable businesses as you will find anywhere. They turn over millions of dollars and will do everything possible to keep their players happy, well looked after and secure.

The honesty of the randomization of cards dealt is pretty much confirmed: I simply don't believe that the world-class experts who play online would tolerate even the slightest suspicion in their minds. They would just leave.

If your intention is primarily to play cash games online (opposed to tournaments), then visit one of the online sites which offers to repay you a percentage of the house rake. You can find these online if you search for "Rakeback Poker Sites". Having chosen which site (or sites) you would like to try, see if you can join them through a rakeback site.

Since virtually all online Poker sites take 5 per cent rake, or commission, from the pot post-flop, you give this away to the site when you win that pot. With a rakeback site, you can earn up to 30 per cent of this raked money back and, even if you are playing relatively low-stake Poker, this can soon add up. The rakeback site gets a commission for getting you signed up, and they then pay you your percentage of the rake at the end of a set period of time, or once you have amassed a stated minimum sum. This is well worth spending ten minutes arranging, since it could, potentially, save you hundreds, or even thousands, of dollars.

Once you have picked an online Poker site and signed up, you will need to register your details, deposit some money from a credit card (ensure that the card you use protects you against online fraud – and that your own computer defences are in place), and explore the site. Pick a screen name by which you will be known online. Some sites offer you the chance to pick an avatar: a cartoon figure, photograph or symbol to represent you online. My advice is to pick something anonymous and unremarkable. It is preferable for people not to remember you if possible.

You should be offered a good sign-up bonus but, as with online casinos, expect the bonus to be released slowly, as you play on the site. Most sites allow the bonus to be released only for your first month of play; some more generously retain your bonus cash for as long as it takes you to play through the funds required for its release. You can monitor the terms of the bonus and your progress towards earning it through a section of the site usually entitled "My Account". Here, you will be able to keep track of transactions, sign-up bonuses and loyalty bonuses.

Most sites offer players points for playing and these points can, in turn, be changed into cash, entries for events and, on some sites, for products and services offered by affiliated companies. Most sites offer similar levels of reward for action in cash games or tournaments. Don't imagine that, if you play low-stake Poker, this will amount to a lot of money, but it is a bonus which is very welcome, especially if you find that your bankroll has depleted somewhat.

Many of the sites offer new players the chance to play in free-rolls (events which are free for you to enter) and these tournaments not only offer you the chance to become familiar with the software and the standard of your opposition, but also to win a sizeable sum. Many of these free-rolls offer between $500 and $5,000 in prize money, and may take place weekly or monthly. As a new player to the site, you will certainly be offered the chance to play in one of these events.

The Lobby

The Lobby area of an online Poker room is where you choose your games, stakes, style of Poker, or whether to play a cash game or tournament, visit the cashier to withdraw or deposit funds, or change settings to ensure the site is as friendly to you as it can be.

From the Lobby, you can view which games are running, which tournaments are registering entries, and who is playing. The advice in this section is geared towards the most popular form of game online: Texas Hold 'Em. But if your game is Seven-Card Stud or Omaha, you can adjust this advice to suit your own personal tastes.

Types of Game

Cash, or Ring, Games

You can choose to play cash games, either at full tables (nine or ten players) or at short tables (five or six players), and even Heads-Up games (two players). The stakes, which are usually displayed in the form of the size of the blinds, will be as low as 0.01c/0.02c and may be as high as $100/$200. If you feel that you are a decent player, my advice is to start at stakes of 0.25c/0.50c or 0.50c/$1. At these stakes, your buy-in will be $50 or $100. You may think this is too small a game for you to play in, but I urge you to start off here as it will give you a good indication of what you can achieve on any given site.

Sit & Go Tournaments

These are usually one-table tournaments which begin as soon as the field (of six or ten players) is complete. You can find Heads-Up games too, which only require two players to agree to play.

The Poker site usually charges between 5 and 10 per cent entry fee for these events, so if you enter a $30 Sit & Go event you will probably pay $33. For a Heads-Up event, you might pay only $31.50. This entry fee should be displayed clearly at the time of entering.

Generally, the prize money is distributed as follows:

Heads-Up events:	winner takes all.
5/6-player events:	70 per cent for first place;
	30 per cent for second place.
9/10-player events:	50 per cent for first place;
	30 per cent for second place;
	20 per cent for third place.

Multi-Table Tournaments

These events, which are sometimes called "Scheduled Tournaments", usually offer fields of unlimited size and start at a pre-arranged time. Be aware of different time zones when signing up for events – 8 p.m. Eastern Standard Time can be early morning in central Europe. By the way, if you sign on for an event but then decide, before it begins, that you not want to play in it, you will be able to sign yourself out again and the site will reimburse you all your entry fees.

Most MTTs offer a guaranteed prize pool, which means that even if there are very few entrants, the casino still promises to pay out a set of minimum prizes. If the field gets bigger than they expect, the overall prize pool will increase.

As a general rule, the top 10 per cent of the field will get into the money, with the top 30–50 per cent of the prize pool paid out to those players who reach the final table. Depending upon the structure of the event, these ~~games~~ can last anywhere from 2–3 hours, right up to 10–12 hours. However, if you make it that long, you will be in big money, so you probably won't care that you are tired, stiff and hungry!

For each of these styles of game, I will provide you with some key tips to get you started. However, if you want to succeed you must study your game in detail.

Satellites

These events can take the form either of a Sit & Go tournament or an ~~MTT~~. For a usually small entry fee, you play a tournament where the winner, or leading players, gains entry to a bigger event. For example, if there is a monthly online ~~MTT~~ on your site with a prize pool of $100,000 – and there usually is – then the entry fee may be about $200. If you cannot afford that entry fee, you can try to qualify via a satellite. The site may offer a Sit & Go satellite where ten players each pay $20 (plus a $2 entry fee) to enter and the winner gets the $200 entry fee to the main event.

There are even super satellites, where you might pay $2 (plus a 20c entry fee) to enter a ten-player Sit & Go and the winner of this event wins a $20 entry to the standard satellite. Players have been known to enter tiny online satellites for huge land-based Poker events, such as the World Series of Poker (WSOP) in Las Vegas. World Champion, Chris Moneymaker, proved it could be done in 2003, when he parlayed a $39 super satellite entry into the main event entry ($10,000) and then won the whole thing – a title which paid him 2.5 million dollars!

Settings

Whatever style of game you choose to play, at whatever stake, once you reach your chosen table you will be able to adjust a number of options to make your playing environment best for you.

Table Display

Most sites will allow you to size your table as you wish, from an eighth of your screen size right up to full screen size. I recommend about one quarter of your screen size. You may make the adjustments either through a menu of options, or by re-sizing the window via your mouse.

Dialogue Boxes

The vast majority of Poker sites have a dialogue box which displays information about which deal is being played, who won the deal, who has bet what, and so on. This box also doubles as a chat box, where players can type messages to each other.

I have a very important tip for you here: **turn off the chat facility**.

I say this for a number of reasons. Firstly, most people who play online Poker get pretty stressed. The last thing you need is to get into an argument with another player about the actions either he or you decided to take. Often people are rude and insulting, and some are clever enough to know just what to say to wind you up. Don't get involved in this;

don't even listen to them. Secondly, if you are thinking about typing messages, you are not focused on the game. You need all your concentration on the next hand and should be observing the action carefully to pick up information about your opponents. Chatting, or even watching the chat box, is a pointless distraction.

Card and Background Designs

Most sites offer the facility to change the background of the display of the Poker table, as well as the colour or design of the cards.

Sounds

Personally, I do not need an electronic representation to remind me what shuffling a pack of cards sounds like, or bleeping warnings to tell me that it is my turn to act. I turn off the sounds; you can alter them on your site to whatever is your preference.

Auto-Post Blinds

There is very little that is automatic in Poker – there are so many options which may be right for any given situation. However, to keep the flow of the game going, it really helps if everyone has clicked this box at the table. This ensures that, when it is your turn to place the blinds, the computer does it for you automatically. The next hand can then start immediately and no one is kept waiting.

Other Control Buttons

You will find that within the game you have many control buttons, or tabs, which you can use. These may include "Check/Fold" when you are in the big blind, "Fold to any

Bet", "Call any Bet", etc. My advice is not to use any of these buttons at any time. You should be thinking about every decision at the Poker table and the use of these buttons tells the other players that you have made your mind up before anyone else has taken action. The fact that you pre-set these actions on a particular hand can help your opponents work out that you have a very weak hand, and they can then take advantage of this information. At the same time, if you then pause before acting, they know you have a hand worth thinking about.

Play-Money Tables

Just as you use play money in an online casino, which allows you to try out the games and test the software, so you can also practise with play money in online Poker. The problem, however, is that Poker is a game where the score is kept by the size of your stack. If you are not playing for real money, no one pays much attention and the action is wild and unrealistic. By all means play at a play-money table just to experience the playing conditions, but do not consider it as practice for your Poker at all. Instead, log in to a low-stake game, for, say, $20, and play some low-stake Poker. At least here, even though the standard may be very poor, you will get some proper Poker action.

Having looked at the start-up procedure, and your options as a player, let's now look at each form of the game and put together some really important tips. If you are new to the game online, this is the absolute minimum information you require, and I strongly advise that, for the price of one modest raise, you order a copy of *The Mammoth Book of Poker*, in which I offer detailed advice on all aspects of the online game. If you are a regular low- or mid-stake player online, use these tips to check that you are not making any fundamental mistakes. While Poker is an individual game, where skill, daring and intuition play a huge part, none of this is worth anything to you if you don't know the basics. So, use these next pages to ensure that you know your stuff. You may be surprised at what you discover.

Key Information and Playing Tips for Cash Games

Table Selection

Before logging into a particular table, utilize the information in the Lobby. Table selection can make a huge difference in influencing whether you enjoy a winning or losing session.

Study the information provided about each table before deciding which to join. The key statistics here are those concerning the average size of pot, and the number of players seeing the flop. Contained within these two figures is information about how loose or tight, how passive or aggressive, the table has been in recent hands. This is how to interpret it:

a) A large pot size, combined with a low percentage of players seeing the flop, suggests that the game is tight and aggressive, with players raising regularly pre-flop, and only one player calling, or re-raising.

b) A large pot size, combined with a high percentage of players seeing the flop, suggests that this is a loose/ aggressive game, where players are raising pre-flop, and receiving many callers.

   c) A small pot size, combined with a low percentage of
   players seeing the flop, suggests that players are not raising
   before the flop and, if there is a raise, only one player is
   calling. This could be described as a tight/passive game.

   d) A small pot size, combined with a high percentage of
   players seeing the flop, suggests a loose/passive game,
   where many players are calling pre-flop, there is not
   very much raising and, when a player does raise, other
   players tend to fold.

I would always favour joining a table in the c) or d) sections.
This would allow me to raise pre-flop and frighten away
players, and also to call with marginal or speculative hands
(such as suited-connectors) and expect to see the flop cheaply.

A table with the characteristics of a) would be a high-pressure
situation where every raise you make may be tested with a re-
raise, and where you would rarely get to see a flop cheaply.

I have spoken to hundreds of online Poker players, asking
them, among other things, how they select their tables. Not
a single one told me that they studied these statistics before
playing, or chose their table for any sensible, logical reason.
Usually, they admitted, they joined the first table they saw
at the stake they wanted to play.

If you follow the information provided on the site, you
have a distinct advantage over your opponents. That advantage
will translate into profits, into money. Isn't it worth spending
an extra 2–3 minutes studying the site before playing?

Seat Selection

You reach the table and find that you have a choice of two
seats. Where should you sit? If you have notes on the players

(see page 428) or you observe them for a few minutes, you may be able to detect the aggressive player, who raises a lot, and the weaker players, who often call and frequently fold. If you can, use this information to seat yourself correctly.

As a general rule, you want:

- Aggressive players to your right, so they have to act before you decide what to do, and commit any chips to the pot.
- Loose, passive players who fold and call a lot to your left, so that if they raise you know they are strong and you can, usually, fold, saving yourself further money. If they call, you have a good chance of milking them for profits; if they are wont to fold regularly, then you can raise them off the pot pre-flop, or subsequently.

Full Table or Short Table?

There are major differences between playing at a full table of nine or ten players, and playing at a short table of five or six players. This difference also occurs when you start off with nine other players, but four leave, and you find yourself playing five- or six-handed.

The more players there are at a table, the more likely it is that there will be good starting hands, and that the flop will connect and make stronger hands. In short, the more players there are, the higher the value of the average winning hand will be.

At tables where there are only five or six players, the values of the hands increase because it is less likely that there will be big hands elsewhere. When you come down to three-handed play or Heads-Up play, cards which you would normally have folded may instantly become playable.

Here's a very simple example:

You hold K, J.

If you were at a ten-player table and you saw these cards, sitting in, say, mid-position at the table, your standard action would probably be to fold or to call.

If you were at a six-player table, in mid-position, your standard action would be to call or raise.

If you were playing Heads-Up against a single opponent, your standard action would be to raise.

The fewer the players at the table, the stronger this marginal hand becomes.

Remember also that, at a short-handed table, the blinds come around to you much more quickly. If you are playing at a $1/$2 table, this means that every six hands you are losing $3. This is why you must be more aggressive and pro-active when playing at a short table than at a full table.

Stake Selection

Play at a stake which your bankroll can support easily. You should have an absolute minimum of ten full buy-ins on your bankroll. That is to say, if you are planning on playing in a 0.5c/$1 game, where the maximum buy-in is $100, you should have $1,000 in your bankroll. You need a big bankroll to play without economic pressures influencing your decisions, even for a low- to mid-stake game.

This policy is recommended because even the best players in the world have losing sessions, sometimes many in a row. If you lost half your bankroll in one session, you would have every right to feel concerned. As a result, you might buy-in for less than the maximum, shy away from making raises when that is the correct play, and refuse the chance to call a big bet which might well be a bluff. These would all be poor decisions influenced by economic worries.

If, on the other hand, you lost three sessions in a row and you still had 70 per cent of your bankroll remaining, you could relax in the knowledge that Poker players always go through wide fluctuations of success and failure, and you would still have plenty of chips to weather it. With your thoughts focused on the correct strategy, you would make the right decisions as often as possible.

There is a persistent myth among online Poker players that lies at the root of thoughts such as: "I am being unlucky against bad players, who call loosely and hit their outs, so if I play against better players, at a higher stake, this won't happen so often and I'll be more likely to win."

You must resist these thoughts because they are quite false. If you are losing because loose players are calling for draws and hitting them, this is a short-term trend and will probably start to end soon. When you start winning pots against these weak players, you can build up your bankroll.

More importantly, you want the weaker players to call you loosely. You have to accept that occasionally they will hit their hands (I've suffered months of them hitting every draw possible), but in the long run they are putting their money in the pot at unfavourable odds: usually in the 30–35 per cent range. You want this, because the upside is the 65–70 per cent of hands you will win in the long run.

If you move up to a higher-stake table, you will probably encounter a generally stronger style, which means that less of your opponents' money will be on offer to you at favourable odds. In short, it will be tougher to win – and at higher stakes too. It is a doubly awful proposition.

Be aware that the gradations of stake can (they do not always, by any means) mark a substantial change in average ability. I know players who regularly play in $1/$2 and $2/$4 games who are full-time poker professionals. They win, perhaps $1,000 per week, playing multiple tables at these stakes. You don't want to be facing them. As you move to mid–high stake games, such as $5/$10 and $10/$20, you will still find the odd rich amateur, but you will also encounter players who are semi-professional or professional online players, and you will find these games very tough.

I recommend 0.50c/$1, and $1/$2 games when you feel confident and successful. Ideally, you should start at a lower stake, build up your bankroll over a period of weeks or months and then test the water carefully at the new higher stake. Every week, I receive numerous emails about how players have built up a sizeable bankroll, moved up to a higher stake, and lost the lot in days. This is a common occurrence and indicates that increasing stakes is far more significant than just the cash at risk.

If you choose to play Limit Poker, then the relative size of stake is that much higher. However, until you are confident that you are winning on a reasonably consistent basis, do not increase your stake.

There is one final reason for being wary of increasing your stake: the levels of stress it creates. As with casino gambling, Poker is supposed to be fun. If you become over-desperate about the money you are staking, it will affect your decision-making process and make winning even harder. Stay at a level where you feel relaxed: disappointed when you lose (but not unhappy); satisfied when you win (but not expecting to pay off your house mortgage or debts with the money).

A key tip: **Always buy in for the maximum when you join a table.** This is because doing so allows you to exploit to the full any massive hand you may encounter. It shows that you are there to play and that you mean business. It means that mid-stacks will always be a little afraid of you, because you could make them broke.

If a player joins a mid-stake table and buys in for the minimum, you know that he is playing scared and you should make a point of bullying him. If a player joins the table with an odd amount of money, like $97.54, then you should suspect that this is the end of his bankroll and, again, he is playing scared. Do not give away this type of information yourself.

Know Your Table; Multiple Tables

Many online Poker players have more than one table on their screens at any one time. Some Poker pros have four or five tables all running simultaneously. There is a crucial element here. When you first join a table, you are at a significant disadvantage, because you have very little information about the style of your opponents. You should play very tight for the first 20 minutes to half an hour as you build up a picture of who is weak and who is strong, who is raising a lot and who is a loose caller. Without that information, your money-making decisions will be little more than guesses.

If you find that you are good at rating your opponents accurately and quickly, then I think it can be a good idea to play two tables. I would recommend that you play one for the higher stake you plan to play, and the other for a lower stake. If you are lucky enough to get two good hands simultaneously, you can ditch the low-stake table and focus on the high-stake table. The advantage of playing two tables is that, if you play a tight style – which is strongly recommended for profit-making online play – you will fold a lot of hands. Playing at two tables stimulates you more and, ultimately, this can keep you more disciplined than sitting woodenly in front of a single table. Beware, however, of opening multiple tables before you have assessed your opponents carefully at your first table.

Almost all sites have the facility to review the hands played, and to see cards which, at a live table, would have had to be shown – for example, after a showdown at the end. Online, your losing opponent's cards may be mucked (discarded) without showing, but you can see what they were calling you on by reviewing the hand. This is an important skill, since this is how you build up a picture of how your opponents play. The knowledge can then be directly exploited in making winning decisions, winning you money and, just as importantly, saving you money when you are losing the hand.

Take Notes

All top sites offer the facility to make notes on other players. This is vital. The more information you have on an opponent, the better your chances against him. The pros can remember all of this and use it against opponents years later when they meet them again. For the average player, the ability to jot down notes about your opponents is brilliant.

You can usually access the note-taking software by right-clicking, or double-clicking, your opponent's name, or avatar. Make the notes useful to you, rather than recording abuse or frustration. Something like:

"Calls a lot of raises loosely; against odds, will not fold top pair; never seems to bluff."

The moment you see this note you will know that, in past encounters, this opponent is a fish, and one who will not be taken off a decent hand. So, if you raise and he calls, you miss the flop and you make a Continuation Bet which he calls again, you can be pretty certain he has something and you may not be able to bluff him off the hand. Equally, when you pick up a really good hand, you know that you can milk this opponent for maximum chips, because he'll keep calling with anything.

"Very tight, folds most small blinds, raises X2 with AA. Raises X5 with 66 – and 44."

This note tells a different story: your opponent plays only big hands and, it seems, the stronger they are, the less he raises. With low pairs, he raises big pre-flop to try to push you away – you have noted that twice.

I had a note like this for a player recently and he raised in the small blind. I held AJ in position in the big blind, and I folded immediately. He showed his hand, and it was AK suited! I kind of knew that already, because of the note I had taken. This probably saved me a lot of money.

Bear in mind that such notes are site specific. If you leave this site and move to another one, you lose all your notes and have to start again. When I first started playing online, not all sites offered note-taking, so I filled book after book with player notes. It really helps and I attribute a lot of my winnings online to good note-taking.

No-Limit Texas Hold 'Em Playing Tips – Cash Games

These tips can also be applied to Limit Poker, and all forms of No-Limit game.

1   **Whatever your actual style, begin by projecting a tight image.** Use the first 15–20 minutes at the table to

assess your opponents and get a feel for the game. During this time play only premium hands, such as mid- and high pairs, AK and AQ. Try to make your first bet a raise or a re-raise. I like to enter the vast majority of hands I play with a raise, and this is especially true of the first hand you play. You want to win this first hand, to show that you are there to win the hands you enter. This presents a very strong image which, no matter how you choose to mix up your style later, will stay in the minds of observant opponents.

2 **Position is crucial.** Your position at the table, in relation to the button (and other opponents), is absolutely vital. As a general rule, the closer to the button (and therefore to being the last player to act on every subsequent round), the more daring you can be.

If you are at a ten-player table and you pick up A8, would you play this hand and, if so, would you call or raise?

In general, if you picked up this hand in early position (first, second or third to act), you should fold these cards. In mid-position (fourth, fifth or sixth to act), if no one else has raised, you might call with these cards. If you were in late position (seventh or eighth to act), and no one had raised, you might well decide to raise on this hand, persuade the blinds to fold, and take down the pot there and then.

Ninth and tenth to act will be the small blind and the big blind and, since these positions will be the earliest positions after the flop, you should only play very strong hands in these positions.

Everyone plays differently, and it is right to mix up your game somewhat, to make it harder for your opponents to read your style. However, this example illustrates how, in early position, if you call on marginal hands, you may get yourself into trouble. After all, if someone raises after you have called with A8, will you call? I hope not. You should muck your hand, but you have still wasted the price of a lame bet.

Take a hand like AJ.

AJ is always over-rated by inexperience players – it's not that good. If the player on your right raised before you, would you call? It would depend on his image, the information you have on him, but, generally, you might call, or even consider re-raising.

If the player raised sitting over you (to your left), would you call? You probably shouldn't. You will have to act before he does from now on, and this will make playing this hand very tricky. You should fold.

These two simple examples should illustrate how important your position is in relation to the button and the other players involved in the hand. Never lose sight of the importance of your position.

3   **Avoid playing marginal hands.** The biggest leak for most players online is playing too many hands, and becoming trapped with marginal hands. Of course, it is horrible to sit folding hand after hand, but sometimes this is what is required. If playing Poker was easy, fun and profitable, everyone would do it, and goodness knows where the money would come from. As it is, to play winning Poker requires patience and discipline. This isn't really that hard, if you have some degree of self-control.

Assuming an average nine-player table, playing cards such as K9, Q10, Q9, K8, J8, A7, and below, will lead to long-term losses. Each of these hands can connect with the flop, and still be way behind another player. If you can creep into the action on the button with a call, they may be worth a shot, but to play them in early or mid-position will just lead to trouble.

Calling raises on marginal hands is also, ultimately, very weak play. It is especially dangerous to call reliable raisers on hands such as low aces (A6, A5, etc) and K10, K9, Q10, etc. This is because, if you hit the flop at all, it is quite possible that your opponent has hit it even bigger. The enormous pots I win are on hands like this:

I raise with AQ and my opponent calls me on A8, and the flop comes: A, J, 6.

Having called the raise, you want to see an ace on the flop, but now that it has appeared you may be completely dominated. I push in the money, get called and leave my opponent on a 12 or 13 per cent chance of hitting Two Pair. Furthermore, if, on this unthreatening flop, I choose to check once and try betting later, I may get paid even more, since my opponent may put me on a jack and not an ace.

If you must call raises on weak hands, at least opt for suited connectors, such as 10, 9 or 6, 5. At least if you miss the flop you can fold easily, and if you hit the flop big (Two Pair, Trips, Straight Flush draws), you may win a huge pot if your opponent holds a premium hand.

As a simple rule, if you think that your hand isn't very good and you are wondering whether to call or not, don't. Fold your cards and wait for a better moment.

4 **Remember that you are not on television.** While the Poker programs on television have transformed Poker into a worldwide phenomenon, and brought millions of

players into the card rooms – both live and online – the downside is that it is easy to be seduced by what you see. Remember that televised events only show you the big hands, not the ones where there is one raise, and everybody folds, and not those where everyone folds to the blinds, the flop comes down, there is a bet and the other player folds. These hands make for dull viewing. The programs often focus on experts making marginal plays against players whose games they know very well. That is why you see experts calling raises on low ace hands, and re-raising with a third pair. In addition, much televised Poker is Sit & Go format, where you have to be far more aggressive at all times if you are to have any chance of qualifying for the next round, or winning the event. It's all action, action, action.

Money-winning Poker isn't anything like that. It is fold, fold, fold. That frustrates most people, and they start to play weakly and loosely. This is when the good players clean up. In which group do you want to be?

5 **Never show your cards.** You might even tick the box that offers to "muck all winning hands". If you do not have to show your cards, it is much better just to throw them away. Unless you are very confident that the information you are giving will be beneficial to you, do not reveal your hands. Many players like to show bluffs – this is usually very silly. Yes, it winds up your opponent, rubbing their nose in their error, but it also makes reading their subsequent actions far harder: are they steaming, still hurting from the wound you inflicted on them, or are they playing normally again? Even showing very strong cards when everyone folds to your raise isn't

a great idea. In general, the less you show, the less your opponents know about you, and that is an image that you want to retain at all times.

6 **Back up your raises with strong plays.** While you will not always make this play, the Continuation Bet should be your default action when you have raised and been called. If your opponent does not re-raise you, he is unlikely to have a super premium hand, so you must put him to the test at once. For example, you raise with AK and you get called by a left-hand opponent. The flop comes: 10, 6, 3. As a general rule, you should bet out now. The size of a Continuation Bet is usually between 50 and 75 per cent of the pot. The advantage of making this bet is that, firstly, you may have the best hand; secondly, you may cause a low pair – 44 or 55 – to fold; and thirdly, when you hit the flop and bet out, it will look exactly the same. If your opponent calls, you will have to decide whether to fire again on the turn and, if he re-raises, you will have to decide whether he is bluffing, or whether he has really hit his hand (he may have A10 or K10).

Although occasionally you will be called or re-raised, and this will cost you your bet, in the long run you will force a good number of folds from loose callers and pick up many hands quickly and without stress. You also continue to project a determined image that you are willing to back your raises up with further bets. This, in turn, will limit the amount of raises your opponents are prepared to call. With this established, you can choose to loosen your play to steal more blinds from your now intimidated opposition.

7 With a choice between calling or raising, raise; with a choice between checking and betting, bet.
For most players it is important to keep the game as simple as possible. Use your bets not only to win more money, but also to discover information. If you call, you discover nothing (until possibly the next round of betting), but if you raise or re-raise, you immediately discover how strong your opponent believes his hand to be.

Similarly, at any time where you feel that you will call a bet if an opponent makes one, make the bet yourself first. This has numerous upsides: your opponent may fold, or he may call this small bet rather than raising, or he may raise (suggesting a very strong hand).

8 Raise into draws; do not fish. Again, this is a general rule and you should be prepared to mix up your style from time to time in order to hide the meaning of your actions. However, very few average players are prepared to make this play, even though it is a basic idea which should be in the mind of every player. It is especially important when you are in position.

Your right-hand opponent raises and you decide to call with 10♠, 9♠.

The flop comes: K♥, 7♠, 4♠.

Your opponent makes a Continuation Bet of 50 per cent of the pot. What should you do?

Many weak players would always call, hoping to hit a spade on the turn. If they didn't, their opponent might well bet again, and then they would be calling for an 18 per cent chance of hitting it on the river. If the spade did come, the opponent might not part with another penny.

Far better is to raise your opponent on the flop. By doing so, you achieve several positive effects:

- Your opponent may have missed the flop and be prepared to fold immediately.
- Your opponent may have a king, but without a top kicker, so he may fold, or call. However, when the turn appears, he may not bet again, fearing that you will raise him again. This allows you to see the river without putting any more money in the pot.
- If you hit your Flush, your opponent may not know that you have hit, and he may commit further chips to the pot if he hits Two Pair or makes trips.

This does not mean that you should always raise into draws; good opponents may re-raise you immediately and force you to commit all your chips. Besides, any play that you make regularly becomes readable, and you want to avoid that. But, as with the advice above, this all contributes to your image of being aggressive, solid, dependable and determined. Since these are the players you should fear the most, this is the player you should seek to be.

9 **Don't stretch to defend your blinds.** It is deeply frustrating to have the player on the button raise every time you are the big blind. The temptation is to teach him a lesson and call his raise, or even re-raise, in an attempt to slow him down. If you are committed to your table, then you may have to do this (I favour the re-raise). However, you need not remain glued to the same table if you find a stubborn and aggressive player two places to your right; you can just leave and find a better spot.

Defending blinds is always hard because you are out of position as soon as the flop falls. The small blind position is the worst; fold most hands there. The big blind position seems to offer a discount on calling for the pot but, believe me, raisers are always delighted to see the big blind call. Be the tightest you have ever been in these two positions.

10 **Don't slow play.** If you are playing in an average mid-stake online cash game, I strongly recommend that you almost never slow play a hand. Most players are paying so little attention to what you are doing, they won't fall for the trap anyway and, in the meantime, you have provided your opponents with more time to hit their hands. If you must slow play, it should be when the flop offers no draw opportunities: no matched-suit cards; no connecting cards which threaten a Straight. Even then, terrible things can happen.

You may argue that the slow play is crucial to maximize your winnings when you have a good hand. You're right. But, such play also maximizes your losses when you have a very big hand and are outdrawn. This is simply because when you hold a monster it is almost impossible to lay it down. So, raising pre-flop with AA may lead to everyone folding, but calling with it and checking the flop may lead to you losing everything when an opponent spikes Two Pair on the turn. So, beware.

Incidentally, check-raises are a form of slow playing and, as such, they carry great inherent risk. If you check, planning to re-raise when your opponent bets, everything will go pear-shaped if he merely checks and sees the turn card for free.

When playing online Poker, the simple Value Bet method is the best for the vast majority of the time: when you think you have the best hand, bet out.

11 Don't miss Value Bets. One of the most significant ways that amateur players fail to optimize their winnings is by failing to make a Value Bet at the end. This bet is made when you believe that you have the best hand and want to be paid more, and it also occludes the times when you want to bet into the hand as a bluff to avoid an almost certain losing showdown. For example:

You raise on A♠, Q♠ and your opponent calls. The flop comes: Q♦, 7♣, 4♦.

You make a Continuation Bet and your opponent calls. The turn comes: 3♣.

You bet again, and your opponent calls. The river comes: 2♣.

Should you check, or should you bet?

The temptation is to check. You might be worried that your opponent has trips or even the Flush, but you should not be. Firstly, if you check and your opponent bets, you will call anyway – it's better to be betting out. Secondly, if he has made a Flush, this is a freak occurrence and can't be helped. If he had trips, surely he would have raised on the flop or turn? It is much more likely that he holds something like KQ or QJ. If you bet now, perhaps 15–25 per cent of the pot, you may get a further call from him – and that is where you make your extra money.

If he re-raises you, you can choose to fold, and you have saved yourself having to call what would probably have been an even bigger bet if you had checked the river. Your bet has therefore acted not only for value if you are winning, but as a blocker bet (against a bigger raise) if you are losing.

Value Bets can occur at any time in the hand. These are situations where you believe you hold the winning hand and you should be making your opponent pay to stay in the hand. Simple Poker, sensibly played, will yield good profits against all but the best players. By and large, you won't find these players in the low- and mid-stake online games.

12 **Know the basic odds.** So many players ignore even the most basic odds at the Poker table. Certainly, Poker is not an entirely odds-based game: that is why it is so popular. However, you should at least know the basic odds, and the simplest way to calculate them is the "Rule of 2 and 4". This is how it works:

You wonder whether you should call a bet made by an opponent. You have four cards to a Flush: what are the odds of hitting it?

Calculate your Outs (the cards which you believe will win the hand for you), and then, if there are still two cards to come (the turn and river), multiply this figure by four and it will give you the rough percentage chance of hitting your card.

If there is only one card to come (the river), multiply the number of Outs by two, and this again provides you with a rough percentage chance.

So, with nine Outs to hit your Flush, on the flop you have a 9 x 4 = 36 per cent chance of hitting your Flush (it's about 35 per cent really); on the turn, you have a 9 x 2 = 18 per cent chance of hitting your Flush. Now you can calculate whether you think it is worth your while to call (or raise).

Of course, you have to consider what action your opponent may take on the next round of betting and whether or not you will get paid more if you do hit your Flush. If you think you will, then you can calculate the cost using "Implied Pot Odds" – what you think you might win if you hit your hand. But, beware: I have heard the phrase "Implied Odds" used as an excuse for a whole multitude of dreadful, costly decisions.

13 Bad beats. I've saved this for last and, appropriately, it is also number thirteen. A bad beat is when, against the odds, an opponent hits his miracle card and ends up beating you off the hand. These occur all the time at Poker, hour after hour, day after day. You get good runs avoiding them, and bad runs when every single draw hits for your opponents and none hit for you.

A terrible beat is when an opponent hits a real long shot to make his hand – perhaps hitting running cards on the turn and river to beat you, or one of two cards that could save him. These are far more rare and they are incredibly frustrating, especially if you know that you are a better player than this opponent and he has just grabbed a whole bunch of your valuable chips through plain dumb luck. However, if you react badly to these situations you may cost yourself more money than the bad beat you have just endured.

Stay calm. Try not to break anything. I do know the pain and frustration and sheer unbelievability of it. It's impossible, unreal, beyond belief! I've been there, and so have all experienced Poker players. Do not think you are uniquely unlucky – you are not. It happens to everyone for a greater or lesser extent of their entire Poker-playing

> **More money is lost by players reacting badly to a bad beat than by the bad beats themselves.**

careers. If you can stay calm and continue to play in a patient and disciplined manner, you will overcome the bad beats and still emerge a winner. You wanted that bad player to call your bet with only a tiny chance of winning because, when he does it next time, and the next time, and the time after that, you will win his money. This occasion, he got lucky; subsequently, he is well against the odds to do so.

Many players get so angry with loose, fishy players that they start raising more, calling more bets, trying to bully the bad player off hands. They forget all their hard, patient work and just go mad. This is known as going "On Tilt", and it is one of the most costly mental states in which to find yourself. If you have been driven completely crazy by your opponent's terrible play and miracle cards, click the "Sit Out Next Hand" box, get out of your chair and have a cold drink, breathe in some fresh air, thump a pillow. Then, return to the table and plan, patiently and carefully, to trap that opponent. If the opponent gives away all your money to another opponent, stay calm; if he leaves the table with your money, stay calm. If you lose control, you will lose your money.

A string of bad beats, even terrible beats, can last for hours, days, weeks, or even months. This is completely within the expected variance of probability and should not be considered any reason to doubt the honesty of the online Poker room.

Keep remembering: you want your opponents to make bad calls against you – that is how you make easy money. However, they will hit their cards sometimes and you must be prepared for that. Do not let their luck change your resolution to play tightly and aggressively and in a disciplined manner.

By the way, this brings me to another crucial point: **Do not assume that your superior skill will result in profits quickly.**

When I play cash games online, I usually play low–mid stakes, because I know that with my style of Poker I will make consistent profits. I prefer an unstressed, relaxing, enjoyable game to a really tough, battling-every-hand-style game. Often, quite objectively, I reassure myself that I am the strongest player at this modest table. But, that does not mean that I will clean up. The cards may be cold, I may get unlucky for two or three big hands, an opponent may be better than I estimated or – and this is a frequent occurrence – my premium hands are diluted by multiple callers. For example:

I hold AA. If I get one caller, I am at least 82 per cent on to win this hand. But, if I get three callers, I am barely 50 per cent on to win. With four callers, I'm odds-against to win the hand. So, if you are at a table where everyone calls everything, your great cards are less strong than usual and you may have to adjust your style to win. Be patient: loose, passive, lame players will lose their money eventually. Make sure that it is to you, when you have ground them down and extricated all their chips from them.

Remain patient through good times and bad – the most patient player will end up with the biggest profits.

Key Information and Playing Tips for Sit & Go Tournaments

Sit & Go events are a brilliant way to practise your tournament Poker since they require almost constant aggression. They are, in effect, Final Tables in a big tournament, so if you go on to make the latter stages of an MTT, you will be well prepared for the intensity of the action.

You choose the event you want to enter from the Sit & Go section of the Lobby. There is usually a choice of entry fees, ranging from $1 up to $1,000. The most popular events range between $10 and $100. Once the table is complete, the site will automatically open a new window and the game will begin.

Take great care when choosing your game, because most sites offer a variety of playing speeds. Although the terminology varies, the styles are usually the same:

• Standard NL Sit & Go	Blinds rise, perhaps every 10–12 minutes.
• Speed, or Fast Sit & Go	Blinds rise, perhaps every 8 minutes.
• Turbo or Super-Turbo Sit & Go	Blind rise, perhaps every 3–5 minutes.

The faster the blinds rise, the quicker the event will be, and the less skill is involved. People who opt for the Turbo or Super-Turbo games are just taking a straight gamble and nothing else. The players who opt for the standard games are hoping that their skill will improve their chances of winning.

If you think that you are a decent Poker player, never, ever play Turbo, or Super-Turbo, Sit & Go events – you are wasting your skill and relying purely on luck.

Note that the entry fee for these events is usually 10 per cent of the stake for full tables and 5 per cent for Heads-Up events.

The prize money is usually paid to the top three players at a 9/10-player table and to the top two players at a 5/6-player table. At Heads-Up tables, the winner takes all.

If you find that you are regularly finishing in the money in these events, you may decide that Sit & Gos are the right form of the game for you to play to make good profits. Remember, however, those entry fees – they all add up, and eat into your overall profits.

In case you do decide to play a Turbo event, the best piece of advice I can offer you is this: start off aggressively and get even more aggressive.

- Don't call at any time; only raise.
- Don't call a raise with a low or mid-pair; either re-raise all-in, or fold.
- Be aware that most players will bet, or raise all-in, on the flop any Straight or Flush draw; be prepared to call them down with top pair and a good kicker.
- Take notes just as diligently for Sit & Go events as for cash games – you can usually see who is playing each event before you have to sign on. Once you find a regular group of predictable players, you have a good chance of cleaning up frequently.

Best Strategy for Online Sit & Go Events

There are many different styles of play that may succeed at this format and your choice will depend to a large extent on the relative playing styles of your opponents. The better you know your opposition, the more you can mix up your game and vary your style of play. However, there is one technique which most experts acknowledge is the best default strategy for Sit & Go formats. Despite the fact that it should be well known, the players I encounter playing Sit & Gos seem to do exactly the opposite. If you can find groups of these players, your chances of winning are enhanced still further.

Break the game into four sections, and follow the guidelines for each of these sections:

1 During the first quartile, play very tight, entering the betting only if you can see a cheap flop with cards which could create big hands (such as suited connectors, or with premium starting hands). Use this time to assess your opponents and decide who seems most likely to be timid, or over-aggressive. Do not play marginal hands, or call down players with hands which may be winning. To win a pot at this stage of the event is far less important than at later stages.

2 Once you reach the second quartile, expect to have lost one player already. Most competitors are over-aggressive early on and frequently bust themselves out of a tournament. You cannot win an event in the first quartile, but you can lose it.

During this second stage, use your tight image, established by folding the vast majority of hands during the first quartile, to increase your raise frequency when in position. Aim to steal blinds – which will have risen two to three levels since the beginning. Do not fight too hard on marginal hands.

If there are short-stacks to your left, be more prepared to pressure them. They may choose to re-raise all-in, but you should not be too afraid to call them – these players are, generally, desperate.

3   In the third quartile, if you are doing well, you can retain a modestly tight/aggressive image and select your hands carefully. However, be aware of the blind size. Statistically, your chances of hitting several premium hands in a row is very small, so you cannot expect to rescue a low chip count with good cards. Instead, the moment that you reach the stage where you hold less than ten big blind bets, you must start pushing in your stack at any time you believe that you have good fold equity (a good chance that your opponent[s] will fold, added to the chance you have to win the hand). For example, the blinds are at 50–100, and you have 960 chips left.

The player on the button raises to 250 and you hold KJ . This is the right time to re-raise all-in. You still have enough chips to make him consider a fold with mid-sized aces. You may have the best hand and, even if he holds a monster, like A, you still have close on a 40 per cent chance of winning the hand anyway. All this adds up to well over a 50 per cent chance of taking down the pot, and that is why you must push immediately.

If you allow yourself to be blinded away, when you do make a move you will have no fold equity left, because it will be too cheap for an opponent to fold to your bet/raise. Now, you rely solely on your hand standing up at showdown. This is why you must push aggressively the moment that you become short-stacked. If you get knocked out, that's too bad, but at least go out fighting and with the odds in your favour.

Towards the end of this third quartile, you will often be left with the prize-money places and the bubble (the last place which pays no prize). This is a prime time to up the aggression since no one wants to go out of a tournament on the bubble. The player to attack is not always the shortest stack, but sometimes the second shortest. If this player feels that, by playing passively, he can slip into the money, then he will be more inclined to pass to your raise than the shortest stack, who may feel that his only chance of making the money is to take you on. This is an important and often-overlooked tactic. If you continuously attack, you will find that, most of the time, people curl up and concede to you, so desperate are they not to be knocked out. If you can exploit this situation to the full, you will not only make it into the money regularly, but you will also find yourself in the chip lead, giving yourself maximum chances to win the event.

I believe that winning should always be your target; prizes for second and third place are often pretty small and you should be aiming for the big one.

Remember also that hand values increase as players leave the table. Do not stick to premium hands, but play any two cards with potential strongly whenever you are in position.

As a general rule (to be adapted to the situation as you find it), do not take your foot off the gas in these situations since, with the blinds high and moving around the table fast, if you choose to pass a few marginal hands you may find that your stack is greatly reduced after only a short time. Keep being aggressive and, if you run into some huge hands, it is just bad luck. Studied aggression is, without doubt, the best tactic in the second half of a Sit & Go event.

Never let yourself be blinded away to extinction – that is a feeble way to exit a Poker tournament.

Remember that even a hand like 10, 4 has a decent chance against even a monster hand like A (31.5 per cent), and that is why you must push while you still have sufficient chips to induce a fold from a mid-strength opponent.

4   In the final stages of the Sit & Go, when you have made the money positions, most players loosen up and become quite freely aggressive once again. Remain in courageous mood and remember that hand values increase dramatically the fewer players there are. Queen-high hands are well above average in Heads-Up play and you should be inclined to raise with them. If the blinds are too high to allow for any meaningful betting exchanges early on, just be prepared to play an all-in game. small and mid-Pairs are worth an immediate all-in bet, raise, or re-raise.

Note also that for every blind you steal when Heads-Up, you gain double that size of swing. If the blinds are 400–800, if you can steal those blinds you win a total of 1,200 and deprive your opponent of 1,200. That is an overall swing of 2,400 – a massive amount when there is likely only 9,000–10,000 chips in play.

To win a Sit & Go – and even more so, a multi-table tournament – you will need to be lucky as well as exercising aggressive, but studied play. In a standard 9/10-player Sit & Go, you will probably have to win at least three 50–50 chances, or "races" as they are known (hands like 99 versus AK), as well as possibly winning against odds hands 40–60, or even 30–70 hands (such as AQ versus AK). If you don't win these, you won't win the event. However, since this is the same for everyone, your duty is to try to persuade your opponents to fold when you are behind (by raising strongly), and to call when you are ahead (by suggesting weakness or indecision).

Beware switching from Sit & Gos to cash games. The styles are very different and to take such an aggressive style into a cash game could cost you a lot of money. Make sure you calm yourself down before playing a cash game. It is especially difficult to adapt between styles if you are playing two tables simultaneously: a Sit & Go and a cash game. I have found from experience that unless you are very focused, you can make the wrong play at both tables and knock yourself out.

Key Information and Playing Tips for Multi-Table Tournaments (MTT)

Multi-Table Tournaments are certainly the cheapest way to experience plenty of Poker action, often against quite good players. For an entry fee as low as $1 (and if your site offers weekly Freerolls – as many do – then no money at all), you can play for hours, with a good starting stack of chips and plenty of chances to try out your moves.

One of the reasons why so many young players have become very good at tournament Poker so quickly is because of the ability to practise online, against good players, hour after hour after hour. Whereas traditionally you would have to seek out smoky Poker clubs and illicit gambling dens, now anyone 18 years old can start to play from the comfort of their own home. The interesting thing about a big MTT is that you will encounter really terrible players, who seem to have no idea at all, and very wily players who seem to know what you have and how best to extract the maximum from you. This experience is priceless.

Tournament Selection

There are a number of different styles of tournament from which to choose and each has its own characteristics. Knowing the effect on your fellow players is very important in deciding how you should play.

Freerolls

As the name suggests, this is a free chance to play in a tournament. These events usually draw big crowds of less experienced players wanting to try their hand at a MTT. Because no one has paid an entry fee and the field seems so enormous, you will usually find that play is very loose from the first hand onwards. Since the prize money is often quite small, unless you are playing purely for practice, it makes sense to be pretty aggressive with any decent hand early on and try to build a big stack of chips. Your real aim should be to take control of your table and stay in that position to challenge for the cash prizes. If you play with an average or short stack and then get eliminated after three hours of play for no prize, it can be quite depressing.

Satellites

The key to these tournaments is discovering which positions pay anything at all. In a MTT satellite, anyone from the winner only, to the top 20 players, is usually seen gaining a seat in the main event. Sometimes, the player just below the qualifying position wins a small cash prize (the remains of the entry fees that are not sufficient to pay for a seat in the main event). Since you gain nothing for finishing outside the prize sector, remember that reaching the final 20 or 30 players out of a large field may be a personal achievement but it gets you no closer to winning a seat in the big event than if you had been knocked out on the first hand. Be prepared to be bold and take risks to build your stack.

Events with Re-Buys

You will find many online MTTs offering re-buys – either one, two or an unlimited number – for the first hour of the event. If you fall below a certain chip level, or get wiped out, this allows you to re-buy chips to re-build your stack. Players like these events as it gives them carte blanche to be hyper-aggressive in the early stages (trying to build a big stack), while knowing that they cannot be eliminated because, for the first hour, they can always re-buy.

In addition, if there are 200 players entered at $10 per player (forming a prize-pool of $2,000), by the time the re-buy period ends there could easily be $6,000 in the prize-pool, making it a highly worthwhile tournament to enter.

In tournaments where there is a single re-buy, or perhaps two, players will start off being moderately aggressive.

In tournaments where there are unlimited re-buys, players will start off very aggressively, especially if the re-buy costs less than the original entry. This will include all-in plays when they are on Straight and Flush draws. This knowledge does mean that you will be presented with opportunities to get all your money in early on against such players, with a 60–65 per cent chance to take down the hand.

In tournaments where there are unlimited re-buys, but these costing the same as the tournament entry, or for a higher price, you will see players being less aggressive.

Knowing this, you have the choice of being quite conservative, but playing your premium hands very strongly, or going wild with the rest of the field. I favour the more conservative approach because, more often than not, I can build a good stack, not have to re-buy and then play for a greatly inflated prize pool, all for the price of my original entry. If not the most fun, this approach is certainly the most cash efficient; it will mean that you are enjoying the best possible value for money for the entry fee.

Events with Add-Ons

An MTT with an add-on allows you to purchase additional chips at the end of the Add-On Period, which is usually the first hour. For a price often less than the original entry fee you can buy a proportion of the original starting stack, and sometimes the same amount, to add to your stack.

If you enter an event with an add-on, unless you are well ahead of the average chip count you should take the add-on, since most others will, or you will be left playing a short-stack game from an early point in the event. So, when you choose to play in an event with an add-on, factor the price into the entrance fee, and ensure that you are happy to pay it.

Events with Rebuys and Add-Ons

Most events which offer re-buys will also offer an add-on. Expect play to be wild and super-aggressive for the first hour. Usually, after the re-buy and add-on period has ended, everyone settles down. The blinds are often relatively small considering how many more extra chips are in play, and there is time to consolidate. However, less experienced players often do not change gear, and continue playing recklessly. This is the moment when, if you are patient, you can pick up a lot of chips from undisciplined players.

Free-Out Events (Events Without Re-buys or Add-Ons)

This is the purest form of tournament, where you start with, say, 2,000 chips, and if you go all-in, even on the first hand, and lose, you are out. In these events, the winning tactics are to follow the style of play recommended for Sit & Go events, but to extend the duration of the quartiles.

All decent online Poker sites will show you the state of the tournament at any given time, usually by pressing an on-screen button saying "Tournament Stats". This will show you how many players are remaining, in what position you stand, and what the average chip-stack should be. This is great information to have, because you can use it to adjust your playing style. Whenever you fall below the average chip-stack, your thoughts should be on becoming more aggressive and trying to create action for yourself. If you fall to within ten big blinds, then you must attempt to double through, even if it results in being eliminated. The reason for this aggression is threefold:

1   If you allow yourself to become too short-stacked, you lose the ability to raise opponents off the pot. The moment you become reliant on picking up a premium hand, you are relying solely on luck – you have lost control.

2   If you leave yourself short approaching the bubble, everyone will attack your stack, perhaps even ganging up on you to eliminate you from the event.

3   Even if you do make it into the money, it is rarely worth cashing in the lowest positions. You want to be

able to challenge for the final table where the real money will be paid out. It is better to go out ahead of the race for the bubble, than to be clinging on for dear life just to make it into the money.

Not only will having a positive, winning attitude help you to put yourself in with a chance of making the big money, but it will also help you throughout the event, because you must be fearless. If you are afraid of going out of an MTT, then you will not play good Poker.

Playing Tips for Freeze-Out MTT – No-Limit Texas Hold 'Em

In the **First Quartile**, play tight and do not threaten your stack unless you can apply high pressure on opponents. Many experts fold even very strong cards during this period, as they believe that there is so little point to winning small pots at this stage if there is any risk of diminishing their stacks. Any situation where you believe you might be in a 50–50 race should be folded cheaply. Races are for later in the event where, when you win, it transforms your position.

Keep observing your opponents and, if you do raise, keep the raise big (X4 or X5) to ensure that you gain information if they do call you. You should be developing a tight image at the table.

During the **Second Quartile**, keep studying the average chip count and become more aggressive if you fall too much below that. It is easy to let everyone overtake you during this stage. Remember that you will have to take on 50–50 hands if you are to progress to the later stages of the event, but at this stage taking on short-stacked opponents allows you to increase your stack if you win, but not be knocked out if you lose.

The **Third Quartile** is the key section of the event. Firstly, remember that the value of the chips has increased and any mid-sized pot you win now could be very significant. Also, do not be afraid to call or raise bets for seemingly massive sums. Everyone has big stacks now and raising 2,000 chips at this point of the game is no more dramatic than raising 100 chips during the first quartile. Often, less experienced players become afraid to commit so many chips to the pot, and they call instead of raising. You must resist this temptation, and continue to be bold.

There is also the additional factor that, as well as steadily increasing blinds, most events introduce Ante Bets at this stage, increasing the size of the pot before anyone has even seen their cards. This puts a premium on stealing blinds and not allowing too many players to see the flop. Ante Bets usually start at 50 chips per player, making 450–500 chips in the pot even before the blinds, and they continue rising with the blinds. This whittles down your stack even more. Never think that tournament Poker is relaxing: you have to be on top form and highly focused at all times.

Assuming that you are not short-stacked (if you are, you must start to play hyper-aggressively and seek a double through), this is the moment to increase your aggression slowly but surely. Your generally tight image must now be transformed into a player who re-raises with decent hands in position, and raises big when on a nut Straight (the highest possible Straight) or Flush draw. Players who are approaching the bubble short-stacked should be bullied and raised and put to the test. You should be able to judge who is folding in a lot of hands and who is prepared to stand up to you. Pick opponents carefully and pressurize them.

Keep in mind that very short-stacked players may be prepared to call lightly just to give themselves a chance to double through and remain in the event. Psychologically, the players most likely to fold to a big raise, or re-raise, are those who are just above what might be described as a short stack. These players will be feeling reasonably confident that, if they play tightly, they can squeeze past the bubble and into the prize money. They will be very reluctant to risk that position by taking on an aggressive player (particularly if they have noticed that you have been tight up until now).

This choice of opponent can be very lucrative to you. It is a prime tip to help you gather chips. It is, of course, dependent upon these players being in a suitable position for you, but if you can exploit them the fold equity you hold against them is massive.

Do not be afraid to go out just ahead of, or on, the bubble. You do not want to be struggling among the low prize winners when you probably have a better than 50 per cent chance of making it to the big money if you act aggressively now. There will be plenty of timid players just glad to make it to the money and it is those players whom you must pick on to gather chips.

Bear in mind that the lower prizes are usually little more than your entry fee money back, or a small premium. This is not why you should play MTTs; if that is your aim, play low-stake Sit & Gos and settle for any paying position. If you enter a MTT, go for the big prizes, because the reason why you enter a tournament with several hundred, or even several thousand, players is to have a shot at a meaningful prize.

As a general rule, to play an opposite style to that which prevails at your table is good Poker policy. And, so it is in a

MTT. If players appear nervous or timid, that is the time to raise aggressively. If players seem relaxed and confident, with healthy chip-stacks, beware of attacking them without premium hands. However, also be aware that if you are relatively short-stacked, they will attack you aggressively on marginal hands.

The **Fourth Quartile** action can get quite stressful, and it is certainly exciting. I advise keeping your eyes firmly on the top prizes and not minding if you are eliminated while trying to build a really convincing stack for the final table. Unless you are incredibly lucky, both with cards and the action that you are shown with them, you cannot reach a Final Table without great aggression, good luck and utter determination.

If you succeed in reaching the Final Table, study the payout schedule to discover what positions pay the biggest premiums. You often find that the bottom five or six players receive relatively little, while the really big payouts come to those in the top four or five. If that is the case, you might choose to set your sights on the top area finish and, if the cards favour you, then aim for the title. This is a typical payout table for a mid-range, say $30 entry fee, tournament:

1st	$1,450
2nd	$970
3rd	$815
4th	$570
5th	$415
6th	$220
7th	$175
8th	$150
9th	$110

The big jump occurs between fifth and sixth places. The top five places should therefore be your prime aim. If you become short at the final table and have a genuine chance of hanging on until you hit fifth place, you might choose to do that. However, the difference between ninth and sixth is really not that great, so be aggressive early on and try to double your stack and get in a really strong position.

If you make it to the last few players, kept focused on how the hand values steadily increase as the number of players decreases, and keep up the pressure on your opponents at all times.

Remember that winning big money in a MTT is a long shot. These events are primarily a good way to enjoy a good game of aggressive Poker for a set buy-in. If you are new to MTTs, start by trying to make the top third of the field. Then, move on to making it past the bubble and into the low payouts. Once you have achieved these goals, you should be prepared to be more aggressive towards the bubble area and really play hard to make it into the money with sufficient chips to make a run for the Final Table.

If you play just one MTT a week online, it is easy to over-value its importance. Bear in mind that professional players don't just enter one event. They are prepared to play in multiple events. If they get knocked out of one, they take two minutes to get over it, and dive straight back into the next one. A MTT is a highly speculative Poker proposition and one which, for the vast majority of the time, will not result in winnings. However, make the big money just once, and you have set yourself for entry fees and cash games for months, if not years, to come.

Remember:

- Most sites schedule a five-minute break, either every hour, or every two hours. Use that time to eat, re-fill your drink and take some exercise. It really can make a big difference to your performance.

- Keep checking your stack in relation to the average. Be aware of the need to change gears, increasing aggression whenever you become short. The moment you approach ten big blinds, start pushing strongly. Never let yourself fall below about eight big blinds. Get all your chips in quickly and hope, either to bully your opponents into folding, and stealing their blinds, or to get a call and double through.

- As a general rule, you want your chips in the pot first at all times in tournament Poker. Leave your opponents to make the tough decisions. Avoid calling lots of bets and hoping for miracle cards. Betting first gives you far more ways to win the pot.

General Quick Tips for Online Play

- If you play on more than one site, choose your site depending on the time of day. In Europe, if you play in the morning, you can often find American players who have been online all night long; Far Eastern players can be found in the same situation when you play in the evenings. Use every possible method to gain an advantage over your opposition.

- Use your first decent withdrawal of profits to invest in a comfortable chair. You are going to be sitting in it for hours on end. Protect your back and stay comfortable.

- Drink – soft drinks preferably. A lack of water dulls the brain, while plenty of liquids enhances concentration. This is a scientific fact.

- Exercise. Ensure that you get up out of your chair and walk around, stretch and swing your arms, every hour, even for just one minute. It will make a big difference.

- If you must chat, do not insult the lousy players at your table. You want to keep them there to win their money. Compliment them or say nothing. Never get into an argument, because this distracts you from the really important business in hand.

- Take your ego out of the equation. Even the best players make fools of themselves sometimes – that is in the nature of the game. Stay positive and confident, but don't believe that, just because you have won a few sessions, you are God's gift to Poker.

- Resist the temptation to move up a level in stakes just because you have won a couple of sessions at your current stake. Poker players experience wild fluctuations in fortune and winning a couple of sessions proves nothing about your relative strengths and weaknesses.

- Do not play online Poker while you are working. You will neither work efficiently, nor play well. Reserve some time for Poker and focus on it with 100 per cent of your concentration.

- Show discipline when you are badly beaten on numerous occasions. Review the hands carefully and check that you bet the right amount at the right time and did not provide free cards or offer your opponent the correct odds (i.e. by betting too small an amount you may have offered your opponent the correct odds to call your bet, stay in the hand, and hope to hit the crucial cards they needed to beat you; if you had bet more at the right moment, this would have dissuaded a wise opponent from paying such a large sum to call your bet and remain in the pot).

- If you are being beaten against the odds by loose opponents, accept that runs of bad luck can occur at any time and sometimes last for thousands of hands. Providing you are getting your money in correctly, when ahead, in the long run you will end up in profit.
- Cards look better the fewer you see: if you have a run of terrible cards you may become tempted to start playing hands which are, in truth, marginal. Playing these hands will allow patient opponents to take advantage of you. Good players wait for these opportunities to make money from undisciplined players.
- In cash games, if you win a couple of decent-sized pots and find yourself with more chips than anyone else, the temptation will be to play more pots. In tournament play, this is sometimes right, as you try to pressurize your shorter-stacked opponents, but in cash games, if your style is to be tighter/aggressive in comparison to the other players at your table, then mixing up your style just because you have a few chips does not make sense. You spoil your table image and, unless you get lucky, leak chips. This is a double-whammy: your respect is lost and you feel that you should play catch-up.
- Poker should be fun; if it is upsetting you, costing you too much money, or causing you to become aggressive and/or paranoid, take a break.

NB At the time of writing, all gaming sites based in the United States are of dubious legality and it remains illegal for US citizens to gamble online. However, during 2009, two bills have been presented to legislators in attempts to reform this situation. It may well be that US and global operators can once again target the world's potentially biggest online Poker audience legally.

27
Live Poker Rooms

TO PLAY POKER in a card room demands that you have a good, solid knowledge of the style of game you want to play, that you have had experience with friends, or online, and that you have money which you are prepared to lose.

This short section deals with your options when you play Poker in a casino, or club, card room, what to expect, and how best to prepare. If you want to update and improve your Poker knowledge, then there is a *Mammoth Book of Poker* which, since I wrote it, I recommend to you!

At the end of the twentieth century, many casinos had abandoned their card rooms in favour of using the space for more Slot machines. The revenues from half-empty Poker rooms were so low it wasn't even worth paying the staff to operate them. With the advent of global television coverage of Poker, the demand to play the game when in a casino (and the attendant action that casinos discovered it encouraged), persuaded casino owners to re-instate their card rooms and promote the action available on their properties. Now, all over the world, leading casinos have made way for Poker tables – from high-stake cash games to low-stake tournaments – all designed to encourage more players through their doors and, from their point of view, hopefully onto the tables and the Slots.

Casinos now sponsor huge tournaments, attracting hundreds, and even thousands, of players from all over the world to descend on their properties. Poker players bring friends and family with them and it is these people, as well as the insatiable desire for another gambling opportunity, that fills the casinos with players at the tables and on the Slots.

Home Game Versus Card Room

No matter how successful you are in your regular home games, you will probably find that there is a massive difference between your regular school and the crowd you encounter in a card room. To start, you won't know anything about your opponents' styles or tactics which, after playing against people whose games you know very well, will seem very strange.

Unless you encounter a privately arranged game within a card room, you won't find any strange Poker variations either, so there will be no wild cards, card swapping, or special side bets. You will probably find that the game is taken more seriously than you are used to and that the standard is higher than you might expect. This is not to say that the lower-stake games (and some of the higher stakes too) are not inhabited by a selection of loose, passive, fishy players who lose session after session, but among them will be plenty of professional players and semi-professional players.

You will also note that, unless you strike it lucky with a jolly crowd at your table, the atmosphere will be quieter and more serious than in your home games. You may find this reduces your pleasure in playing: Poker isn't always a sociable game.

Playing in a Card Room for the First Time

Take your time to observe the action in any card room in which you plan to play. If possible, chat to some of the players and seek their views about the overall standard, which games to avoid and which players to watch out for. Talk also to the card room staff – the manager if possible – and see what he/she recommends as a good starting place for you. Within a few hours of playing there, you will pick up the vibe and start feeling at home but, for that first visit, you want to judge where you play well.

If the card room is busy, you may need to place yourself on a waiting list with the card-room staff. When a seat becomes free, you will be called to the table.

Which Game to Play

The best advice here is to stick to a game as close to the one you are used to as possible. If you venture into new territory – maybe because it is the only game going – it is very unlikely that you will succeed. You will present a nervous, indecisive table image, and you will make it easy for the sharks to pick you off.

The fundamental decision to make is which game to play. These are the usual options (although every card room has its own variations):

Limit Texas Hold 'Em

The game will be described by bet size, usually starting at $1/$2 and moving up through $10/$20 to $50/$100 and higher. The lower figure represents the size of bet and raise available to players pre-flop and on the flop, the second figure the size of bet and raise on the turn and river. The number of raises is usually limited per round. If you are used to playing No-Limit Texas Hold 'Em, you will find that a Limit game seems slow and far more mathematical. The value of the hands plays a far higher role in deciding the outcome, since pressurizing raises cannot be made.

Many semi-professional and professional players opt for Limit Poker since they realize that it offers far more pot control than a No-Limit game and allows their fluent knowledge of pot and drawing odds to guide them to the correct mathematical decisions. The problem with encountering these players is that they rarely make a mistake and it is from opponents' mistakes that most amateur players make their money.

No-Limit Texas Hold 'Em

The world's most popular Poker game has overtaken many card rooms now and the lower-stake games usually encourage less experienced players. Whenever you play in a new club or card room, even if you rate yourself as a good player, I urge you to start off in a low-stake game just to get the feel for the style of play. You may find that the club or card room games are far tougher than those you are used to; players are more aggressive pre-flop, allow fewer flops, and back up raises with testing Continuation Bets and re-raises.

Once you have the feel of the standard, and your place within it, then you can branch out to higher-stake tables.

Omaha

This variation, with four hole cards, of which you must employ exactly two to create your hand, is another form gaining in popularity. There are standard versions, as well as High/Low variations, and some card rooms offer tables where the High/Low variation is played in alternate rounds with NL Texas Hold 'Em.

Seven-Card Stud

Considered by professional players to be the most skilful variation of Poker, and one where the skill rises readily to the surface, these games can be very testing indeed. Versions from standard to Hi/Lo are usually played.

In one well-known card room in Las Vegas, the manager told me that the regular game consisted of full-time Poker pros just waiting for the tourists to arrive. When they did, they left soon afterwards, every last ounce of flesh ripped from their fishy bones. The really worrying thing was how friendly and welcoming these pros were to every new player who joined their table. Remember that at Poker the games start even before the cards are dealt.

Razz

Razz is not normally played as a stand-alone game (it is more commonly found as part of the H.O.R.S.E. variation

– see below), although I have seen it offered independently on occasion. It is normally played for ace-to-five low, so-called "Lowball Poker". The object is to make the lowest possible five-card hand from the seven cards you are dealt. In Razz, Straights and Flushes do not count as high hands, and the ace always plays low. The best possible Razz hand is 5-4-3-2-A, known as the "Wheel" or the "Bicycle". Also played sometimes is 2-7 Razz.

Stud and Draw Games

You will still find the original Poker games. Some card rooms have a long-established Five-Card Stud game as well as a Five-Card Draw game. They tend to be inhabited by old-timers who enjoy the psychological elements of the game more than all the newfangled variations. Beware these characters: they know their game and they are experts at reading their opponents.

H.O.R.S.E.

A combination of variations – Texas Hold Hold 'Em, Omaha Hi/Lo, Razz, Seven-card Stud, and Seven-card Stud Hi/Lo – is usually played in tournaments and is considered the ultimate test of a Poker player's all-round ability, but it can also be found as cash games where the game changes after each circuit of the table. However, these games are becoming increasingly popular both online and in card rooms as cash-game alternatives. If you are an all-rounder, you will find that you test all your skills at these tables. Once again, these games tend to attract the strongest players. Beware playing if your knowledge of some variations is weaker than others as you will find that opponents soon discover this and start to pressurize you quickly.

Key Tips for New Players

- **Appear confident.** Experienced players, usually local
  to the casino or card room, lie in wait for the tourists,
  hoping to pick up easy money from gamblers on short
  stays who are over-eager, loosened with alcohol and
  wanting to play fast and loose. The first people they pick
  on are those who seem inexperienced and lacking
  confidence. This is why it is so important to take time to
  pick your table and game, play for a stake which does not
  worry you at all, and project an air of calm patience and
  focused determination. If you can do that, the better
  players will show you some respect.
- **Buy-in for the maximum.** If you buy-in for the full
  available amount, this shows confidence in your own
  ability, that you mean to play for a sustained period, and
  that you are not afraid to push in your stack when you
  believe the moment is right to do so. If, on the other
  hand, you buy-in for the minimum, this prevents you
  from making scary raises on your opponents, forces you
  into playing short-stack Poker, and projects an air of fear
  or even desperation. Far better to buy-in for the
  maximum at a minimum stake table, than only a
  proportion of it at a higher-stake table.
- **Play tight for the first 45 minutes at a new table.**
  You want to play Poker – that's why you've come to the
  card room. It will go against your instincts to play so few
  hands, because you've come here for action. However,
  some discipline early on can set you up, not only for the
  rest of your stay, but also for future visits, because word
  on players spreads like wildfire around the locals and
  regulars. Whatever your default style, discipline yourself

to play tight for the first 30 minutes to an hour. Make sure you turn over only big hands and that you fold any marginal situations. This sets up the image that you are not out of control, or over-eager to play, but that you will wait for your moments to push forward. If you see few cards during this time and appear very tight, you can use this to your advantage later, when you can start to raise and re-raise players off the pot on semi-bluffs, expecting them to show you respect after your early showing. It is very easy to blow all table image very quickly and then it makes reading your opponents' hands more difficult and, strangely, you become more, not less, reliant on holding good cards.

- **Players you want to avoid:** Very focused players, who are clearly not sitting at the table for enjoyment. Complete drunks, who slow up the game and ultimately frustrate everyone, making reads harder to come by and inducing you to play over-aggressively. Players who are of retirement age who seem very friendly among each other, but unfriendly to new arrivals – these may be the locals waiting to pick you off. Avoiding the bad games can be worth far more to you than a run of brilliant hands. Game selection both in live games and online rates as one of the most important skills at Poker – if you want to win!

- **Players you want at your table:** Loud, happy players, who are drinking, but who are not yet completely drunk – these players are there to play and they will almost certainly play way too many hands and bluff more frequently than is sensible. They are there to have fun, and they don't care if they win or not. Players who have friends around them, who are showing their cards to the onlookers. Players who show their cards all the time, especially when there is no need: this is a sign of insecurity. Players who seem nervous, are biting their nails and chewing their lips: this might be a false tell but, almost always, it is not – they feel out of their depth and they are showing it. If you are playing Limit Poker, then younger players present are often just learning the game and are using the limited stakes to ensure they do not lose too much in the process. Beware younger players in No-Limit games, because these are often successful online players who are preparing for more live play and tournament play by practising their mathematical games for cash. They may not be that experienced but they will be very aggressive and these are players who are tough to play against.

- **Seat choice.** If you have been watching and doing your research, and you join a table which is just starting, you may get the chance to pick your seat. Given that choice, you should aim to have aggressive players to your right so that you can act after them, and calling, passive players to your left so that you are unlikely to be raised, or squeezed, out of the pot.

- **Remain aware of game conditions.** Stay alert to the changing conditions at your table. You may join a table perfect for you, with the players seated in about the right positions, your image firmly established in their minds, and the betting and pot size completely within your control. However, if one weak player leaves and is replaced by a player of greater skill, or just of a very different style, the dynamic of the game can change quickly. As the number of players at your table falls, so the value of the hands increases, and experienced players will know this and adjust their play immediately. Be prepared to leave the table if you feel that your spell has been broken. There are plenty of other games available, and you can always return to your original table, having eaten a meal, or stretched your legs.

- **Straddle Bets.** Most card rooms permit Straddle Bets in many games, and you need to keep an eye out for these situations, because you can be pressurized into making them, and embarrassed if they take you by surprise. Imagine you have bought into a mid-stake NL Hold 'Em game, where the blinds are \$5/\$10, and the maximum buy-in is \$1,000. To your dismay, on the first hand, the player in first position makes a bet, before the cards are dealt, which represents a doubling of the big blind – \$20. The next player bets \$40 and the next \$80. These are blind Straddle Bets designed to increase the pressure on players in the later positions. They are sheer gamblers' bets, but the effect on you is enormous. Just to call to join the hand will cost you 8 per cent of your stack and to raise you may feel that you need to bet about \$200 – 20 per cent of your entire stack.

  Incidentally, if you don't want to straddle, don't. If the player to your right tells you that everyone makes this bet, just shrug and say: "Not me". You may get a few frowns, but no one is allowed to tell you how to bet your chips and the fact that you've refused to bow to their demands shows you have a mind of your own. However, if you are unhappy with the game, just stand up and seek another table.

- **Tipping.** You want the card-room staff on your side, so watch the level of tips offered to the dealer when you

win a pot and mimic it. If you are playing low-stake
Poker, $1 will be ample when you win the pot, or even
50c if the pot is won after one bet only. For higher-stake
games, observe the common policy and follow that.

- **From online to live – watch out for tells and facial
  expressions.** Here, I mean your own. I've done it myself
  and been pretty ashamed to notice my lack of discipline.
  You move from online Poker to the real thing and, so used
  are you to banging the table, pulverizing the mouse and
  sliding down your chair in despair as the flop misses you for
  the 500th time that, come the moment you are in the real
  world, you forget yourself and show all that emotion.
  Younger players in particular often show their emotions
  broadly and obviously, from the slumping of shoulders and
  sitting back in their chairs, exhaling loudly and shaking their
  heads when flops miss, to sitting up attentively and ham
  acting when they hold big cards and have hit the board.
  Don't believe that people cannot be this poor at hiding their
  reactions to Poker situations, because every time I play, I am
  amazed how often I see this.

- **Key tells.** There are thousands of both obvious and very
  subtle tells which can be studied for live play. There are
  many books on these but, usually, experience is the best
  way of learning individual tells. One key factor: does the
  player providing you with what you read as a tell know
  you are watching him? If he does, then the tell may be
  deliberately misleading. A tell given when a player is not
  aware that you are watching is far more reliable. To get
  you thinking along the right lines, here are just a few of
  the best known tells which, despite their notoriety, still
  crop up regularly:

- Weak is strong; strong is weak. For most players (not the professionals or the true experts) the most common tell is to act weak when you are strong and strong when weak. Amazingly, despite this being so well known, it is still the most common and reliable tell there is. And, it works against most players, which is why it is still perpetuated by so many players, including the very good ones.

- Flop staring. This is a sign that the player has missed the flop; if he had hit, he would not be drawing attention to himself. However, the fact that he continues to stare suggests that he has a draw and is assessing what outs he might have to win the hand.

- Fast calling. Not a certainty, but often a drawing hand, as with a made hand, a raise might be considered to protect against drawing players.

- Chip reaching or touching. A player who starts to fiddle with his chips, or count out chips, even before you have acted ahead of him, almost certainly has no desire to continue in the hand. He may be hoping that you check to provide a free card for a long-shot draw, but he is most unlikely to raise. If he wanted to raise, he would want your money in the pot first.

- Chip directing and player stares. Any move made by a player which directly plays back at a bettor or raiser, or indeed the only other player left in, suggests a bluff or semi-bluff move. The focus on the opponent is intended to intimidate, but if the player has such a good hand why would he want to do this? Instead, he would bet quietly and hope that he continues to see action.

28
Casino Comps

WHEREVER YOU play, I want you to remember this: you are doing the casino a big favour gambling at their establishment. They will make money from you in the long run and, if you don't gamble sensibly, they will make a lot of money. In return, if they want your business, they should make you feel welcome.

Outside of the United States, unless you are gambling absolute minimums, slowly, the casino should be looking after you. This will range from a friendly welcome from dealers and supervisors, to free drinks and perhaps cigarettes and cigars.

If you are a mid-range player, then you should expect to be offered a meal in the casino's restaurant, with fine wines and a chance to entertain friends.

As a high roller – as a rough guide, we are talking about players who stake a minimum of $10,000 per session (with perhaps several sessions per day) – on top of all the other hospitality, well-run casinos and clubs should offer you a limo (or a taxi), invitations to special events and parties, accommodation on site, or even at a local top hotel, and a personal welcome whenever you play.

Casinos attached to hotels should offer you big discounts on your stay and, the higher your bets, the grander the accommodation should be. A real high roller will stay exclusively in the best suites, pay for nothing and may even be flown around the world just to gamble.

If the casino in which you play is well run, you will not need to do anything to benefit from these privileges. Good management should spot your excellent action and a host or manager should approach you to offer you benefits. If they don't, and you want a meal or to entertain a friend, then speak to the casino manager.

In Las Vegas, above all places, what you gamble makes you who you are. If you are a low roller, or a hobby gambler, no one pays much attention to you; if you are a mid-stake player, you'll enjoy some modest benefits. As the size of your bankroll increases – win or lose – so will the casino's desire to keep you happy and playing on their premises. You are what you bet – nothing more, nothing less.

Player's Card

In the US, and especially in Las Vegas, unless you are an exceedingly high roller, or even a "Whale" (a $500,000-in-a-weekend player), you will generally need to enrol in the casino, or casino group's, Player's Card scheme. The advantage of a Player's Card that covers all properties within a company's holdings is that you can visit several casinos and have all your action rated on one card, allowing you to claim your benefits at the hotel where you are staying. This makes it more likely that your food and accommodation will be covered during your stay.

If you are loaded you might want to experience the high life for a long weekend in Vegas – I've witnessed it from the sidelines. The Whales arrive by the casino's private jet (some casinos have private 737s and 757s too, to collect their favourite clients from around the world). The limo meets the plane's passengers often on the tarmac. For the true high roller there is no need to join the general public: they enter their hotel through separate VIP doors (no standing in line to check in), play in private rooms, relax in villas with private pools and gold where gold really should not be, grand rooms and 24-hour butler service. Their wives and girlfriends hold parties, hit the nightlife and go shopping at the most glamorous addresses – all on the casino's tab.

For us mortals on the Strip, casinos usually expect a minimum of $25 per bet at Blackjack, Craps, Baccarat and other Table Games before they start rewarding you. If you plan to play these games at $25–$100 per bet then, when you first play at a table, ask a supervisor for a Player's Card. You will need identification – that's all. Usually, within half an hour, you have your card. Every time you join a new table, show this card to the supervisor so that he can rate your level of play, your time of arrival and when you leave. The casinos have a simple equation based on how much, on average, they expect to win from your play, and what small percentage of this they offer back to you in comps. These may range from free meals, free accommodation, upgrades to suites, shopping sprees and limos. These days, almost everything is decided by the computer; the supervisor has very little personal discretion.

If you follow the guidelines in this book, you will lose less (and win more) than the casino expects, and your comps will represent an asset to your gambling funds. To enjoy a stay in Vegas, leave with a modest profit, and pay no hotel bill – that's the high life for me.

Incidentally, the supervisor's job is probably the most depressing of all. He spends all day sorting out Player's Cards, comps and line passes, dealing with moaning gamblers and complaining clients. So, if you have a problem with anything, ask for the pit boss or the duty manager. Make a point of complimenting the supervisor; make him or her your friend and let the top brass take the heat. This works really well in Vegas, because the top guys have the influence and can make things happen, and those lower down the food chain really appreciate a little respect and praise.

If you are playing an average of $100 or more per bet, then you will likely find yourself with a casino host – a (usually) friendly man or woman who will organize transport, sort out meals and comps generally, and arrange special treats like rounds of golf and suite upgrades. If you are a regular player, contact your host when you make a booking and everything will be sorted out for you, saving you check-in lines, and getting you into the action as quickly as possible.

Downtown, the casinos will rate you for lower stakes and offer you more in return for your action. However, a suite in a downtown casino may not be as pleasant or comfortable as a standard room in a grand Strip casino and, in terms of entertainment, outdoor areas and variety of games played, the choice may be very limited.

In off-Strip, out-of-town casinos, which cater mainly for Vegas locals, the comps will be modest, but you will get looked after well. Many people find those casinos the most friendly of all. In local casinos the qualification rate is usually lower and some of the smaller venues will rate you for any money you gamble at all. However, don't expect the comps to be as exciting: you may be on for a $10 food voucher, a baseball hat, or a pack of cards.

Player's Card Tips

- Never play for a higher stake simply to qualify for comps. You may win, but you may lose and if you lose it may be such a big loss that it wipes out your bankroll for the entire stay. Just bet as normal and, if you qualify for comps, that's a bonus.
- If you do play at a Vegas Strip property, ask if your Player's Card is valid elsewhere and, if so, play there to benefit from the accumulated action.
- Ask the supervisor for a Line Pass. This entitles you to jump the queue (there's usually a separate very short line) at the hotel buffet and restaurants. At peak times, this can be a real boon, as lines can stretch for a quarter of a mile! Also, if you ask for a Line Pass, the supervisor may be so amazed you haven't asked him for a free meal he may offer you a complimentary meal.
- When playing at other casinos, even if you do not bother to apply for a Player's Card, if you have been playing for an hour or more, at a stake of $25 or more

per bet, ask the supervisor if the casino can buy you breakfast/lunch/dinner. Often he will be happy to give you a voucher to cover your costs. A free meal always tastes sweeter somehow.

- Be aware that some bets do not qualify for rating. For example, at Craps your Odds Bets (which offer no edge to the house whatsoever) will not be counted towards comps. This is why you sometimes see crazy people betting $25 on the Pass Line and $5 on the Odds, just to qualify for comps. However, financially, you would do far better to place $5 on the Pass Line and up to $25 on the Odds and forget the comps.

Slots Club Card

There's no reason not to enrol in a Slots Club. It might cost you five minutes of your time, but the welcome offers you receive (from gaming credits to free buffets) will be worth your time. After that, providing you insert your card every time you play the Slots, your action will be rated and you will earn points. In turn, those points can be exchanged for cash, comps (complimentary meals, etc) and even room upgrades and free stays. Even if you play 25c Slots, you will still accumulate the same as a modest win by the time you finish your session.

The second-grade casinos which, perhaps, have seen better days, often offer better odds on their Slots and usually much better deals on their Slots Clubs, since they want to attract more business. This means that the points earned will be worth more and you may earn them quicker. You may also be offered some tempting-sounding introductory deals. One well-known mid-range casino offers players an hour to play as much as they like, and all the winnings can be kept and the losses repaid. This sounds like a great deal, and it is — up to a point. However, any losses will not be returned for a calendar month, so you have to return to the casino to do that. While it is being sorted out, which, inevitably, takes time, you may be tempted to play some more. Sometimes, winnings from these kinds of deals are paid out in casino credits, which must be played only in that casino — and so on. Just be careful to check the small print on these deals.

Slots Card Tips

- The benefits you accrue from a Slots Club card are not based on how much you win or lose, just on your play through — the amount of money you stake. If you have a winning session, you have your Slots Club points to cash in as well — a double bonus.
- Playing with a Slots Card does not make it less likely you will win. The computer doesn't know what a Slots Club card is anyway.
- Playing with a Slots Club card does not mean that you will get reported to the IRS if you win. The casinos will report any win of $1,200 or greater regardless of whether you have a card or not. Otherwise, they won't.
- Check you take your card with you when you leave your machine. Regular players attach it to themselves via a coiled wire, like a telephone cable. If you fail to insert your card and you play through a lot of money, it won't be registered. If you do lose your card, apply at the Slots Club desk and it can be replaced. Don't wait — stop what you are doing and get your card replaced as soon as possible.

29
Visiting Casino Cities

THERE ARE NOW casinos all over the world. The "gaming" industry, once a pariah, both in investment terms and community planning, is now welcomed everywhere. Even within the United States, where Las Vegas and Atlantic City used to be the only towns in which to gamble seriously (and legally), many States have now legalized gambling, and casino resorts keep appearing. Licences in the UK and Europe have become far more readily available and casinos everywhere, from tiny islands to mega-cities in the developing world, are attracting billions of dollars of gaming revenues.

There are great cities, with wonderful casinos, all over the world, but there are three which, in my opinion, stand out as fantastic destinations for gamblers and their families.

Las Vegas

Without doubt, this is the number one gambling city in the world and an amazing place for a vacation, both for gamblers and non-gamblers. It's tacky, vulgar, gaudy, distasteful... It immerses you in a world where normal values are suspended and replaced by hedonistic greed, hope over logical expectation, and a battle to the financial death between you, the player, and the biggest, fiercest opponent you've ever encountered. And it is wonderful.

Even if you are on a modest budget, the grand hotel resorts on the Strip are well worth the extra money for a room. The charm of Vegas is that, when you are winning – even if it is $100 – you feel like a king. You have a luxury room, staff wanting to help you, people welcoming you. If you are losing, you can still feel privileged, tucked inside stadium-sized beds topped with luxury linens, and carpets so deep-pile you could lose a small dog. The outdoor areas are wonderful too. Since Vegas is hot most of the year, lying by the pool is a real pleasure. Long-legged cocktail waitresses bring you cooling cocktails; the shade of olive trees and the distinct tinkle of music and fountains will sooth your ears. You can be massaged, exercised and pampered in a private cabana, and return to the chill of the air-conditioned casino, feeling like a million dollars. If you go to Vegas and you don't enjoy the high life, it is a waste of a trip: play online instead and save the airfare, hotel costs and food tabs.

Downtown, in what used to be called "Glitter Gulch" but is now really Freemont Street, you have more old-style casinos, looser Slots and more favourable game rules. The "Freemont Street Experience" is four blocks of hotels and casinos covered by a blanket of millions of LEDs. Programmed with cartoons and images, every 15 minutes in the evening it lights up the street and brings punters pouring out of the casinos to witness a truly amazing modern spectacle. It is highly recommended for, at the very least, an afternoon/evening excursion.

Vegas must be one of the few cities in the worlds where you stay in a hotel and go out to another hotel – but, with so many gourmet restaurants, fabulous shopping experiences and tourist activities, that's what you do. Bellagio's fountains, Paris's Eiffel Tower, TI's maritime extravaganza – all can be admired and enjoyed from the street at no cost. Meanwhile, the nightclubs and bars are buzzing, the outdoor terraces high above the Strip, or just off-Strip, afford spectacular views for the price of a cocktail.

And, don't forget the rest of the surrounding area. The Hoover Dam and the Grand Canyon are both within reach and make for memorable excursions. Some of the golf courses are among the best kept anywhere in the world, and the theme parks and adrenalin rides do, literally, take your breath away.

Vegas Visit Tips

- **Leave your credit cards at home.** Take what you can afford to lose and leave yourself no chance of being lulled into changing more money. I've made the mistake – just about every gambler I've ever known has made this mistake – please don't make it yourself. Vegas is a truly seductive place, and it is your hard-earned cash which is being wooed. Protect yourself and stay out of temptation.

  Whether you are in Vegas solely to gamble, or for a more general vacation, the key to a successful stay is to enjoy a multitude of activities and not become tied to the emotional roller coaster of gambling. No matter how well you play, you could hit three terrible sessions in a row and leave yourself very short. In that position, the last thing you will want to do is to spend money on treats for yourself. That is why this tip is so important, to guarantee you a good time.

- **Divide your bankroll into sums for each separate session.** If you are planning to spend four days in Vegas, have twelve independent bankrolls – three for each day. Lock away everything else in your room safe, or put it on deposit with the casino. If I had just $1 for every time a gambler has told me that he has lost his entire bankroll on the very first evening he arrived in Vegas, I'd be a high roller myself.

- **Set sensible targets and have modest expectations.** If you want to gamble and you don't mind what happens, relax and enjoy it. If you care whether you win or lose, follow the advice in this book to the letter. It is the correct advice statistically for almost every decision you will face.

  When playing Slots, if you aim for a big jackpot, the chances you will return home with nothing are very, very high. If you aim to make 20 per cent profit on your stake, you might just do it – but only if you are disciplined and lucky.

  If you play Table Games, aim to make between 25 and 50 per cent profit at any given session (see the individual chapters in this book for a realistic expectation). Lock away this profit if you make it, and do not touch it during the session. If you do this for even one quarter of your sessions, you will have a good chance of making a really big score on one of them and coming home in profit.

  Remember, the more you try to win, the more likely it is that you will lose *everything*.

- **Enrol in Player's Card and Slots Club schemes.** They cost you nothing, provide modest benefits and can give a welcome bonus if things are going poorly.

- **Vegas is a tips town.** Be prepared to offer tips to dealers, bell boys, waitresses, etc. It's the way the town works.
- **If you have a problem, pick your adversary.** Do not take it out on the dealer, cocktail waitress or supervisor. They have no authority to help you much, and they suffer abuse and moaning and complaints day in, day out. Call for a pit boss, or shift manager. Be extra polite (they are not used to that and it will help your cause), and be firm and clear with your complaint.

  Never panic if you think you have been misled, or a winning bet has been taken away, or someone else claims that the chips you think are yours are really theirs: the eyes in the sky will sort it out for you perfectly, every time. Just be patient.

- **Use jet lag to your benefit.** If you have travelled from the East Coast, or from Europe, enjoy the jet lag. Ignore the clocks, get up in the morning when you wake up – usually very early – and take a nice walk along the Strip in the cool of the day. It's the best time to explore Vegas on foot. Walk to a distant hotel and have a big American breakfast, shoot a little dice, and then wander back to your own property via the town waking up to a new day of scorching temperatures and exciting action.

- **Book treats in Vegas before you arrive.** Depending upon your budget:
  - Book up a fancy meal in a grand restaurant in one the major Strip hotels.
  - Book tickets to see a show (Cirque du Soleil's shows in Las Vegas are breath-taking and far exceed any you might catch elsewhere since all their shows in Vegas play in purpose-built arenas).

- Book a massage, reserve a private cabana by the pool, put aside a shopping budget.
- Book a helicopter flight over the Strip at night, to the Hoover Dam, or one that lands in the Grand Canyon, serves you breakfast and rides you home again, over the Dam and over the Strip – it's worth every penny.
- Pre-book the club pro to play with you on an amazing golf course – it's expensive but a wonderful golfing memory.
- Rent a classic car, or a dream car – drive it for a day and a night, and up the Strip at Sunset.
- Book treats before you go, or you may miss out on all these fabulous experiences.

- **Do your research before you go.** Once you arrive in Vegas, there'll be no time for research. If you are a Slots player, go online and find out which casinos have the best deals and make it your business to seek out great welcome deals to Slots Clubs, the loosest Slots, Slot tournaments, etc.

  If you like Table Games, learn the correct strategies from this book, take notes, and look up online which casinos currently offer the best rules and payouts for the games you want to play. You will enjoy this work in advance of the trip – building the excitement – and it could save you, and win you, thousands of dollars.

- **Never try to cheat the casinos.** It's a bad idea anywhere, but in Vegas they'll take you out, arrest you, and lock you up in a very hot, very desolate prison for ten years if you take computer-aided cheating equipment into the casino. Track cards, follow your instinct, but never be tempted to join anyone who thinks they can beat the house. It'll be a scam, or will get you arrested.

- **Never forget they are out to get you – and every penny you possess.** However exciting, however glamorous, however friendly –Vegas makes billions of dollars per year. Some of this money comes from hotels, food and beverages, but gaming is still the number-one earner. Keep your eye out for scams because, despite the cameras (and Vegas is a very safe city), there are plenty of pickpockets, chip stealers, snake-oil salesmen and con-artists out there. Above all, don't let your own personal weakness ruin your vacation. Keep an eye on your finances at all times.

Monte Carlo (Monaco)

The principality of Monaco is located between the South of France and Italy. It's tiny, expensive, picturesque and, for the most part, as glamorous as it gets. But, despite being world-renowned as a gambling "Mecca", beware – all is not as it seems. Monte Carlo is not a wonderful place to gamble: the limits are high, the staff generally surly, and the action slow and pretty staid.

This is not to say that it's not worth visiting. It certainly is, but you'll need to be wealthy to enjoy its charms. The top hotels are truly luxurious and offer wonderful accommodation, lovely restaurants and, if you pick carefully, beautiful sea and marina views. The famous Casino Square is awash with beautiful people admiring each other's Ferraris and Lamborghinis and looking very tanned, and you can dine on the terrace of the Hotel De Paris and watch everyone pass by. Just off the main square are numerous restaurants and bars for a light lunch or early evening drinks. Up at the top of the hill is the old town, full of expensive shops selling tawdry nick-nacks and expensive designer goods, and the Changing of the Guard may lack the gravitas of the

London version but has the distinct advantage of being in the sun. Away from the Marina and old town, the principality can look quite jaded and grey, the multi-millionaire tax dodgers all holed up in their faceless apartments.

There are few Slot machines, and those which you can find are notoriously tight. The rules for Blackjack and other games are usually quite restrictive, and if you hit the busy summer weekends you are unlikely to get near a table anywhere without a fight. The Italians are usually pretty wild gamblers and enjoy taking a long time to make their (wrong) decisions at Blackjack.

Here is a selection of the casinos on offer, all within walking distance of each other. However, to reach the Sporting Club and Monte Carlo Bay Hotel, you may prefer to take a taxi. Many casinos only open at 2 p.m., and some not until 4 p.m., and all expect, at the very least, smart casual attire.

The Casino de Monte-Carlo, located at the bottom end of Casino Square, is worth a visit just to experience the stunningly beautiful and refined gaming rooms, the hushed tones and the vaulted ceilings. Table minimums usually start at 50 euros for Blackjack and other Table Games, and slightly lower for Roulette, which is a mainstay. Be aware that, not only will you have to pay to get in (and show identification), but in the summer months much of the action moves to the Sporting Club, which also offers live music and concerts, fine dining and, obviously, sports.

One insider tip: if you enjoy the sensuous and erotic, ask about the secret nightclub beneath the casino. A gilded lift will take you into another world.

Casino Cafe de Paris is a more modern and relaxed casino, with the best selection of Slots in Monaco.

Sun Casino calls itself trendy and expects guests to dress as such. Some Slots and various Table Games.

Monte Carlo Bay Hotel and Casino boasts that it is one of Europe's only casinos using cards and ticket-paying Slots. It claims to have 145 Slots, and be open from 2 p.m. until 2 a.m. each day.

Monte Carlo Grand Hotel was formerly Loewes Hotel – the tunnel beneath which sees the Formula One cars roar through on Monaco Grand Prix day. It is modern in the 1960s style, but the small guest rooms do enjoy lovely Mediterranean views, and the rooftop terrace and pool is as glamorous as it comes. Expect to see deep tans, hairy chests, too much gold jewellery and a lot of mobile phone calls answered in the pool by cigarette-smoking grande dames!

Expect High Prices

Expect to pay high prices for accommodation and meals, even just light snacks and drinks.

Monte-Carlo SBM

Monte-Carlo SBM operates most of Monaco's casinos and many luxury hotels, as well as nightclubs and the Monte-Carlo Golf Club and the Monte-Carlo Country Club. High-rollers should contact SBM in advance. They look after you brilliantly if you're in town to gamble, and gamble big.

Poor Player Benefits

At the time of writing, there is no Slots Club or Player's Card scheme in operation in Monte Carlo, so average bettors will not gain any benefits, and even getting a free drink may prove difficult.

Treat Yourself to a Helicopter Transfer

The closest airport to Monaco is Nice. A great way to arrive in (and depart from) Monte Carlo is by helicopter and, if you book in advance, you can stroll from your plane to the heliport and be whisked over the mountains and into Monte Carlo, enjoying the million-dollar views as you go. It's an extravagance, but well worth it.

Avoid Grand Prix Month

May is a lovely time to visit the South of France and Monaco. However, the weeks preceding and following the Monaco Grand Prix (usually mid-May) are very busy and prices of everything rise astronomically.

London

As well as being by far the most interesting and complex city to visit, London also offers some great opportunities to gamble. Above all, however, London is one of the great arts centres of the world and boasts some of the finest restaurants on the planet, beautiful parks and awe-inspiring architecture and design. Unfortunately, like Monaco, London has also become very expensive so, unless you are prepared to live very modestly, expect to pay top international prices.

The history of gambling in London goes back many centuries. The most famous club in town was Crockfords, owned by William Crockford and located on the prestigious St James' Street, just minutes from Buckingham Palace. This casino still exists, but not under the same name. A new Crockfords club now stands in Mayfair, on Curzon Street. William Crockford was such an icon in gambling circles that when he died, just before a big race on which he had taken many thousands of pounds in wagers, his colleagues propped up his body in the top floor window of his club to reassure everyone that their bets were safe and would be paid. Latterly, people have speculated that his casino cheated players with rigged games – as has been suggested about other famous gambling haunts, even as late as the mid-1960s. However, in London now you can be pretty certain of a fair gamble as the British Gaming Board oversees all casinos with a rod of iron.

In terms of gambling, London remains a Table Games casino town, as Slots are still tightly regulated. There are a few Slots in most casinos, but they are mainly limited to jackpots of £1,000, although there are plans to change these rules in the near future.

Most Table Games start at minimums of £5 per bet (£2 per chip at Roulette), but the minimums are often increased in the evenings to £10, and sometimes even £25.

At the time of writing, London boasts some 45 casinos, with more planned to open soon. There are two main types of casino in London:

Standard London Casinos

These are the casinos into which you walk, either without any identification, or once you have shown your passport or ID and enrolled. They tend to be the bigger, more modern casinos, where stakes are lower and the casino is busy most of the day (and night). Having said that, you will rarely find more than ten Roulette wheels, the same number of Blackjack tables, and perhaps one or two Three-Card Poker, Caribbean Stud Poker and Mini-Baccarat tables (or Punto Bunco, as it is known in the UK).

The Empire in Leicester Square is a mid-size example of such a casino; it also hosts the World Series of Poker London heat.

The Victoria (often known as The Vicky, or The Vic), on the Edgware Road, is most famous for its Poker Room and the very high standard games which are played there. Some of the best players in the country gather for high-stake cash games and London heats of big Poker tournaments. However, most days see a low-stake tournament game available to ordinary players.

The Golden Nugget in Shaftesbury Avenue, just off Piccadilly Circus, is packed with Chinese gamblers from nearby China Town.

All these casinos will, generally, offer you free drinks at the tables where you are playing (a tip of anything from 50p to £5 is appreciated by the cocktail waitresses). You may also be able to get toasted sandwiches and other snacks served at your table. If you are a mid-stake bettor – say, £25 per hand or higher – you can expect to be invited to eat at the casino restaurant. These restaurants are usually excellent, offering a wide range of cuisines to cater for the many different nationalities that gamble in London.

Grand London Casinos

These casinos are the reason why you should come to London to gamble, since you will play in some of the most beautiful gaming rooms in the world. The finest casinos will allow you to play if you apply to them by fax or email in advance, if you know a member of the club, or if you apply at the door, looking well-dressed and wealthy. Sometimes, they will try to charge you a joining fee, but you should resist, telling them that you have come to gamble and that should be good enough for them. Once in, prepare to be beguiled by grandly proportioned rooms, fine art, chandeliers and gold leaf. These casinos will, generally, allow you to order from the bar (or be served at the gaming tables) all on the house – and the quality of wines, champagnes and cocktails is superb. The barmen, sommeliers and waiting staff have often been with the club for years and they truly know how to look after you. If you are betting at mid-stakes (in terms of these clubs, perhaps £50 per hand), you can expect to be treated to a fantastic dinner or lunch, and higher rollers will get VIP invitations to sporting events and special performances.

The atmosphere inside these clubs is very different from most casinos. It is more like gambling in someone's drawing room than in a casino. Unless you happen to catch a busy and excited group inside, the atmosphere is usually hushed and, if like me, you get excited hitting a big hand at Blackjack, your celebrations will echo around the room. Mostly, the dealers and supervisors welcome a bit of a distraction; the eerie quiet must get to them eventually...

Crockfords in Curzon Street, was created by David Gray – one of the great perfectionists of the London casino scene. Now sold on, the club is still very grand, boasting a lovely circular bar and gaming tables in a grand sunken room. The Punto Bunco table takes up one end of the room and, when the table is in play, it is an impressive sight indeed. The restaurant serves wonderful food and is overseen by some of the best staff in London.

Like many of the grand casinos in London, Crockfords has only a small gaming area: three Blackjack tables, three Roulette tables, Three-Card Poker and Caribbean Stud Poker, plus a full-size Punto Bunco table.

Also opened by David Gray just around the corner in Hertford Street, is the more modern **Colony Club**. More relaxed, bigger and attracting a younger crowd, this is a glamorous casino to visit, also with a first-rate restaurant, serving excellent oriental cuisine. This casino is larger, with roughly six tables of Roulette and Blackjack, plus the usual extra Table Games.

Fifty, in St James' Street, is in the original building occupied by the famous Crockford's Club. In the late twentieth century, the owners decided to renovate the building and, in association with English Heritage (a body which supervises restorations of important buildings and gardens), the casino has now been returned to its former glory, painted and decorated in the original colours and designs of the era. The bar and restaurant have developed a strong reputation.

Les Ambassadeurs Club in Hamilton Place – again in Mayfair – has long been associated with very grand gaming. The casino has recently been updated and has a funky modern feel, but the restaurant, with its excellent cooking and wonderful service, remains an enclave of peace and serenity amidst one of the busiest parts of town.

The Ritz Club is a tiny, beautifully formed gem right next to the hotel of the same name. Set underground in what used to be the private ballroom, the decor of the gaming rooms, bar and restaurant is exquisite. It has very few tables but, if you can, try to get in to see the perfect little example of grand London gambling.

Aspinalls, next door to Crockfords in Curzon Street, is a very grand club with, once again, an excellent restaurant. Attracting a younger, more fashionable crowd, it bills itself as a private club, demanding membership, but check with their front desk if you really want to play there. The decor alone is wild and worth a look.

Finally, the **Palm Beach** on Berkeley Street is an accessible grand casino, set in a huge high-ceilinged building. It is one of the very few grand casinos to have any Slots and, even here, the number is limited to one dozen. The Palm Beach now offers up to six Poker tables and provides both cash games and tournaments daily.

Research Membership or Visiting Rights Before Your Trip

If you plan to play in one or more of what I call the Grand London casinos, research online and apply for membership in advance. If the casino suggests that a membership fee is payable, explain that you are visiting London and that you are there to gamble – most clubs will welcome you.

The standard London casinos are open to everyone, usually upon production of valid ID, such as a passport.

Good Benefits, but No Player's Cards

London casinos do not use Player's Cards or (because there are very few Slots available) Slots Club cards. In the standard casinos, ask a supervisor for free drinks and dining options; in the grand London casinos, you will be looked after handsomely. As ever, the more you gamble, the more you can expect to be entertained on the house.

Genteel – and Quiet – Atmosphere

The grand London casinos usually have a very quiet atmosphere. If you prefer more lively surroundings, then head for one of the bigger standard casinos, such as The Victoria, or perhaps, The Palm Beach.

Glossary of Gambling Terms

action	the amount of gambling activity provided by a player
baccarat	Table Game, also known outside the US as Punto Bunco
betting right	betting on the Pass Line at Craps, with the table
betting wrong	betting on the Don't Pass Line, against the table
break, bust	to go over 21 at Blackjack
burn (a card)	to discard a card, or cards, before dealing from a shoe
cage	the cashier's cage is where chips are exchanged for cash, cheques are cashed and credit is held
caller	a Bingo or Keno supervisor who calls out winning numbers
cash out	button marked as such appearing on Slot machines for redemption of remaining credits, either in cash or with a printed credit ticket
changeur	usually in French casinos, an employee who changes notes into chips
cold	a cold table, or cold dice – performing consistently badly for the players
comp	short for complimentary. The benefits of meals, accommodation, etc, offered to players by casinos
corner bet	a bet covering the intersection of four numbers on the Roulette layout
coup	the deal of a hand at Blackjack, Baccarat and other card-based Table Games
cut card	also known as a marker card, this is used to cut off a portion of the deck at Blackjack, and mark the end of the playable cards at Baccarat; also inserted as a cut for other card games
dealer	in Europe called a croupier; all Table Game staff are usually called dealers, except for certain Craps staff
deuce	a 2, either on card, or dice
double/ double down	at Blackjack, to match your original bet with a second one when your hand is favourite to win

edge	the advantage for the player, or "house edge" for the casino
even money	a payoff at 1–1
floorman	(American) a supervisor of several tables, overseeing dealers
gaming	the polite term the gambling industry likes to use for gambling – so it does not sound like gambling
hard total	Blackjack term for a hand not containing an ace
hardway	Craps term for making total with both dice showing the identical result
high roller	a big bettor, for high stakes, although not as big as a "whale"
hit	to take another card at Blackjack
hole card	in Blackjack, if the dealer takes both his up card and his second card before dealing the remaining players' hands; thus the second card, held face down, is known as the hole card
host	a casino employee who looks after big bettors and high rollers
hot	referring to dice: opposite of cold; the table where the dice are winning consistently
house	the casino, or gambling, establishment
insurance	a bet separate from the main game of Blackjack, wagering that the dealer will have a ten card with his ace showing and make Blackjack – not a good bet
junket	a group of usually mid–high rollers visiting a casino
kibitzer	a spectator of card games/gambling games
layout	the betting pattern printed onto baize (sometimes glass or Perspex) onto which bettors place their wagers
loose	loose Slots are those which pay more generously, opposed to "tight"
marker	a house cheque used within a casino to mark the use of funds
muck	to discard, or throw away
nickel	(American) a $5 chip
off	a Craps term to indicate that your bets are not in play for a particular roll

paint	slang term for picture, or court, cards
parlay	to double the size of your bet, or to add your winnings from the previous coup to the next bet
pigeon	a poor, exploitable gambler
pit	an area inside a group, circle or square of gaming tables
place numbers	the numbers established as point numbers on the Craps layout: 4, 5, 6, 8, 9 and 10
plaques	extra large denomination chips, much larger than usual, usually oblong in shape and used for high denominations in many European casinos
press	to press is to increase the size of your bet
proposition bets	bets placed in the centre section of a Craps layout, on Hardway Bets, or Next Roll Bets – almost always these are terrible bets to make
push	a stand-off, or tie
quarters, quarter chips	(American) $25 chips
rails	the grooved area, usually wooden, around the top edge of a Craps table, where players can stack their chips and store drinks, etc, beneath – beware thieves who remove your chips during a hot roll
rating	on production of your Player's Card, the floor manager will rate your play – when you sat down, how much money you changed, the size of your stake, when you left – from this, the resort will calculate your benefits
roll	a single roll of the dice, but also a series of successful throws resulting in a "hot roll"
rush	a series of good cards, or successful bets
shoe	a card holder, usually containing 4–6 decks of shuffled cards, from which the dealer can distribute cards to players and himself without the next card being revealed
shooter	the player throwing the dice at Craps
slots	general term for all machine-based gambling, from modern-day one-armed bandits to Video Poker and multi-game machines
soft total	a Blackjack term for a hand containing an ace

stiff, stiff hand a Blackjack hand totalling between 12 and 16, likely to break if hit

systems usually, betting methods supposedly capable of thwarting the house edge, and which never work; sometimes, strategy to make the best plays

table games general term for all gambling games played at tables, as opposed to at machines (Slots)

table limits the maximum single bet, or combined bets, permitted at a particular Table Game

taken down a bet which is removed from the layout legally, most often at Craps

tapped out losing your entire bankroll at the table

ten card a card which counts as ten; usually in Blackjack – 10, jack, queen or king

toke usually used by casino personnel: a tip

trey a 3

up card in Blackjack, any card that is dealt face up, most particularly the dealer's card which is showing

vig, vigorish a gambler's term for the house edge on any given game; often used to describe the commission on Sports betting

wager a bet

wild symbol a symbol on a Slot machine that counts as any symbol which creates a winning combination

working at Craps, the opposite to "off", indicating that bets are in play and can be won or lost on the next roll of the dice

Glossary of Poker Terms

add-on	in a Poker tournament, you may be offered the opportunity to add to your chips by buying extra chips after the first session of play
advertising	the act of showing one or more of your hole cards to show that you have a strong hand when you say you do; done probably to mislead subsequently; occasionally, the showing of a bluff to encourage more action from opponents
aggressive	a tendency to bet out and raise/re-raise rather than just to call or check
all-in	to place all your remaining chips into the pot
ante	bet made before the cards are dealt on each hand
ATM	a mildly abusive description applied to a player who appears to be dispensing cash to anyone who cares to call
bad beat	a hand where you lose to a player against the expected odds.
bad beat story	a lengthy dissertation of a supposedly very unlucky occurrence when the "expert" storyteller has been beaten by a mindless fool who has hit miracle cards to beat him – usually not that bad a beat; always much less interesting to the listener than to the storyteller
bet	to make the first movement of chips on any betting round
big blind	the bigger of the two Ante Bets placed before each hand of Texas Hold 'Em
big slick	slang term for AK in the hole
bluff	to attempt to steal the pot by representing a hand stronger than the one actually held
board	the table; the community cards showing on the table
boat	a full house
bubble	the position in a tournament that is one off the money – the worst place to be eliminated.
burn	to discard; the dealer "burns" the top card before dealing the "flop", "turn" and "river".

button	the dealer button which denotes the position of the dealer; also sometimes referring to the player in that seat
buy-in	the exchange of cash for chips; the amount required to sit at a given table
call	to match the highest bet made to date
calling station	like an ATM, a loose, forever-calling player
cap	the limit some casinos and card rooms put on the number of raises per round permitted in Limit games
cash in	to leave the table, and exchange your chips for cash
check	when no other player has bet, to check is to make no bet at that stage (sometimes indicated by tapping the table)
check-raise	a play that is usually strong; to check at first and then, once an opponent bets, to raise him
chip, chips	also known as "checks", these are circular plastic or clay discs which represent different financial values and which are used instead of cash in almost all Poker games
community cards	the flop, turn and river cards dealt face up in the middle of the table
continuation bet	a follow-up bet by a pre-flop raiser once the flop has appeared – designed to re-enforce the appearance of great strength
dead money	a disparaging description of those competitors in a tournament whom you consider to have no chance of winning, who are therefore contributing to the overall prize pot generously
dealer	the player who deals (or for whom a paid dealer deals) the deck, before this honour moves on to the next player in a clockwise direction
deuce	a two
dog	short for underdog
donkey	a poor player
down cards	your "hole" or "pocket" cards
draw	to improve your hand with the community cards

early position the two- or three-player positions closest to the left of the dealer; the first players to decide what to do

fifth street the fifth and final community card, also known as the river

final table the last table of ten players (sometimes eight) in a tournament when all other players have been eliminated

fish a player who stays in pots hoping to catch the right cards to create a winning hand – but against the odds

Five-Card Stud an old variation of Poker where you are dealt five cards and there is then betting – not popular these days

flop the first three community cards

flush five cards of the same suit

flush draw when you have four cards of the same suit and you are hoping that the subsequent card(s) will produce a fifth card to complete the flush

fold to throw away, or muck, one's cards

fold equity the extra value a big bet carries because of the chance that the opponent(s) may fold rather than continue to contest the pot

fourth street the fourth community card, also known as "the turn"

free card to allow the turn or river card to appear without there having been any betting and calling

gut-shot draw a Straight draw that can be filled by only one card: you might hold QJ and the flop comes 9, 8, 2: only a 10 can make your Straight

heads up head-to-head play at a table containing only two players

high roller a player who competes for very high stakes

hole cards/ in the hole the player's two secret cards, dealt face down

home game Poker played at home

H.O.R.S.E. a style of Poker game where five variations are played in succession: Hold 'Em, Omaha, Razz, Seven-card Stud, Seven-card Stud Hi/Lo Eights or better

house, the the casino or club in which you are playing

implied pot odds	the potential pot odds given that the chips currently in the pot are likely to be added to by further action; there will be further betting and therefore more chips in the pot by the end of the hand
kicker	card or cards not involved in the formation of a Poker combination, but still part of the five-card Poker hand
late position	player(s) closest to the dealer's right, last to act on each round of the betting
lay down	to concede or give in; often a good play in Poker if you feel you are beaten
leak	a small, but consistent, error which, over time, leads to consistent losses
limp in	to call a small bet in "late position" when you are unlikely to be raised
loose	a loose player is likely to play too many hands, remain in pots for too long and make speculative plays which will result in chips being lost
mid-position	in the middle of the table between the big blind and the dealer
MTT	Multi-Table Tournament; an event featuring more than one table of action in simultaneous play
muck	to fold, or discard
no-limit	a game with no maximum limits on the amount which can be bet
nut, nuts	the best possible hand; a "Nut" Flush would be an ace-high Flush, with no chance of a Straight Flush
off, off-suit	cards of different suits
out, outs	card or cards which will complete your hand and improve it, usually to winning status
overcard	card, or cards, which are higher than those showing among the community cards
palooka	an inexperienced card player
passive	a player who tends to check and call opposed to betting and raising
pigeon	similar to donkeys, palookas and fish
pocket rockets	AA "in the hole"

position	a player's location at the table, measured in terms of the order in which action must be taken on each round of the betting
pot	the collection of chips (sometimes cash) which will be awarded to the winner of the hand
premium hands	the best cards possible as starting hands (in Hold 'Em: AA)
rainbow	board cards which are all of different suits, offering no Flush draw possibilities
rake	the amount, usually a small percentage, taken out of each pot by the casino, card club or online Poker site as payment for hosting the game; there should be no rakes in home games
raise	increase the size of the biggest bet at the table
re-buy	in a tournament, when you lose all your chips early on you may be offered the opportunity to pay the entry fee again for another chance and another set of starting chips
represent	to give the impression of a very strong hand from all your betting actions
re-raise	To raise over an opponent's raise – considered a very strong, intimidating move
respect	on the basis of his powerful betting actions, to believe that your opponent has a good hand and is acting accordingly
river	the fifth and final community card
rock	a player who chooses only the best hands to enter the action and bets only when he is sure that he holds the best hand
rush	to be on a roll, a sequence of successful plays
satellite	a qualifying event for a big Poker tournament
school	a regular Poker game, acknowledging that you never stop learning; a Poker School
semi-bluff	a bet or raise made without the, currently, best hand but with the potential to improve to the best hand if a successful draw is made

set	three-of-a-kind; "trips"
shorthanded	a Poker game containing five players or less; the value of hands often changes as a result of having fewer players at the table
short stack	when you have less than the average amount of chips in front of you
showdown	when a bet or bets is called after the river card, all players must show their hole cards; the best hand wins
side pot	a secondary (sometimes tertiary) pot, formed because one player is all-in and cannot bet any more into the pot, contested by the remaining players
Sit & Go	a one-table (occasionally more) tournament, most often played online, which begins the moment the required number of players are signed up
slowplay	to give the impression of weakness or uncertainty by checking or calling bets rather than raising them
slow-rolling	to turn over a winning hand slowly after another player believes that he has won; poor form at the Poker table
smooth call	to call, rather than to raise, with a strong hand which, at a later date, you intend to raise your opponent; a trapping call to disguise strength, possibly to induce further callers into the pot
stack	a player's chips, either literally or, online, metaphorically
stealing	to bet or raise when opponents have shown comparative weakness in the hope of taking down the pot there and then; often used in the context of a button raise in an attempt "to steal the blinds"
straight	five cards of mixed suits in sequence
suited	of the same suit
super-satellite	a satellite event from which the winner(s) gains a seat in a satellite
table image	the personality that you have displayed in order to create an image of your style of play; may well be misleading/designed to trap opponents into misjudging your future actions

tell	a physical indication, often subconscious or unrecognized by the player himself, by which other players may gain an insight into the strength of a player's hand
tight	likely to enter only a few pots with very good or premium hands; opposite of loose
tilt, on tilt	usually a sign of frustration or anger, a player may go "on tilt" by playing too many hands of poor quality and subsequently showering opponents with chips
trap	to mislead an opponent into believing that you have a weak hand – perhaps by checking or calling when a bet or raise would normally be called for
treys	pocket threes
trips	a "set"; three-of-a-kind
turn	the fourth community card; sometimes known as "fourth street"
underbet	a bet which, considering the size of the pot and the preceding action, appears too small
under the gun	the player first to act after the blinds in Hold 'Em
value bet	to bet a hand you believe to be winning to extract the best value from your opponent; a bet made at the end of a hand which, over time, will lead to profit
W.S.O.P.	the World Series of Poker – the world championships of the game, held each summer in Las Vegas